Trading Index Options

Trading Index Options

James B. Bittman

McGraw-Hill
New York   San Francisco   Washington, D.C.   Auckland   Bogotá
Caracas   Lisbon   London   Madrid   Mexico City   Milan
Montreal   New Delhi   Singapore
Sydney   Tokyo   Toronto

Library of Congress Cataloging-in-Publication Data

Bittman, James B.
    Trading index options / by
    James B. Bittman
        p.   cm.
    ISBN 0-7863-1230-0
    1. Stock index futures.   2. Options (Finance)   I. Title.
    HG6043.B58   1998
    332.63'228—dc21   97-39222

McGraw-Hill

A Division of The **McGraw·Hill** Companies

7 8 9 0 DOC/DOC   0 2

ISBN 0-7863-1230-0

The sponsoring editor for this book was *Stephen Isaacs,* the editing supervisor was
John M. Morriss, and the production supervisor was *Suzanne W. B. Rapcavage.* It was
set in Garamond by *Electronic Publishing Services, Inc.*

Printed and bound by R. R. Donnelley & Sons Company.

McGraw-Hill books are available at special quantity discounts to use as premiums and sales promo-
tions, or for use in corporate training programs. For more information, please write to the Director of
Special Sales, McGraw-Hill, Professional Publishing, Two Penn Plaza, New York, NY 10121-2298. Or
contact your local bookstore.

This book is printed on recycled, acid-free paper containing a minimum of 50%
recycled de-inked fiber.

Dedicated to

Harrison Roth   and   James W. Yates
1931–1997   1940–1996

Men who loved options almost as much
as they loved their families and friends
and almost as much as they were loved

Contents

Acknowledgments

This book was made possible by significant contributions from many people. The entire manuscript was edited by Lisa Harms, whose clear thinking and clear writing contributed greatly to the book's organization and clarity. Marty Kearney also reviewed the entire manuscript. His comments, based on his knowledge of trading, motivated me to rewrite many examples so that different or more important points were emphasized.

The OP-EVAL3™computer program that accompanies the text is both a valuable trading tool and easy to use, thanks to James Karls, who wrote the program. His knowledge of trading contributed greatly to a program design that provides necessary, easy-to-understand information for traders. Long after this book has been read, the computer program will continue to be used.

Jim Adams and Mark Straubel of CBOE Compliance offered valuable advice on the entire manuscript. Many of the technical subjects are more clearly explained because of their careful attention to detail. I am also indebted to Dan Verr of CBOE Strategic Planning who prepared the strategy graphs in Chapter 2.

Laurel Sorenson and John Rusin offered valuable assistance on Chapter 17, "Thinking Like a Trader." Laurel's choice of words and writing style enlivened a difficult subject. John's 30 years' trading experience provided many of the specific insights that makes this chapter valuable. Someday, John, I hope you will teach me your forecasting technique!

Stephen Isaacs, my editor at McGraw-Hill, was a pleasure to work with. Despite the delays and technical problems encountered during manuscript preparation, he maintained his enthusiasm and patience.

John Power, CBOE Vice President and executive director of The Options Institute, was very supportive of my efforts during the writing process. I would also like to thank the entire staff of The Options Institute. It is you who make this a great place to work. Our mission is to teach options, how they work and why they are valuable investment and trading tools. The courses you offer are a quality product, and you make it fun at the same time.

Disclosures

The examples in this book are hypothetical. They do not represent and are not intended to represent real people, real situations, or actual trading advice on particular indexes. The examples presented are meant to be realistic, but they are for illustrative purposes only.

In order to simplify computation, commissions and other transaction costs, margin requirements, and bid-ask spreads have not been included in the examples used in this book. These factors will impact the outcome of stock and option strategies and should be considered in real-world situations.

Options involve risk and are not suitable for everyone. Prior to buying or selling an option, a person must receive a copy of *Characteristics and Risks of Standardized Options.* Copies may be obtained from your broker or from OP-EVAL, Suite 200, 2501 N. Lincoln Avenue, Chicago, IL 60614. The investor considering options should consult a tax advisor as to how taxes may affect the outcome of contemplated options transactions. A prospectus, which discusses the role of The Options Clearing Corporation, is also available without charge upon request addressed to The Options Clearing Corporation, 440 S. LaSalle Street, Suite 908, Chicago, IL 60605. Past performance is not a guarantee of future performance.

Introduction

IS THIS BOOK FOR YOU?

If you are an index option trader and you want to improve your skills by learning how to analyze option prices, plan trades, and find new tools that improve the decision-making process, then this book is for you. This book and the accompanying software will:

- Explain option price behavior
- Teach you what you need to know about volatility
- Show you a method for evaluating option prices and selecting the "right" strategy
- Demonstrate a new way of thinking about and *using* several intermediate and advanced strategies
- Provide a computer program to assist your analysis
- Give you an understanding of trading psychology

For every trade you must (1) state a specific goal, (2) have realistic expectations, (3) plan for several position management alternatives, and (4) keep the principles of trading psychology firmly in mind. *Trading Index Options* will teach you how to complete these four essential steps every time you trade.

This introduction will first explain why index options were created and why they are so attractive to many traders. Second, it will summarize the goals and outline of this book.

WHY INDEX OPTIONS EXIST

Index options and index futures contracts were born out of the tremendous growth and concentration of institutionally managed money.

Investment funds range into the hundreds of billions of dollars. Managers of these funds could easily state the problem: How could $10 million, $50 million, or $100 million be invested in or withdrawn from the stock market quickly and economically? But the solution was harder to come by. Purchasing or selling that much in individual stocks could trigger exaggerated price moves, an event commonly referred to as "market disruption." It would also potentially violate a fund's guidelines for diversification. Market liquidity and portfolio concentration are major concerns for managers of these gigantic investment funds.

If only a way could be found to commit enormous sums to the market quickly, economically, and in a diverse manner. Then the details of specific stock selection and portfolio balancing could be worked out later.

In response to this need, two financial vehicles—index futures and index options—were developed. These products enabled money managers to trade the *market*, not individual stocks. The word "trade," however, is a misnomer, because trade connotes an air of speculation. What actually began to happen was that large sums of investment capital were being invested efficiently and economically.

The demand for this service of facilitating large purchases and sales was being met by professional trading firms, known as arbitrageurs, who attempted to profit from price differences between the index futures and options contracts and the underlying portfolio of stocks. The arbitrageurs established highly efficient operations to transact large, diversified portfolios of stock at a moment's notice if they perceived that futures or options were "mispriced." With the hope of making above-average returns, these arbitrageurs assumed the risk of losing money from market disruptions.

In the beginning, arbitrageurs did make above-average returns, because these new financial products had wide bid-ask spreads, a situation known as "inefficient pricing." But profit-seeking capital was attracted to the new opportunity, and increased competition from more arbitrageurs entering the market caused bid-ask spreads to narrow. Now there is an efficient, competitive market. As a result, opportunities exist for all who want to trade these instruments.

WHY TRADE INDEX OPTIONS

There are many reasons to trade "the market" rather than individual stocks. It has long been said that three factors determine a stock's performance: (1) the direction of the overall market, (2) the industry, and (3) the individual company. Many analysts believe that the largest factor is the direction of the overall market, which, some argue, accounts for as much as 70 percent of the performance of an individual stock. The second most important factor is commonly believed to be the industry, its trends and fundamentals; this is thought to influence 20 percent of a stock's performance. The specific fundamentals relating to a particular company are considered by many to account for only 10 percent of a stock's price action.

What is the implication of this 70%–20%–10% theory? Simple: If the market is rising, then it is relatively easy to jump on board with the purchase of a few individual stocks, especially if positions are taken in the leading industry group. Of course, positive results are not guaranteed. If the overall market is declining or going sideways, however, then it is difficult to find those few stocks that are trending up. Trading the market itself—with index options—allows a trader to take a position more easily, no matter what the trend.

There are other reasons to trade the market rather than individual stocks. First, it is often more difficult to predict the impact of macro events on individual companies than on the overall market. A government report that indicates a growing economy and little inflation, for example, could be interpreted as a positive for the overall market, but not necessarily for an individual stock.

Another advantage of trading the market is the way index options are constructed. As will be explained in Chapter 3, many index options have a higher element of leverage than options on individual stocks. This means that the profit or loss from an index option when the index moves 1 or 2 percent may be equal to or greater than the profit or loss from trading an option on an individual stock that moves 5 to 10 percent. Consequently, there is a "frequency of moves" argument in favor of trading index options. While there are always a few stocks making big moves, most stocks are trading sideways at any given point in time. Consequently, given the fact that index options are more highly leveraged, index option traders may find more market movements of sufficient size to justify making trades.

A final point: People discuss "the market" much more often than specific stocks. And, just as often, a trader may have a forecast for what the market, rather than a particular stock, will do. As a result, it is frequently easier to act on general ideas by trading the market with index options than by trading individual stocks.

MARKET PARTICIPANTS AND THE USE OF OPTIONS

The financial markets consist of three distinct types of participants: investors, speculators, and market makers. Options are valuable tools for all three, although the trading techniques used by each group are significantly different.

As explained in detail in *Options for the Stock Investor* (McGraw-Hill, 1996), options give investors an increased range of investment alternatives, that is, more risk profiles from which to choose. The concepts presented in that book also apply to the use of index options for investors with portfolios that closely follow an index on which options are traded. If index options are used in a nonleveraged manner, they offer insurance and income enhancement alternatives that are different from traditional investing in stock portfolios.

Speculators, for whom this book is written, differ from investors in several ways. First, investors seek the long-term benefits of stock ownership, whereas speculators attempt to profit from short-term market moves. While there is no absolute rule regarding time frame, investors tend to hold for a minimum of 6 months and a maximum of several years. In contrast, the minimum holding period for speculators is a few hours. A maximum of a few weeks seems to be the norm.

Other distinctions between speculators and investors are the use of leverage, the variety of strategies employed, and performance measurement. The practice of trading "on margin" and the use of margin loans to leverage profits—at the risk of leveraging losses—is the realm of speculators. The use of margin debt, however, is typically anathema to conservative investors. Also, investors tend to use only bullish or neutral-to-bullish strategies, because their primary goal is to benefit from stock ownership. Basic income enhancement strategies (writing covered calls) and insurance strategies (purchasing protective puts) are the strategies most commonly used by investors. Speculators, however, trade both market sell-offs and rallies and often use a wide variety of strategies. Investors typically measure performance relative to the market, while speculators have absolute profit targets regardless of market direction. Since speculators take leveraged risks in bull and bear markets, their goal is to make a "high" return every year. A high profit target for the speculator is the compensation for the leveraged risk being assumed.

Investors and speculators also differ in their motivations for trade selection. Although both use fundamental and technical analysis, investors tend to rely more on fundamental considerations, while speculators tend to rely more on technical analysis. Also, since many investors tend to use options for insurance or income enhancement over longer time periods, they do not require as in-depth an option price analysis as speculators, who need to know as much as possible about an option's price, including the current level of implied volatility, a subject explained and used throughout this book. Speculators also need a specific forecast for the time frame of a trade, while investors can be less precise.

Finally, investors and speculators differ in their psychology. "Instinct," "discipline," and "win some, lose some" are concepts both employ. But, given the differences in holding period, method of trade selection, and types of strategies used, these terms mean different things to investors and speculators. Table I-1 summarizes the differences between investors and speculators.

Table I–1 Decision Making: Investors versus Speculators

	Speculators	Investors
Method of profiting	Time short-term market moves	Benefit from long-term stock ownership
Time horizon	Min.: Few hours Max.: Few weeks	Min.: Several months Max.: Many years
Use of leverage	Yes	No
Strategies employed	Bullish, bearish, neutral, basic to advanced	Bullish, neutral, basic
Type of analysis	Greater emphasis on technical analysis	Greater emphasis on fundamental analysis
Nature of forecast	Specific forecast for time and price of underlying	General forecast of long-term funda-mental outlook

THE GOALS OF THIS BOOK

This book is for index option traders and is written with five goals in mind. The first goal is to explain how option prices behave so that appropriate trading decisions can be made. The second goal is to explain risk in a way that is useful for traders. Third, a variety of strategies from simple to complex are presented so that traders can take advantage of the flexibility of index options. The fourth goal is to demonstrate how to use OP-EVAL3™, the option-pricing and strategy-graphing computer program included with this book, to analyze option prices, set profit targets for specific trades, and implement trading decisions. Fifth, several elements of trading psychology are explained. This is the hardest part of trading, but in addition to matching strategies with market forecasts, it is essential that traders think and trade in a disciplined way.

These five goals are discussed in five sections, each of which develops your ability to be a successful index option trader.

THE OUTLINE OF THIS BOOK

Section 1, "Basic Concepts and Strategies," starts with Chapter 1, "The Basics of Index Options." This brief chapter reviews definitions, contract specifications, and index option mechanics. Experienced index option traders may skip this chapter, but equity option traders should be sure to understand the unique aspects of cash-settled index options, especially American-style index options. Chapter 2, "Diagrams of Basic to Advanced Strategies," explains this important method of analyzing profit potential and risk. Although a traditional review of profit and loss diagrams of basic strategies starts this chapter, an interesting variety of intermediate and advanced strategies conclude it. Chapter 3, "Option Values and How They Change," explains short-term option price behavior conceptually. Experienced option traders may want to skim or skip this chapter, but beginners will need this preparation for the more advanced discussions in later chapters.

All option traders must master the concepts presented in Section 2, "Option Price Behavior and Volatility." Understanding how and why option prices change is vital. Interpretation and evaluation of option prices are important skills for traders to develop. Without them, a realistic forecast for strategy results simply cannot be made. Chapter 4, "OP-EVAL3™ for Index Options," explains the option-pricing and strategy-graphing computer program that accompanies this text. This program is useful for graphing strategies, studying option prices, making relative price valuations, and making option price forecasts for a given market forecast. Chapter 5, "The Greeks," completes the explanation of option price behavior begun in Chapter 3. Delta, gamma, vega, and theta are defined, and their usefulness in anticipating option price behavior is explained. Warning! Chapter 5 is very technical, and many readers will want to come back to this material after reading the chapters on trading strategies.

Chapter 6, "Volatility," is intended to answer the most commonly asked questions about the V word, a topic that is often a source of frustration and confusion. The goal is to discuss volatility conceptually, not mathematically, so that the subject is comprehensible and not intimidating. The four types of volatility are defined, and their relevance to valuing options and making trading decisions is discussed. The advanced subject of volatility skews is also introduced.

Chapter 7, "The Importance of Futures Prices," discusses the interaction of the stock market, the options market, and the futures market and how supply and demand conditions in one can affect price behavior in the others. A unique aspect of index options, as opposed to options on individual stocks, is that it is sometimes difficult to determine the "price of the underlying." Index option traders who understand futures prices know how to deal with this problem. The goal of Chapter 7 is to give off-floor traders a better understanding of how markets interact so that potential opportunities can be identified and potential traps avoided.

Section 3, "Trading Strategies," reviews several strategies and the essential elements of trade planning, strategy selection, and strategy tracking. Chapter 8, "Buying Options," focuses on long option strategies. Managing trading capital and the use of OP-EVAL3™ to develop realistic expectations about various alternatives are important topics in this chapter. Chapter 9, "Selling Options," explains the differences in market forecasting, trade planning, capital management, and risk monitoring for strategies involving short options. Chapters 10 through 13 discuss vertical spreads, straddles and strangles, ratio spreads, and time spreads. In these chapters a strategy is defined first, and its mechanics at expiration are reviewed. The delta, gamma, vega, and theta of the strategy are discussed next so that the strategy's short-term price behavior can be anticipated. Each chapter is concluded with a sample trading situation. In Chapter 14, "Case Studies," three traders are followed as they state their market forecast and then choose a strategy after analyzing some alternatives.

The focus of Section 4, "Managing Positions," is the flexibility of index options. To take advantage of this flexibility, traders must learn to use a variety of strategies and how to shift between them when the market forecast changes. This section shows how complex strategies can be used as part of a two-step trading process known as "managing positions." Sometimes, as is explained in Chapter 15, "Alternatives for Managing a Profitable Position," the initial strategy is working well, but the market forecast changes. There is much more to do than simply close a position. At other times, as explained in Chapter 16, "Alternatives for Managing an Unprofitable Position," the initial trade is showing a loss. In these cases, there are also strategies that may improve the situation other than simply taking a loss or holding on in the hope of being saved by a market reversal.

Section 5, "The Psychology of Trading," explores subjective factors that are extremely important but too often ignored. Chapter 17, "Thinking like a Trader," discusses disciplining one's mind, managing trading capital, taking profits or losses, and trading frequency. It also raises questions that should be asked—and answered—before, during, and after every trade, regardless of profit or loss. This is a valuable process for beginning and experienced traders alike, because it provides a method for developing and maintaining systematic thinking and acting. And this method helps traders reach their goal: improving results, day after day, year after year, in rising or falling markets.

Trading
Index Options

Section 1

Basic Concepts and Strategies

One

The Basics of Index Options

INTRODUCTION

Experienced option traders may be familiar with basic definitions and concepts, but there are several commonly used option terms that have different meanings when used in regard to index options. The first purpose of this chapter, therefore, is to review the important differences between options on individual stocks—equity options—and options on stock indexes—index options.

The second purpose of this chapter is to provide a list of many of the available index options, together with their underlying indexes and ticker symbols. Very few index option traders, even experienced ones, fully appreciate the range of contracts that are available to trade. Options on several broad-based market indexes and several market sector indexes exist.

BASIC DEFINITIONS

Call options give buyers the right to buy some underlying instrument at a specific price (the *strike price*) until a specific date (the *expiration date*). *Put options* give buyers the right to sell. Option buyers are not obligated; they have rights. Option sellers, however, are obligated to fulfill the terms of the contract if an assignment notice is received. A simple way of remembering the terminology is this: option owners are active; they exercise. In contrast, option sellers are passive; they are assigned. Call sellers, when assigned, are obligated to deliver the underlying instrument, that is, sell. Put sellers, when assigned, are obligated to accept delivery and pay for the underlying, that is, buy.

Indexes As Underlyings

An *index* is a consistent way of measuring the performance of a group of stocks, and differences in index construction can cause different price action even if two indexes have the same component stocks. Some of the methods of calculating index levels are price weighting, market capitalization weighting, modified equal-dollar weighting, and aggregate market value. Calculation of index levels is beyond the scope of this book, and it is not necessary that index option traders know the mathematics. However, it is important to be familiar with the price behavior of an underlying index on which you are trading options, because different indexes behave differently. A five-point move may be a common occurrence in one index, for example, and it may be a rare occurrence in another index. Do not make the mistake of thinking that all indexes behave the same!

A unique aspect of index options is that the "underlying" does not exist in the same way that individual stocks exist. Although futures contracts on some indexes and a few mutual funds aim to replicate the performance of some major indexes, neither of these instruments can be delivered against option positions, even if the same indexes are involved. Instead, the concept of cash settlement was developed to resolve the rights and obligations involved with outstanding in-the-money index options at expiration.

In a *cash settlement* an exerciser of a call option receives cash instead of stock, and the assigned call writer pays cash instead of delivering stock. A put exerciser receives cash but does not deliver stock, and the assigned put writer pays cash but does not buy stock. The details of cash settlement will be explained after some other terms have been reviewed.

Index Option

An *index option* gives the buyer the right to receive a cash payment equal to the in-the-money amount, if any, times the index multiplier. The seller of an index option is obligated to pay this amount if an assignment notice is received.

Expiration Date and Strike Price

The *expiration date* is the date on which an option will cease to exist. An option owner must exercise the right contained in the option contract prior to expiration or the right to do so expires. Typically, the third Friday of the expiration month is the last day that exercise is possible. In order to give brokerage firms time to make adjustments for any contingencies following the close of business on Friday, the actual expiration date is the Saturday following the third Friday. Some index options, such as index options with end-of-quarter expirations, expire on different dates, but these exceptions are few.

Generically, the *strike price* is the price at which a transaction in the underlying is created. For options on individual stocks, for example, an XYZ February 50 Call is the right to buy 100 shares of XYZ stock at a price of $50 per share until the expiration date in February. Since index options are settled by cash payment instead of purchase or sale of the underlying security, the strike price of an index option is a reference point, the level of an index that determines whether an option is in-the-money, at-the-money, or out-of-the-money. These terms are defined next.

In-the Money, At-the-Money, Out-of-the Money

The terms "in-the-money," "at-the-money," and "out-of-the-money" have the same meaning for index options as they do for equity options. *An index call is in-the-money* if the index level is above the strike price of the call; *an index call is out-of-the-money* if the index level is below the strike. For puts, the opposite relationship is true. *An index put is in-the-money* if the index level is below the strike price of the put; *an index put is out-of-the-money* if the index level is above the strike. *At-the-money* refers to an option whose strike price is equal to or approximately equal the index level. Figure 1–1 illustrates when calls are in-the-money, at-the-money, or out-of-the-money. The curved line in Figure 1–1 illustrates that a call option's value tends to increase as the underlying index increases in price from below the strike to at the strike to above the strike. Figure 1–2 illustrates when puts are in-the-money, at-the-money, or out-of-the-money, and the curved line illustrates that put values tend to increase as the underlying index decreases in price.

Intrinsic Value and Time Value

The total price of an option has two components: intrinsic value and time value. These terms are used in the same way for index options as they are for stock options. The *intrinsic value of a call* is the amount by which the index is above the call's strike price. The *intrinsic value of a put* is the amount by which the index is below the put's strike price. *Time value* is that portion of an option's total price in excess of intrinsic value. Figure 1–3 illustrates the concepts of intrinsic value and time value for calls and puts.

Figure 1–1 Call Options: In-the-Money, At-the-Money, Out-of-the-Money

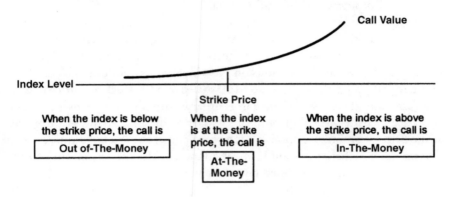

Figure 1–2 Put Options: In-the-Money, At-the-Money, Out-of-the-Money

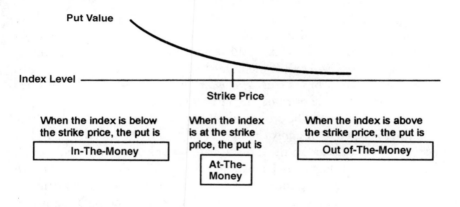

MULTIPLIERS: STOCK INDEX VERSUS FUTURES

Index option prices are quoted in amounts to the nearest sixteenth of a dollar up to $3 and to the nearest eighth of a dollar above $3. This is similar to the way stock options are quoted on a per-share basis. The actual cost of an index option is determined by multiplying the quoted price of the index option by its multiplier. An *index multiplier* is the amount by which the quoted option price is multiplied to arrive at the actual market price of an option. In listed option markets in the United States, with a few exceptions, index options have a multiplier of $100.

Consider a call option on General Motors stock. If the quoted price of a GM January 50 Call is $2, this means $2 per share. The actual cost to purchase

Figure 1–3 Put Options: In-the-Money, At-the-Money, Out-of-the-Money

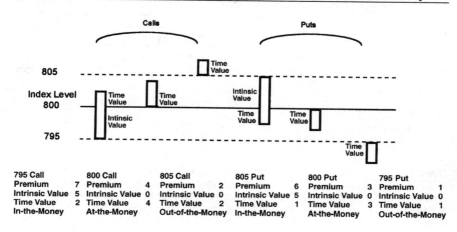

795 Call		800 Call		805 Call		805 Put		800 Put		795 Put	
Premium	7	Premium	4	Premium	2	Premium	6	Premium	3	Premium	1
Intrinsic Value	5	Intrinsic Value	0	Intrinsic Value	0	Intrinsic Value	5	Intrinsic Value	0	Intrinsic Value	0
Time Value	2	Time Value	4	Time Value	2	Time Value	1	Time Value	3	Time Value	1
In-the-Money		At-the-Money		Out-of-the-Money		In-the-Money		At-the-Money		Out-of-the-Money	

the option is $200 plus commissions and other transaction costs. To get from the $2 quoted price to the $200 actual market price, the multiplier of 100 is used. Each XYZ option covers 100 shares.

Now consider a call option on the S&P 100 Index, more commonly known as the OEX. In the case of an OEX January 800 Call quoted at 12, the actual market price is $1,200. This is calculated by multiplying the quoted price of 12 by the index multiplier of $100. This illustrates why some traders say that trading OEX index options is like trading options on a high-priced stock.

Think about it! With General Motors stock at $50 per share in the example above, the 50 Call traded for $2, or $200. The OEX index at 800 is like an $800 stock with an 800 Call trading for $12, or $1,200. Index options were designed to be similar in structure to stock options, and some traders find it helpful to think of them as such. Nevertheless, there are many differences in trading index options.

Virtually all stock index options have an index multiplier of $100 and are traded at exchanges regulated by the Securities and Exchange Commission (SEC). Options on stock index futures, however, have different multipliers, and these options are traded at futures exchanges, which are regulated by the Commodity Futures Trading Commission (CFTC). In the case of options on S&P 500 futures contracts traded at the Chicago Mercantile Exchange, the multiplier is $250. Consequently, an S&P 500 futures option quoted at 15 would cost $3,750 to purchase. This price is calculated by multiplying the stated price of 15 by the index multiplier of $250. Table 1–1 illustrates

Table 1–1 Underlying Dollar Values of Stock Options, Index Options, and Futures Contracts

	Option Type		
	Stock Option	**Stock Index Option**	**Stock Index Futures Option**
Quoted price	$15 per share	15	15
Multiplier	100	$100	$250
Actual market price in dollars	$1,500 (15 × $100)	$1,500 (15 × $100)	$3,750 (15 × $250)

Note: Stock options and stock index options are traded at four option exchanges, the American Stock Exchange, the Chicago Board Options Exchange, the Philadelphia Stock Exchange, and the Pacific Exchange, which are all regulated by the Securities and Exchange Commission (SEC). Stock index futures options are traded at futures exchanges, which are regulated by the Commodity Futures Trading Commission (CFTC).

how options on different underlying instruments have different multipliers and, as a result, different actual market prices.

EXERCISE AND ASSIGNMENT: EQUITY OPTIONS

For options on individual stocks, the "underlying" is simply the underlying stock, and the act of exercising an equity option creates a stock transaction. The exerciser of an equity call pays cash in the amount of the strike price plus commissions and receives 100 shares of the underlying stock for each option exercised. The exercise of a call on an individual stock results in a long stock position unless the exerciser holds a short stock position, in which case the stock purchased is delivered against the short position. If the short stock position exists on a share-for-share basis with the equity calls being exercised, then the exercise of those calls closes out the short stock position and eliminates any market exposure.

An exerciser of a put on an individual stock delivers 100 shares of the underlying stock for each put exercised and receives cash equal to the strike price less commissions. If no stock is owned, exercising an equity put creates a short stock position. If, however, stock is owned on a share-for-share basis with the exercised equity puts, then those shares are sold and the long stock position is closed.

Conclusion: Exercise or assignment of an option on an individual stock creates a transaction in the underlying stock, and the market exposure of an unhedged equity option is replaced by a position in the underlying stock.

EXERCISE AND ASSIGNMENT: CASH-SETTLED INDEX OPTIONS

Cash settlement means that an option exerciser receives cash and an assigned option writer pays cash. The amount of cash transferred from option writer to option owner equals the option's intrinsic value times the index multiplier. After the transfer, neither the buyer nor the seller has any remaining market exposure.

Conclusion: Exercise or assignment of an index option does not create a transaction in the underlying, and the market exposure of an index option position is eliminated.

Table 1–2 compares the different impacts that exercise and assignment have on equity option positions and index option positions.

AMERICAN-STYLE VERSUS EUROPEAN-STYLE INDEX OPTIONS

American-style and European-style index options differ in several ways: when they can be exercised, when their expiration settlement values are determined, and whether or not they can be covered.

Exercise Time

Options that are *American-style exercise* may be exercised at any time prior to expiration, so writers of these options must be aware that early assignment is possible. In order to exercise an American-style index option prior to expiration, the same procedures for exercising equity options must be followed, and proper notifications must be made prior to established deadlines.

Options that are *European-style exercise* may be exercised only on the last day prior to expiration. Consequently, early assignment of short positions in European-style options is not a possibility.

Since all options on individual stocks traded in the United States are American-style, the unique aspects of European-style options are of little concern to traders of these options. There are, however, both American-style exercise index options and European-style exercise index options in the United States. Consequently, index option traders need to know the differences between the two exercise styles and how to pair a particular strategy with the right index option.

Assignment is random. Be it an option on an individual stock or an option on an index, when an American-style option is exercised early, a random process known as *assignment* results in the selection of an option writer to fulfill the

Table 1–2 Exercise and Assignment: Equity Options versus Index Options

	Equity Options			
	Long Equity Call	**Short Equity Call**	**Long Equity Put**	**Short Equity Put**
Opening transaction	Buy equity call (pay cash)	Sell (or write) equity call (receive cash)	Buy equity put (pay cash)	Sell (or write) equity put (receive cash)
Position	Long call	Short call	Long put	Short put
Action/event	Exercise	Receive assignment notice	Exercise	Receive assignment notice
Consequence of the action	Buy stock at strike (pay cash)	Sell stock at strike (receive cash)	Sell stock at strike (receive cash)	Buy stock at strike (pay cash)
Final position	1. Long stock, if no short-stock position existed	1. Short stock, if no long-stock position existed	1. Short stock, if no long-stock position existed	1. Long stock, if no short-stock position existed
	2. Flat, if equal short-stock position existed	2. Flat, if equal long-stock position existed	2. Flat, if equal long-stock position existed	2. Flat, if equal short-stock position existed

	Index Options			
	Long Index Call	**Short Index Call**	**Long Index Put**	**Short Index Put**
Opening transaction	Buy index call (pay cash)	Sell (or write) index call (receive cash)	Buy index put (pay cash)	Sell (or write) index put (receive cash)
Position	Long call	Short call	Long put	Short put
Action/event	Exercise	Receive assignment notice	Exercise	Receive assignment notice
Consequence of the action	Receive cash equal to the in-the-money amount	Pay cash equal to the in-the-money amount	Receive cash equal to the in-the-money amount	Pay cash equal to the in-the-money amount
Final position	Cash: no market exposure (profit or loss depends on initial cost of call)	Cash: no market exposure (profit or loss depends on initial selling price of call)	Cash: no market exposure (profit or loss depends on initial cost of put)	Cash: no market exposure (profit or loss depends on initial selling price of put)

demands of the option exerciser. The process goes like this: An option owner instructs a brokerage firm to exercise a particular option, and that firm notifies the Options Clearing Corporation (OCC), the central clearinghouse and guarantor of performance of every options exchange in the United States. The OCC randomly selects a brokerage firm with one or more customers with a matching short option. The selected firm then chooses an appropriate customer either by random choice or by first in, first out. It should be noted that while the option owner made the exercise notification before the market closed, the option seller is not informed about being assigned until the morning of the next trading day prior to the opening. A specific example of these procedures will be presented later in this chapter.

On expiration day the process is different. At expiration, both European-style and American-style index options are subject to *automatic exercise,* a process by which the Options Clearing Corporation automatically exercises and assigns all in-the-money index options and debits and credits the appropriate funds to brokerage firms' accounts, which, in turn, debit or credit customer accounts.

Reasons for early exercise.   Early exercise of American-style options occurs for rational reasons. American-style options on individual stocks are generally exercised early because of dividend payments. American-style index options are typically exercised early by professional traders who are attempting to profit from perceived arbitrage opportunities between stock index futures and stock index options. A discussion of arbitrage is beyond the scope of this book, but early assignment of index options typically occurs only when an option is deep in-the-money and close to expiration.

Options that are exercised or assigned early *are subject to standard commissions* as if the option were sold or repurchased in the market. Therefore, early exercise is not a method of avoiding commissions and other transaction charges.

Determination of Settlement Value

Index *settlement value at expiration* is the final settlement value of an index at expiration. This value is important, because it is this index level and its relationship to the strike price that determine whether an index option is in-the-money or out-of-the-money and, consequently, whether an exercise or assignment is made and how much money, if any, changes hands. Before the two types of expiration settlements are explained, daily settlement value must be explained.

An index's *daily settlement value* is similar to a stock's closing price. When closing prices for all stocks in an index have been established, an index's daily closing price, or daily settlement value, is calculated using those closing stock prices.

An index's expiration settlement value, however, may be determined by one of two methods. One method is based on closing stock prices, p.m. settlement, and the other method is based on opening prices, a.m. settlement.

P.M. settlement. Afternoon settlement, or p.m. settlement, is the most straightforward method of determining an index's expiration settlement value; it is the same index level as the daily settlement value. Closing prices of stocks in an index are used to calculate the index settlement level. Cash payments and receipts from exercise and assignment are determined based on that index level.

A.M. settlement. Morning settlement, or a.m. settlement, is based on opening prices the morning after the last day of option trading. The last day of trading for options subject to a.m. settlement is typically a Thursday, so Friday opening prices are used to calculate settlement values of those indexes. When opening prices of all stocks in such an index have been established, then the index settlement value is calculated using those opening prices. As mentioned earlier, all index options are subject to automatic exercise, so traders need not worry about exercise notification procedures on expiration day.

Settlement values of indexes on which a.m.-settled options are traded have their own ticker symbols. For example, the ticker symbol for the cash settlement level of options on the S&P 500 Index (SPX index options), is SET. It should be noted that on some expiration days the settlement values of some indexes can be delayed for several hours owing to delayed openings in individual stocks. An expiration settlement value cannot be determined until opening prices for all stocks in an index have been established.

What Does "Covered" Mean?

A *covered call* on an individual stock is a short call that is part of a position in which either (1) the underlying stock is owned, (2) a call with a lower strike is owned, or (3) a call with an equal strike and a later expiration date is owned. A *covered put* on an individual stock is a short put that is part of a position in which either (1) a put with a higher strike is owned or (2) a put with an equal strike and later expiration date is owned.

In any of these cases, an early assignment of a short option can be met by exercising an owned option or by delivering the owned stock, in the case of a short call. There is no risk of overnight market fluctuations, because the obligation of receiving or delivering stock is covered by the owned option or owned stock.

Short American-style cash-settled index options.   The situation is different with short American-style cash-settled index options! These short options are not "covered" by any of the alternatives listed above, because these options are subject to cash settlement and because an assigned option writer does not receive notice of the assignment until the morning after exercise occurs. Consequently, a long American-style index option, which was offsetting a short American-style index option, is subject to overnight fluctuations without the counteracting impact of the short index option, which was assigned. Even if the long option is sold at the opening on the day notification is received, there is risk that the long option could drop dramatically in price. Exercising the long index option on the morning an assignment notice is received does not "cover" the assignment of a short index option, because the amount of cash to be received from exercising is not determined until the end of that trading day, when the daily settlement is determined.

Consider the case of Philip, who purchased an OEX March 825 Call for 14 ($1,400) and sold an OEX March 835 Call for 8 ($800), thus creating the 825–835 Call spread for a net cost of 6 ($600). Assume that on the Tuesday before the March expiration the OEX settles at 860 and Philip's long 825 Call and short 835 Call settled at 35 and 25, respectively. Note that both calls, in this example, settled at prices equal to their intrinsic values. Further assume that on Wednesday morning Philip receives an assignment notice: His short 835 Call has been assigned.

The assignment notice means that Philip's short 835 Call position is closed out and his account is debited for 25, or $2,500. This amount is equal to the intrinsic value of the call and is calculated by subtracting the strike price of 835 from the index level of 860 and multiplying the difference by the index multiplier of $100.

Philip is now left with his long 825 Call. Even though Philip's long 825 Call closed at 35 on Tuesday, there is absolutely no guaranty that it will open at or above that price on Wednesday.

If Philip is able to sell his 825 Call at 35 ($3,500), then he will realize a profit of 4 ($400) on his spread. His 825 Call, purchased for 14 ($1,400) in this case and sold for 35 ($3,500), earned a profit of 21 ($2,100). His short 835 Call, however, was sold for 8 ($800) and closed out by early assignment at 25 ($2,500), thus incurring a loss of 17 ($1,700). The net profit of 4 ($400), therefore, is the difference between the profit on the 825 Call and the loss on the 835 Call.

But suppose Philip cannot sell his 825 Call at 35! Imagine a large adverse market fluctuation in which Philip sells his 825 Call at 15 ($1,500). In this case the result is a total loss of 16 ($1,600), more than Philip's original investment of 6 ($600)!

Make sure you understand the calculations: Philip's original position was long the 825 Call at 14 and short the 835 Call at 8 for a net cost of 6. Selling the 825 Call for 15 results in a profit of 1. Being assigned on the short 835 Call at 25 results in a loss of 17. Consequently, the net loss is 16. This example illustrates the potentially unlimited risk of spreads involving short American-style cash-settled index options.

Short European-style options. Because European-style index options cannot be exercised early, spreads involving these index options truly are limited in risk. Short European-style index call options can be covered by long calls with the same underlying index, same expiration month, and a lower strike. Also, short European-style put options can be covered by long puts with the same underlying index, same expiration month, and a higher strike.

Consider Sally, who purchased an SPX September 870 Put at 17 ($1,700) and sold an SPX September 855 Put for 7 ($700), thus creating the 855–870 Put spread for 10 ($1,000). Sally truly has a position with risk limited to 10 ($1,000), the net premium paid. There is no risk of early assignment of the short SPX put, because it is subject to European-style exercise. Sally can hold the total position until expiration, or she can sell the entire position at any time prior to expiration. She also has the ability to close out one option in the spread and assume the risk of the remaining position. In this case, if she sold the long option first, she must be qualified by her broker to assume the risk of uncovered short index options. This risk is unlimited in the case of uncovered short calls and substantial in the case of uncovered short puts.

OPTIONS BASED ON THE DOW JONES AVERAGES

October 6, 1997, was the beginning of a new and exciting era in the options business. That is when options based on the three best-known Dow Jones averages began trading. Important facts to know about these options are the following.

Ticker Symbols

Options based on the Dow Jones Industrial Average have the root symbol DJX. The symbol for options based on the Dow Jones Transportation Average is DTX, and DUX is the symbol for options based on the Dow Jones Utilities Average.

8000 or $80: What Is the Index?

The DJX Index is defined as one one-hundredth (0.01) of the Dow Jones Industrial Average. The DTX Index is one-tenth (0.10) of the Dow Jones Transportation Average, and the DUX Index is the full value of the Dow Jones Utilities Average. This means that, if the Dow Jones Industrial Average is trading at 7,846, then the DJX Index will be 78.46. If the Dow Jones Transportation Average is 2,886.30, then the DTX Index is 288.63; and if the Dow Jones Utilities Average is 228.75, then the DUX Index is also 228.75.

Strikes, Expirations, and Ticker Symbols

Options based on the Dow Jones averages have expirations on the March cycle. In addition, there will be two near-term expirations available and LEAPS, long-term options, with expirations up to two years. If today is October 5, 1999, for example, there will be call and put series expiring in October, November, and December of 1999, March and December of 2000, and December of 2001.

Strike prices are every 1.00 on the DJX, which is similar to 100 points on the Dow Jones Industrial Average. With the DJX at 78.46 and the Dow Jones Industrial Average at 7,846, for example, option strikes on the DJX are available beginning from 74.00, 75.00, 76.00, etc., up to 81.00, 82.00, and 83.00. For the DTX and DUX, strike price intervals are 5.00. There will be a minimum of five strikes above and below the current index level.

Exercise Is European-Style

The Dow options *cannot* be exercised early! These European-style options can be sold individually or as part of a spread position without concern that early assignment will occur.

A.M. Cash Settlement at Expiration

As described earlier for other index options at expiration, in-the-money Dow options are subject to cash settlement. Also, DJX, DTX, and DUX options are subject to a.m. settlement. This means that, generally, the last day of trading is the Thursday preceding the third Friday of the expiration month. Expiration settlement value is then determined using opening prices for each of the component securities on expiration Friday. Traders accustomed to index options that are subject to p.m. settlement at expiration should review the section above describing expiration procedures for these options.

Table 1–3 summarizes the contract specifications for the DJX, DTX, and DUX options.

OTHER AVAILABLE INDEXES

Few traders are aware of the wide range of available index options. There are both broad-based market indexes and market sector indexes on which options are traded. If a trader believes that health care stocks, retail stocks, or chemical

---

Table 1–3 Stock Index Options Based on Dow Jones Averages

Options Based on the Dow Jones Industrials: DJX Index = 1/100 of the DJIA

Example:	If the DJIA is 8,175, the DJX is 81.75
Strike prices:	Every 1.00: 79.00, 80.00, 81.00, 82.00, etc.
Exercise style:	European (early exercise is *not* permitted)
Last day of trading:	Thursday before third Friday of expiration month
Expiration settlement:	a.m. settlement; opening prices on expiration Friday determine index value for cash-settlement transfers.

Options Based on the Dow Jones Transports: DTX Index = 1/10 of the DJTA

Example:	If the DJT is 2,980, the DTX is 298.00
Strike prices:	Every 5.00: 285.00, 290.00, 295.00, 300.00, etc.
Exercise style:	European (early exercise is *not* permitted)
Last day of trading:	Thursday before third Friday of expiration month
Expiration settlement:	a.m. settlement; opening prices on expiration Friday determine index value for cash-settlement transfers.

Options Based on the Dow Jones Utilities: DUX Index = Full Value of the DJUA

Example:	If the DJUA is 228.50, the DUX is 228.50
Strike prices:	Every 5.00: 220.00, 225.00, 230.00, 235.00, etc.
Exercise style:	European (early exercise is *not* permitted)
Last day of trading:	Thursday before third Friday of expiration month
Expiration settlement:	a.m. settlement; opening prices on expiration Friday determine index value for cash-settlement transfers.

Table 1–4 Popular Options on Broad-Based Indexes

Index Name	Symbol	Exercise Style	a.m./p.m. Settlement	Expiration Settlement Symbol	Exchange
S&P 100	OEX	American	p.m.	n.a.	CBOE
S&P 500	SPX	European	a.m.	SET	CBOE
Dow Jones Industrials	DJX	European	a.m.	DJS	CBOE
Value Line	VLE	European	p.m.	n.a.	PHLX
NYSE Composite	NYA	European	a.m.	NYX	CBOE
NASDAQ-100	NDX	European	a.m.	NDS	CBOE
Institutional	XII	European	a.m.	XSV	AMEX
S&P Small Cap 600	SML	European	a.m.	XSM	CBOE
S&P 500/Barra Value	SVX	European	a.m.	SVS	CBOE
S&P 500/Barra Growth	SGX	European	a.m.	SGS	CBOE

stocks are about to make a move, there is a good possibility that index options in that area are available. Table 1–4 lists several popular broad-based indexes and important contract specifications, such as the ticker symbol, the style of exercise, the method of settlement, the expiration settlement symbol, and the exchange where traded. Table 1–5 contains similar information for popular sector indexes.

SUMMARY

Although terminology is generally consistent for options, there are some technical differences between options on individual stocks and options on indexes. First, all listed index options in the United States are subject to cash settlement. Cash settlement means that index option owners have the right to receive cash equal to the in-the-money amount, if any, and index option writers are obligated to pay this amount. The in-the-money amount is calculated by multiplying the difference between the settlement index value and the option strike price by the index multiplier.

Both American-style and European-style exercise index options exist in the listed options markets in the United States. Options subject to American-style exercise may be exercised at any time prior to expiration, and those subject to European-style exercise may be exercised only at expiration.

The possibility of early assignment means that short, American-style cash-settled index options cannot be covered by long options with the same underlying index in the same way that short American-style options on individual stocks can be covered by long options with the same underlying or by long stock.

Table 1–5 Popular Options on Sector Indexes

Index Name	Symbol	Exercise Style	a.m./p.m. Settlement	Expiration Settlement Symbol	Exchange
Dow Jones Transports	DTX	European	a.m.	DNS	CBOE
Dow Jones Utilities	DUX	European	a.m.	DUS	CBOE
Automotive	AUX	European	a.m.	AXS	CBOE
S&P Banks	BIX	European	a.m.	BBS	CBOE
Biotechnology	BTK	European	a.m.	BTS	AMEX
S&P Chemical	CEX	European	a.m.	CXS	CBOE
Morgan Stanley Consumer	CMR	European	a.m.	CMO	AMEX
Morgan Stanley Cyclical	CYC	European	a.m.	CYO	AMEX
Pharmaceutical	DRG	European	a.m.	DRO	AMEX
CBOE Gaming	GAX	European	a.m.	GXS	CBOE
Goldman Sachs Multimedia	GIP	European	a.m.	GPZ	CBOE
Super Cap	HIX	European	a.m.	HFX	PHLX
Hong Kong	HKO	European	p.m.	n.a.	AMEX
S&P Insurance	IUX	European	a.m.	IUS	CBOE
Japan	JPN	European	a.m.	JPV	AMEX
Morgan Stanley High Technology	MSH	European	a.m.	MHV	AMEX
Networking	NWX	European	a.m.	NVW	AMEX
Phone Sector	PNX	European	a.m.	POX	PHLX
PSE Technology	PSE	European	a.m.	PTO	PSE
Semiconductor	SOX	American	p.m.	n.a.	PHLX
Semiconductor	SXE	European	a.m.	SX	PHLX
S&P Transportation	TRX	European	a.m.	TRS	CBOE
CBOE Technology	TXX	European	a.m.	TTS	CBOE
Utility	UTY	European	p.m.	n.a.	PHLX
Gold/Silver	XAU	American	p.m.	n.a.	PHLX
Computer Technology	XCI	American	p.m.	n.a.	AMEX
Natural Gas	XNG	European	a.m.	NGV	AMEX
CBOE Oil	OIX	European	a.m.	OXS	CBOE
AMEX Oil	XOI	American	p.m.	n.a.	AMEX

P.M. settlement means that closing prices of stocks in the index on the last day of trading are used to determine the expiration settlement value of an index. The last day of trading for p.m.-settled options is usually the third Friday of the expiration month. A.M. settlement means that opening prices on the morning after the last day of trading are used to determine the expiration settlement value of an index. The last day of trading for a.m.-settled options is usually the Thursday before the third Friday of the expiration month. All in-the-money index options in the United States are currently subject to automatic exercise at expiration; therefore, it is not necessary for index option owners to be concerned about exercise procedures on the last day of trading. Index options are available on several broad-based market indexes and several market sector indexes.

TWO

Diagrams of Basic to Advanced Strategies

INTRODUCTION

O
ptions give traders more strategy alternatives and, therefore, more than one way to approach a given market forecast. A good way to understand the many alternatives options offer is to see them graphically. Expiration profit and loss diagrams achieve this objective by showing the maximum theoretical risk of a strategy, the profit potential, and the break-even point. Profit and loss diagrams, however, do not answer every question a trader might ask about a strategy. One question not answered is how a strategy performs over a specific time period prior to expiration. Nevertheless, these diagrams do illustrate much of what a trader needs to know about a particular strategy.

This chapter introduces 22 different option strategies, starting with basic and progressing to advanced. These are, however, not all the possible strategies. Option strategies are limited only by one's imagination.

Although many people have seen the diagrams presented in this chapter, there is a difference between having seen them and being able to draw them yourself. The ability to draw profit and loss diagrams demonstrates a true understanding of how options work and what the potential profits and risks of a strategy are. Many of the strategies presented in this chapter must be established in a margin account and require a margin deposit, but these factors and commissions and other transaction costs are not included in the examples.

CREATING DIAGRAMS

There are six steps to drawing profit and loss diagrams. Because this book is intended for experienced option users, this process will be described only briefly. For those interested in a more thorough grounding in drawing diagrams, the process is described in detail in Chapter 2 of *Options for the Stock Investor* (McGraw-Hill, 1996). Another source for learning is a free handout distributed by The Options Institute, the educational arm of The Chicago Board Options Exchange, entitled "Teach Yourself to Draw Basic to Advanced Option Strategies." This free handout may be obtained by calling 1-800-OPTIONS or 312-786-7760.

The six-step process for drawing profit and loss diagrams is as follows:

Step 1   Describe the opening transaction completely.

An example of a complete description is: "Buy 1 OEX June 1999, 720-Strike Call at 2½." It is not enough to say "buy a call," because this does not provide sufficient information to create a diagram.

Step 2   Create a profit and loss grid on which the diagram will be drawn.

A profit and loss grid consists of a horizontal axis, X, and a vertical axis, Y. The horizontal axis must be sufficiently wide to accommodate an appropriate range of the underlying index. The vertical axis must be sufficiently long to account for potential profit and loss.

Step 3   Select an index level and calculate the option's value at expiration.

An option's value at expiration is its intrinsic value, which is either positive or zero. For example, if an index is 727 at expiration, the 720 Call has a value of 7 and the 720 Put has a value of zero. If a strategy contains more than one option, the value of all options must be determined.

Step 4   Calculate the profit or loss.

For an option that was initially purchased, profit or loss is calculated by subtracting the purchase price from the value at expiration. For the purpose of drawing diagrams it is assumed that a purchased option is sold at its value at expiration. For example, if the index is 727 at expiration, a 720 Call purchased for 2½ has a value of 7. The result is a profit of 4½, or $450, not including transaction costs (value of 7 minus purchase price of 2½). In the case of an option that was initially sold, profit or loss is calculated by subtracting the value at expiration from the selling price. In this case, it is assumed that a sold option is repurchased at its expiration value. Consider the example of a 725 Put sold for 3¼. If the index is 727 at expiration, this option will expire worthless. Its "value" is zero, and the resulting profit is 3¼, or $325, before transaction costs.

Step 5   Plot the profit or loss on the grid.

Chart profits or losses by placing dots above or below the appropriate index levels by the appropriate number of units. Chart a profit of 3 with an index level of 727, for example, by placing a dot three units above the index level of 727 on the horizontal axis.

Step 6   Repeat steps 3 through 5 until the diagram is complete.

Gradually, enough points will be plotted on the profit and loss grid so that a graphical representation of the strategy appears.

TWENTY-TWO STRATEGIES

Each of the following strategies is represented in a corresponding graph. In each graph, the straight line is a diagram of a strategy's profit and loss at expiration, and the curved line is an estimate of profit and loss at some time prior to expiration. Each strategy includes an example; comments about the potential profit, maximum risk, break-even, desired market action, the effect of passage of time toward expiration, and the effect of an increase in volatility; and a note about when the strategy is appropriate and where it is discussed later in the book.

Figure 2–1: Long Call

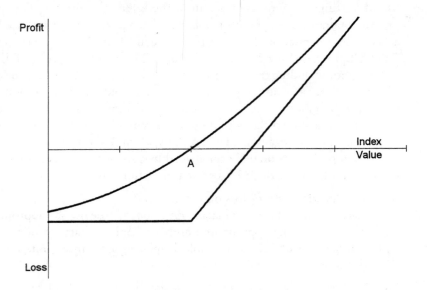

Example: Buy 1 Call, Strike A

Maximum profit potential: Unlimited

Maximum risk potential: Limited to premium paid for the call

Break-even point at expiration: Strike A plus premium paid

Desired movement: Bullish

Effect of passage of time: Negative. Options decrease in value with
                                     the passage of time if other factors remain
                                     constant.

Effect of increase in volatility: Positive. Options increase in value with an
                                     increase in volatility if other factors remain
                                     constant.

Comment: This basic strategy can be an excellent
                                     choice for a short-term bullish forecast when
                                     volatility is low and expected to remain
                                     constant or increase. Successful application
                                     depends on making a three-part forecast:
                                     underlying price movement, time, and
                                     volatility. Buying calls is discussed in depth
                                     in Chapter 8, "Buying Options."

Figure 2–2: Short Call

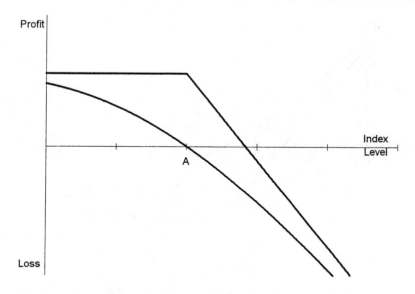

Example:	Sell 1 Call, Strike A
Maximum profit potential:	Limited to premium received
Maximum risk potential:	Unlimited
Break-even point at expiration:	Strike A plus premium received
Desired movement:	Neutral or moderately bearish
Effect of passage of time:	Positive. Options decrease in value with the passage of time if other factors remain constant.
Effect of increase in volatility:	Negative. Options increase in value with an increase in volatility if other factors remain constant.
Comment:	Suited only for experienced index option traders who qualify for the highest level of risk, this strategy is appropriate when a short-term market forecast is neutral or moderately bearish and when volatility is expected to remain constant or decrease. Successful application depends on making a three-part forecast: underlying price movement, time, and volatility. Selling calls is discussed in Chapter 9, "Selling Options."

Figure 2–3: Long Put

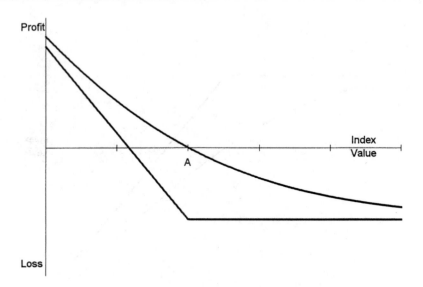

Example:	Buy 1 Put, Strike A
Maximum profit potential:	Substantial. The profit potential is limited to the index falling to zero less the premium paid.
Maximum risk potential:	Limited to premium paid for the put
Break-even point at expiration:	Strike A minus premium paid
Desired movement:	Bearish
Effect of passage of time:	Negative. Options decrease in value with the passage of time if other factors remain constant.
Effect of increase in volatility:	Positive. Options increase in value with an increase in volatility if other factors remain constant.
Comment:	This basic strategy can be an excellent choice for a short-term bearish forecast when volatility is expected to remain constant or increase. Successful application depends on making a three-part forecast: underlying price movement, time, and volatility. Buying puts is discussed in Chapter 8, "Buying Options."

Figure 2–4: Short Put

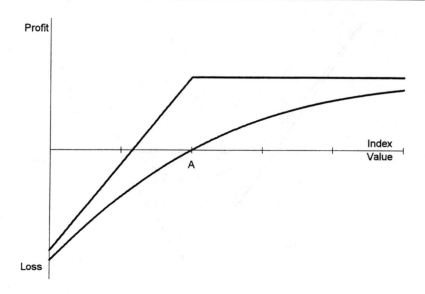

Example:	Sell 1 Put, Strike A
Maximum profit potential:	Limited to the premium received
Maximum risk potential:	Substantial. The potential risk is limited to the index falling to zero less the premium received.
Break-even point at expiration:	Strike A minus the premium received
Desired movement:	Neutral to moderately bullish
Effect of passage of time:	Positive. Options decrease in value with the passage of time if other factors remain constant.
Effect of increase in volatility:	Negative. Options increase in value with an increase in volatility if other factors remain constant.
Comment:	Suited only for experienced index option traders who qualify for the highest level of risk, this strategy is appropriate when a short-term market forecast is neutral or moderately bullish and when volatility is expected to remain constant or decrease. Successful application depends on making a three-part forecast: underlying price movement, time, and volatility. Selling puts is discussed in Chapter 9, "Selling Options."

Figure 2–5: Long Straddle

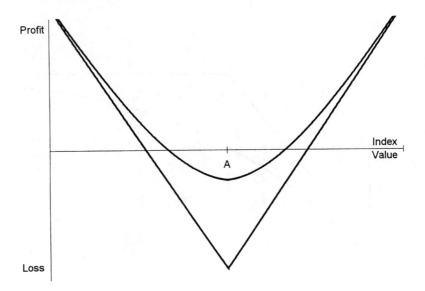

Example:	Buy 1 Call, Strike A, *and* Buy 1 Put, Strike A
Maximum profit potential:	Unlimited in the case of a price rise; substantial in the case of a price decline
Maximum risk potential:	Limited to the total premiums paid
Break-even point at expiration:	Two points: Strike A plus the total premiums paid and Strike A minus the total premiums paid
Desired movement:	A large movement in either direction (high volatility)
Effect of passage of time:	Double negative (long two options). Options decrease in value with the passage of time if other factors remain constant.
Effect of increase in volatility:	Double positive. Options increase in value with an increase in volatility if other factors remain constant.
Comment:	While simple in concept, buying a straddle is difficult to implement. Careful attention must be paid to the three-part market forecast (price, time, and volatility) to determine the profit or loss impact on the total strategy. Buying straddles is discussed in Chapter 11, "Straddles and Strangles."

Figure 2–6: Short Straddle

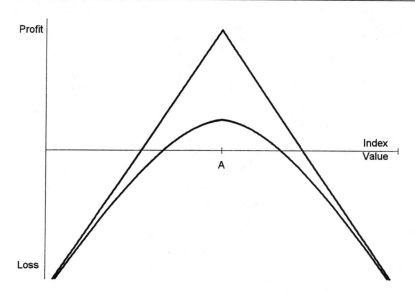

Example:	Sell 1 Call, Strike A, *and* Sell 1 Put, Strike A
Maximum profit potential:	Limited to the premiums received
Maximum risk potential:	Unlimited in the case of a price rise; substantial in the case of a price decline
Break-even point at expiration:	Two points: Strike A plus the total premiums received and Strike A minus the total premiums received
Desired movement:	None (low volatility)
Effect of passage of time:	Double positive (short two options). Options decrease in value with the passage of time if other factors remain constant.
Effect of increase in volatility:	Double negative. Options increase in value with an increase in volatility if other factors remain constant.
Comment:	Suited only for experienced index option traders who qualify for the highest level of risk, selling a straddle is appropriate when a short-term market forecast is for neutral price action and when volatility is expected to remain constant or decrease. Selling straddles is discussed in Chapter 11, "Straddles and Strangles."

Figure 2–7: Long Strangle

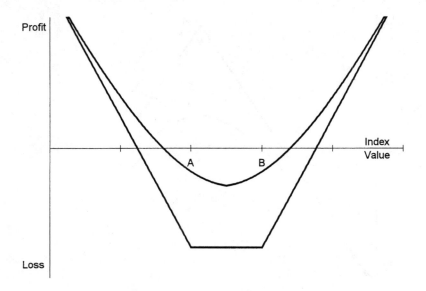

Example:	Buy 1 Call, Strike B, *and* Buy 1 Put, Strike A
Maximum profit potential:	Unlimited in the case of a price rise; substantial in the case of a price decline
Maximum risk potential:	Limited to the total premiums paid
Break-even point at expiration:	Two points: Strike B plus the total premiums paid and Strike A minus the total premiums paid
Desired movement:	A large movement in either direction (high volatility)
Effect of passage of time:	Double negative (long two options). Options decrease in value with the passage of time if other factors remain constant.
Effect of increase in volatility:	Double positive. Options increase in value with an increase in volatility if other factors remain constant.
Comment:	Careful attention must be paid to the three-part market forecast (price, time, and volatility) to determine the profit or loss impact on the total strategy. Buying a strangle is not "better" in an absolute sense than buying a comparable straddle. Rather, there is a trade-off. The strangle is less expensive than a comparable straddle, but the break-even points of the strangle are farther apart. Strangles are discussed in Chapter 11, "Straddles and Strangles."

Figure 2–8: Short Strangle

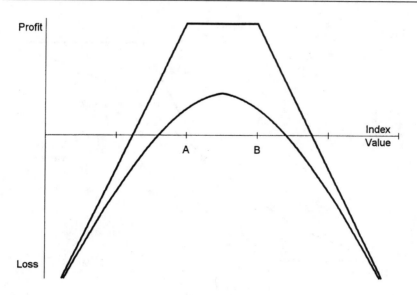

Example:	Sell 1 Call, Strike B, *and*
	Sell 1 Put, Strike A
Maximum profit potential:	Limited to the premiums received
Maximum risk potential:	Unlimited in the case of a price rise; substantial in the case of a price decline
Break-even point at expiration:	Two points: Strike B plus the total premiums received and Strike A minus the total premiums received
Desired movement:	None (low volatility)
Effect of passage of time:	Double positive (short two options). Options decrease in value with the passage of time if other factors remain constant.
Effect of increase in volatility:	Double negative. Options increase in value with an increase in volatility if other factors remain constant.
Comment:	Suitable only for experienced index option traders who qualify for the highest level of risk, selling a strangle is appropriate when the forecast is for neutral price action and volatility is expected to remain constant or decrease. Selling a strangle is not "better" in an absolute sense than selling a comparable straddle. Rather, there is a trade-off. The break-even points for a strangle are farther apart than for a comparable straddle, but a short strangle takes in less premium. Strangles are discussed in Chapter 11, "Straddles and Strangles."

Figure 2–9: Long Call Spread

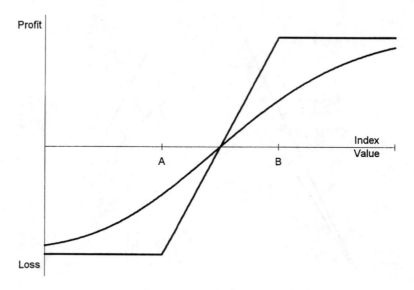

Example: Buy 1 Call, Strike A, *and*
                                  Sell 1 Call, Strike B

Maximum profit potential: Limited to the difference between Strikes A
                                  and B minus the net premium paid

Maximum risk potential: Limited to the net premium paid

Break-even point at expiration: Strike A plus the net premium paid

Desired movement: Bullish

Effect of passage of time: Negative, but less so than with the outright
                                  purchase of a call with Strike A

Effect of increase in volatility: Slightly positive. The call spread value will
                                  increase if volatility increases and other
                                  factors remain constant.

Comment: This can be an excellent strategy for
                                  attempting to profit from a bullish forecast
                                  while decreasing maximum risk and the
                                  negative effects of time erosion and/or a
                                  decrease in volatility. The trade-off is that
                                  profit potential is limited. Traders who use
                                  call spreads with American-style index
                                  options must be careful of the risk of early
                                  assignment of the short call. This is
                                  discussed in Chapter 10, "Vertical Spreads."

Figure 2–10: Short Call Spread

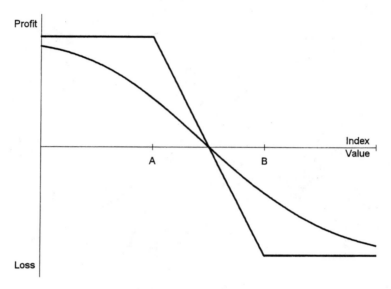

Example:	Sell 1 Call, Strike A, *and* Buy 1 Call, Strike B
Maximum profit potential:	Limited to the net premium received
Maximum risk potential:	Limited to the difference between Strikes A and B minus the net premium received
Break-even point at expiration:	Strike A plus the net premium received
Desired movement:	Neutral to moderately bearish
Effect of passage of time:	Positive but less so than with the outright sale of a call with Strike A
Effect of increase in volatility:	Slightly negative. The call spread value will increase if volatility increases and other factors remain constant.
Comment:	This can be an excellent strategy for attempting to profit from a neutral forecast while decreasing the risk of an increase in volatility. The trade-off is that maximum profit potential and the potential benefit from a decrease in volatility are decreased. Traders who use call spreads with American-style index options must be careful of the risk of early assignment of the short call. This is discussed in Chapter 10, "Vertical Spreads."

Figure 2–11: Long Put Spread

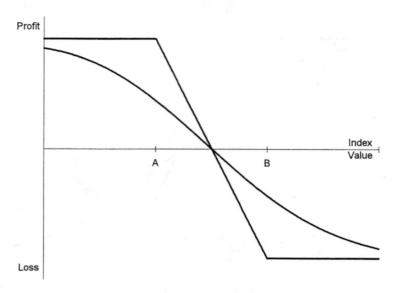

Example:	Buy 1 Put, Strike B, *and* Sell 1 Put, Strike A
Maximum profit potential:	Limited to the difference between Strikes A and B minus the net premium paid
Maximum risk potential:	Limited to the net premium paid
Break-even point at expiration:	Strike B minus the net premium paid
Desired movement:	Bearish
Effect of passage of time:	Negative, but less so than with the outright purchase of a put with Strike B
Effect of increase in volatility:	Slightly positive. The put spread value will increase if volatility increases and other factors remain constant.
Comment:	This can be an excellent strategy for attempting to profit from a bearish forecast while decreasing strategy risk and the negative effects of time erosion and a decrease in volatility. The trade-off is that profit potential is limited. Traders who use put spreads with American-style index options must be careful of the risk of early assignment of the short put. This is discussed in Chapter 10, "Vertical Spreads."

Figure 2–12: Short Put Spread

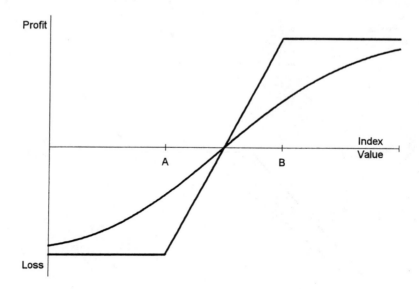

Example:	Sell 1 Put, Strike B, *and* Buy 1 Put, Strike A
Maximum profit potential:	Limited to the net premium received
Maximum risk potential:	Limited to the difference between Strikes A and B minus the net premium received
Break-even point at expiration:	Strike B minus the net premium received
Desired movement:	Neutral to moderately bullish
Effect of passage of time:	Positive, but less so than with the outright sale of a put with Strike B
Effect of increase in volatility:	Slightly negative. The put spread value will increase if volatility increases and other factors remain constant.
Comment:	This can be an excellent strategy for attempting to profit from a neutral to moderately bullish forecast while decreasing both the maximum theoretical risk and the risk of an increase in volatility. The trade-off is that maximum profit potential and the potential benefit from a decrease in volatility are decreased. Traders who use put spreads with American-style index options must be careful of the risk of early assignment of the short put. This is discussed in Chapter 10, "Vertical Spreads."

Figure 2–13: Long Split-Strike Synthetic

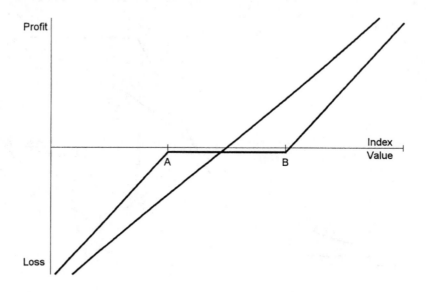

Example:	Buy 1 Call, Strike B, *and* Sell 1 Put, Strike A
Maximum profit potential:	Unlimited
Maximum risk potential:	Substantial—from the short put. (See the discussion of the risk of short puts from Strategy 4.)
Break-even point at expiration:	Strike B plus the net premium paid (or Strike A minus the net premium received)
Desired movement:	Bullish
Effect of passage of time:	Neutral. The decrease of the short put makes up for the decrease of the long call.
Effect of increase in volatility:	Neutral, for the same reason as for the passage of time.
Comment:	The presence of a short, uncovered put makes this strategy appropriate only for experienced traders who qualify for the highest level of risk. The goal of this strategy is to profit from a bullish forecast at a decreased out-of-pocket cost and lower upside break-even point. The trade-off, however, is that risk is increased. This is one example of an option strategy in which "cost" (a small debit in this case) does not equal risk (substantial in this case).

Figure 2–14: Short Split-Strike Synthetic

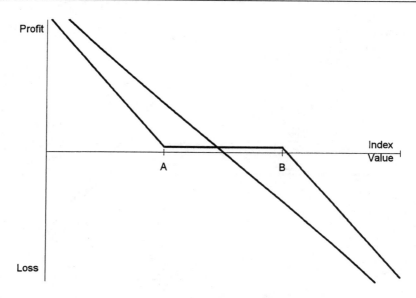

Example:	Sell 1 Call, Strike B, *and* Buy 1 Put, Strike A
Maximum profit potential:	Substantial—from the long put. (See the discussion of profit potential for long puts in Strategy 3.)
Maximum risk potential:	Unlimited—from the short call. (See the discussion of the risk of short calls in Strategy 2.)
Break-even point at expiration:	Strike B plus the net premium received (or Strike A minus the net premium paid)
Desired movement:	Bearish
Effect of passage of time:	Neutral. The decrease of the short call makes up for the decrease of the long put.
Effect of increase in volatility:	Neutral, for the same reason as for the passage of time.
Comment:	The presence of a short, uncovered call makes this strategy appropriate only for experienced traders who qualify for the highest level of risk. The goal of this strategy is to profit from a bearish forecast at a decreased out-of-pocket cost and higher upside break-even point. The trade-off, however, is that risk is increased. This is one example of an option strategy in which "cost" (a small credit in this case) does not equal risk (unlimited in this case).

Figure 2–15: Ratio Vertical Spread with Calls

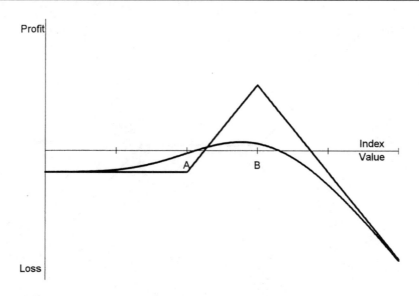

Example:	Buy 1 Call, Strike A, *and* Sell 2 Calls, Strike B
Maximum profit potential:	Limited to difference between the strikes minus the premium paid (if established for a net premium paid)
Maximum risk potential:	Unlimited if market rises; limited if market falls
Break-even point at expiration:	Two points: Strike A plus the net premium paid and Strike B plus the maximum profit potential
Desired movement:	Neutral to slightly bullish with the index near Strike B at expiration
Effect of passage of time:	Slightly positive. The value of a ratio vertical spread will increase with the passage of time if other factors remain constant.
Effect of increase in volatility:	Negative. The value of a ratio spread will increase if volatility increases and other factors remain constant.
Comment:	The presence of a short, uncovered call (the second call) makes this strategy appropriate only for experienced traders who qualify for the highest level of risk. The goal of this strategy is to profit from option time erosion with neutral market price action. Significant time erosion, however, does not occur until very close to expiration. Therefore, it is important to study the price behavior of this strategy with a tool such as the OP-EVAL3™ program before attempting to trade it with real options.

Figure 2–16: Ratio Volatility Spread with Calls

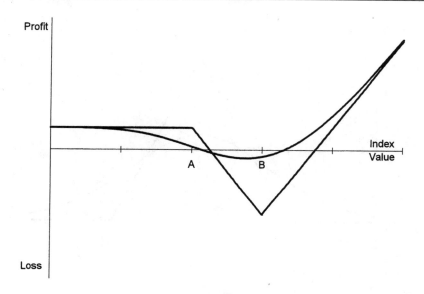

Example:	Sell 1 Call, Strike A, *and* Buy 2 Calls, Strike B
Maximum profit potential:	Unlimited if market rises; limited if market falls
Maximum risk potential:	Limited to the difference between the strikes minus the premium received (if established for a net premium received)
Break-even point at expiration:	Two points: Strike A plus the net premium received and Strike B plus the maximum risk
Desired movement:	Very bullish, above the upper break-even point
Effect of passage of time:	Slightly negative. The value of a ratio volatility spread will decrease with the passage of time if other factors remain constant.
Effect of increase in volatility:	Positive. The value of a ratio volatility spread will increase if volatility increases and other factors remain constant.
Comment:	Although the risk is limited (for European-style options), traders should know the maximum risk before establishing this position. The goal of a ratio volatility spread is to profit from a bullish forecast with less out-of-pocket cost and less time erosion. The trade-off is that the upside break-even point is higher than compared to the outright purchase of a call with Strike A. It is important to study the price behavior of this strategy with a tool such as the OP-EVAL3™ program before attempting to trade it with real options.

Figure 2–17: Long Butterfly Spread with Calls

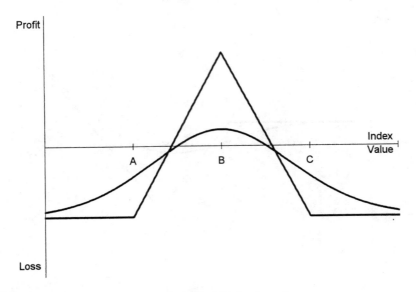

Example:	Buy 1 Call, Strike A, *and* Sell 2 Calls, Strike B, *and* Buy 1 Call, Strike C
Maximum profit potential:	Limited to difference between the Strike A and Strike B minus net premium
Maximum risk potential:	Limited to the premium paid (for European-style options)
Break-even point at expiration:	Two points: Strike A plus the net premium paid and Strike C minus the net premium paid
Desired movement:	Neutral with the index near Strike B at expiration
Effect of passage of time:	Neutral to slightly positive. The butterfly spread value will increase with the passage of time if other factors remain constant.
Effect of increase in volatility:	Negative. The butterfly spread value will decrease if volatility increases and other factors remain constant.
Comment:	This is an impractical strategy for off-floor traders to initiate, because of transaction costs. However, as discussed in Chapter 15, the creation of this strategy is one possible alternative for managing a profitable long option. Significant time erosion only occurs very close to expiration. Therefore, it is important to study the price behavior of this strategy before attempting to trade it with real options.

Figure 2–18: Iron Butterfly Spread

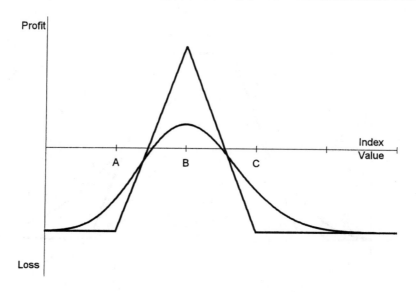

Example:

> Buy 1 Put, Strike A, *and*
> Sell 1 Put, Strike B, *and*
> Sell 1 Call, Strike B, *and*
> Buy 1 Call, Strike C

Maximum profit potential:

> Limited to the net premium received

Maximum risk potential:

> Limited to the difference between Strike A and Strike B minus the premium received (for European-style options)

Break-even point at expiration:

> Two points: Strike B plus the net premium received and Strike B minus the net premium received

Desired movement:

> Neutral with the index near Strike B at expiration

Effect of passage of time:

> Neutral to slightly positive. The iron butterfly spread value will decrease if time passes and other factors remain constant.

Effect of increase in volatility:

> Slightly negative. The iron butterfly spread value will increase if volatility increases and other factors remain constant.

Comment:

> This is an impractical strategy for off-floor traders to initiate, because of transaction costs. Since significant time erosion only occurs very close to expiration, it is important to study the price behavior of this strategy before attempting to trade it with real options.

Figure 2–19: Long Condor Spread with Calls

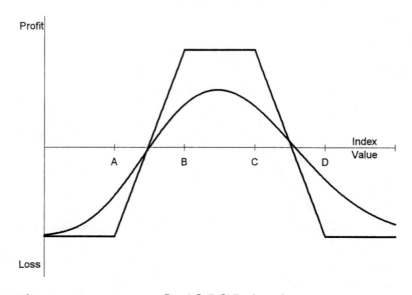

Example:	Buy 1 Call, Strike A, *and* Sell 1 Call, Strike B, *and* Sell 1 Call, Strike C, *and* Buy 1 Call, Strike D
Maximum profit potential:	Limited to the difference between Strike A and Strike B minus the premium paid
Maximum risk potential:	Limited to the net premium paid (for European-style options)
Break-even point at expiration:	Two points: Strike A plus the net premium paid and Strike D minus the net premium paid
Desired movement:	Neutral with the index between Strike B and Strike C at expiration
Effect of passage of time:	Neutral to slightly positive. The condor value will increase as time passes and other factors remain constant.
Effect of increase in volatility:	Slightly negative. The condor value will decrease if volatility increases and other factors remain constant.
Comment:	This is an impractical strategy for off-floor traders to initiate, because of transaction costs. However, the creation of this strategy is one possible alternative for managing a profitable position (Chapter 15). Significant time erosion only occurs very close to expiration. Therefore, it is important to study the price behavior of this strategy with a tool such as OP-EVAL3™ before attempting to trade it with real options.

Figure 2–20: Iron Condor

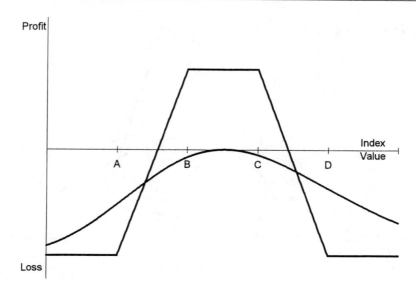

Example:	Buy 1 Put, Strike A, *and* Sell 1 Put, Strike B, *and* Sell 1 Call, Strike C, *and* Buy 1 Call, Strike D
Maximum profit potential:	Limited to the net premium received
Maximum risk potential:	Limited to the difference between Strike A and Strike B minus the net premium received (for European-style options)
Break-even point at expiration:	Two points: Strike B minus the net premium received and Strike C plus the net premium received
Desired movement:	Neutral with the index between Strike B and Strike C at expiration
Effect of passage of time:	Neutral to slightly positive. The iron condor spread value will decrease as time passes and other factors remain constant.
Effect of increase in volatility:	Slightly negative. The iron condor spread value will increase if volatility increases and other factors remain constant.
Comment:	This is an impractical strategy for off-floor traders to initiate, because of transaction costs. Significant time erosion only occurs very close to expiration. Therefore, it is important to study the price behavior of this strategy before attempting to trade it with real options.

Figure 2–21: Christmas Tree Spread with Calls: Variation 1

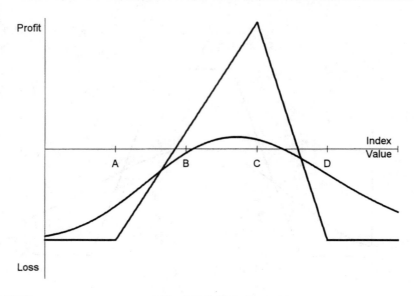

Example:	Buy 1 Call, Strike A, *and* Sell 3 Calls, Strike C, *and* Buy 2 Calls, Strike D
Maximum profit potential:	Limited to the difference between Strike A and Strike C minus the net premium paid
Maximum risk potential:	Limited to the net premium paid (for European-style options)
Break-even point at expiration:	Two points: Strike A plus the net premium paid and Strike D minus one-half of the net premiums paid
Desired movement:	Neutral with the index at Strike C at expiration
Effect of passage of time:	Neutral to slightly positive. The Christmas Tree spread value will increase as time passes and other factors remain constant.
Effect of increase in volatility:	Slightly negative. The Christmas Tree spread value will decrease if volatility increases and other factors remain constant.
Comment:	This is an impractical strategy for off-floor traders to initiate, because of transaction costs. However, the creation of this strategy is one possible alternative for managing a profitable long position, as discussed in Chapter 15. Since significant time erosion only occurs very close to expiration, it is important to study the price behavior of this strategy before attempting to trade it with real options.

Figure 2–22: Christmas Tree Spread with Calls: Variation 2

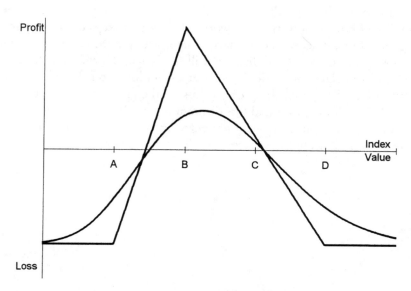

Example:	Buy 2 Calls, Strike A, *and* Sell 3 Calls, Strike B, *and* Buy 1 Call, Strike D
Maximum profit potential:	Limited to two times the difference between Strike A and Strike B minus the net premium paid
Maximum risk potential:	Limited to the net premium paid (for European-style options)
Break-even point at expiration:	Two points: Strike A plus one-half of the net premium paid and Strike D minus the net premium paid
Desired movement:	Neutral with the index at Strike B at expiration
Effect of passage of time:	Neutral to slightly positive. The Christmas Tree spread value will increase as time passes and other factors remain constant.
Effect of increase in volatility:	Slightly negative. The Christmas Tree spread value will decrease if volatility increases and other factors remain constant.
Comment:	This is an impractical strategy for off-floor traders to initiate, because of transaction costs. However, the creation of this strategy is one possible alternative for managing a profitable long position, as discussed in Chapter 15. Significant time erosion only occurs very close to expiration. Therefore, it is important to study the price behavior of this strategy before attempting to trade it with real options.

SUMMARY

The ability to draw profit and loss diagrams demonstrates a true understanding of how option strategies work. There are six steps to drawing these diagrams. First, describe the transaction completely. Second, create a profit and loss grid on which the diagram will be drawn. Third, select an index level and calculate the option's value at expiration. Fourth, calculate the profit or loss. Fifth, plot the profit or loss on the grid. Sixth, repeat steps 3 through 5 until the profit and loss diagram is complete.

Although 22 strategies were presented in this chapter, there are many more possibilities. Option strategies are limited only by one's imagination.

Three

Option Values and How They Change

INTRODUCTION

This chapter explains option values in two parts. First, it demonstrates the analogy between options and insurance. Second, it discusses how option values change as the different inputs change. The conceptual nature of this chapter will provide a good foundation for using the computer program OP-EVAL3™ in Chapter 4.

THE INSURANCE ANALOGY

An option is simply an insurance policy that pays its owner if certain conditions are met on or before the expiration date. If the conditions are not met, the policy expires worthless.

The analogy between put options and insurance policies is, perhaps, easiest to understand. As with an insurance policy paying a claim on an insured asset that is damaged, a put goes up in value if the underlying instrument declines in value. If the underlying does not decline below the strike price before expiration, the put option expires worthless.

Why calls are like insurance policies may be less obvious. Calls are insurance policies that insure participation in a price rise. Calls contain a right to buy, as opposed to a right to sell. Whereas puts insure against the risk of being in the market—the risk of suffering from a price decline—calls insure against the risk of being out of the market—the risk of missing a rally. Although one loss is a "real loss" and the other an "opportunity loss," the put and call options that protect against these events both act as insurance policies in every respect.

Components of Insurance Premiums

Insurance companies consider five factors when calculating premiums. For example, consider automobile insurance. The first consideration is the *value* of the car. If other factors are equal, the more valuable the car, the more expensive the insurance. Second, the amount of the *deductible* affects the insurance premium. The higher the deductible, the lower the premium. The policy's term, or *time to expiration,* is the third factor. The longer the term, the higher the insurance premium. Fourth is *interest rates.* Insurance companies invest the premiums they receive until claims are paid. Consequently, the level of interest rates influences what premiums are charged. Fifth, and final, is *risk.* For automobile insurance, the age and driving record of the driver, where the car is parked, and how many miles per year it is driven are some of the risk factors considered. If other factors are equal, the higher the risk, the higher the insurance premium.

Insurance actuaries take these five components and apply a mathematical formula to arrive at the premium they charge for a particular policy.

Options Compared to Insurance

Corresponding to the five components for insurance are six components for options: the price of the underlying instrument, the strike price, the time to expiration, interest rates, dividends, and volatility.

The index level, that is, the *price of the underlying instrument,* corresponds to asset value. For index options, a higher index level is like a higher asset value. If other factors are constant, the higher the index level, the higher an option value.

An option's *strike price* corresponds to the deductible element in insurance. The deductible, remember, is the amount of risk born by the insured party. An insurance policy with a $1,500 deductible, for example, means that a loss up to this level requires no payment from the insurance company. With options the same concept is true. An out-of-the-money option is like a policy with a deductible: if the underlying index does not move above (below) the strike price of the call (put), then the option pays nothing at expiration. An at-the-money option is similar to an insurance policy with no deductible.

The impact of *time to expiration* on option values is identical to its impact on insurance premiums. The longer the time to expiration, the higher an insurance premium and the higher an option value. While this concept may seem obvious, what is not so obvious is how changes in time affect option values. The subject of time erosion will be discussed in depth in Chapter 5, "The Greeks," but option values do not decrease linearly with the passage of time.

Changes in *interest rates,* the fourth factor, affect calls and puts differently. When interest rates increase, call values increase and put values decline. An in-depth discussion of the impact of changes in interest rates is both beyond the scope of this book and unnecessary, because the impact of interest rates on short-term option values is quite small; therefore, they have little impact on short-term trading decisions. Interest rates do, however, have a greater impact on the values of longer-term options.

The effect of *dividends* on option values is opposite that of interest rates. An increase in dividends tends to decrease call values and increase put values. Fortunately, the effect of typical changes in dividends is small, so index option traders need not be overly concerned with this aspect of option valuation.

The final component of option value, *volatility,* is conceptually identical to the risk factor in insurance. The higher the volatility, the higher an option's value, just as an increase in risk assessment increases insurance premiums. A word of caution about volatility: it is not an intuitively obvious concept. Consequently, traders who are studying volatility for the first time must be patient in order to develop an understanding of this important concept. Chapter 6, "Volatility," discusses the subject in depth. Volatility is also discussed in numerous places in this book.

Table 3–1 summarizes the analogy between insurance premiums and option premiums.

Theoretical option values are calculated using a mathematical formula known as the Black-Scholes option pricing model, which involves advanced calculus. The mathematics of deriving this formula are beyond the scope of this book, but detailed discussion can be found in *Option Markets* by John C. Cox and Mark Rubenstein (1985, Prentice Hall, Upper Saddle River, NJ, 498 pages) and *Options, Futures, and Other Derivatives,* 3rd edition, by John C. Hull (1997, Prentice Hall, Upper Saddle River, NJ, 544 pages). Option

Table 3–1　Components of Insurance Premiums and Options

Insurance Policy	Option
Asset value	Index level
Deductible	Strike price
Time to expiration	Time to expiration
Interest rates	Interest rates and dividends
Risk	Volatility
= Premium	= Premium

values in Tables 3–2 through 3–8 are presented in decimals rounded to the second place rather than in eighths and quarters for the sake of clarity in explaining several concepts.

The following examples review how changes in the inputs to the option pricing formula affect call and put values. Each example is static; only one factor is changed at a time while all other factors remain constant. Dynamic examples will be presented in later chapters.

HOW OPTION VALUES CHANGE

Table 3–2 shows how the six components discussed above are used to calculate theoretical call and put values. In this example, the index level is 800, the strike price is 800, the dividend yield is 2 percent, the volatility is 15 percent, the interest rate is 5 percent, and it is 30 days to expiration. The theoretical values are 14.69 for the 800 Call and 12.72 for the 800 Put.

An important observation to be made from Table 3–2 is that when the index level is exactly at the option strike price, the call value is higher than the put value: 14.69 versus 12.72 in this example. This difference occurs because there is an interest component, i.e., the cost of money, in the call that is not in the put. How option values change as individual inputs change is discussed next.

Change in Index Level

Table 3–3 illustrates how call and put values change when the price of the underlying index increases. A rise in the index from 800 to 801 has a direct effect on the value of the 800 Call, which increases to 15.23. It has the oppo-

Table 3–2 Black-Scholes Option Pricing Formula: Inputs and Outputs

Inputs	
Index level	800
Strike price	800
Dividend yield	2.0%
Volatility	15.0%
Interest rates	5.0%
Days to expiration	30
Outputs	
800 Call value	14.69
800 Put value	12.72

Table 3–3 Effect of Increase in Price of Underlying

	Initial	New	
Inputs			
Index level	800	801	← Increase in index level only
Strike price	800	800	
Dividend yield	2.0%	2.0%	
Volatility	15.0%	15.0%	
Interest rates	5.0%	5.0%	
Days to expiration	30	30	
Outputs			
800 Call value	14.69	15.23	← Call value up
800 Put value	12.72	12.26	← Put value down

site effect on the 800 Put, which decreases to 12.26. Two important observations can be made about these changes.

First, neither the 800 Call value nor the 800 Put value changed as much as the index level. If factors other than the price of the underlying remain constant, then option values change by less than the change in price of the underlying. In Table 3–3, the index increased by one point (+1.00), the 800 Call increased by 0.54, and the 800 Put decreased by 0.46. The relationship of an option's price change to the price change of the underlying is known as *delta;* it will be discussed in detail in Chapter 5, "The Greeks."

Second, after the one-point change in the index level, the relationship of the call's time value to the put's time value remained constant. With the index at 800, the 800 Call's time value of 14.69 is 1.97 greater than the 800 Put's time value of 12.72. With the index at 801 and other factors unchanged, the 800 Call's time value of 14.23 (total price of 15.23 minus the intrinsic value of 1.00) is still 1.97 greater than the 800 Put's time value of 12.26.

Change in Strike Price

Changing the strike price, as noted above, is similar to changing the deductible of an insurance policy. With the underlying index at 800, both the 800 Call and the 800 Put are at-the-money. Raising the strike to 805 decreases the call price, because this call, an 805 Call, is out-of-the-money by five points. The price of the put, however, increases, because an 805 Put is in-the-money by five points. Table 3–4 illustrates how raising the strike price to 805 and leaving other factors unchanged has an inverse effect on call prices and a direct effect on put prices.

Table 3–4 Effect of Increase in Strike Price

	Initial	New	
Inputs			
Index level	800	800	
Strike price	800	805	← Increase in strike price only
Dividend yield	2.0%	2.0%	
Volatility	15.0%	15.0%	
Interest rates	5.0%	5.0%	
Days to expiration	30	30	
Outputs			
800 Call value	14.69	12.27	← Call value down
800 Put value	12.72	15.29	← Put value up

Change in Dividend Yield

Like changes in interest rates, the impact of changes in dividends is minor relative to changes in underlying price, time to expiration, and volatility. This is especially true for index options, because, even though individual companies in an index may change dividend policy, the overall impact on the yield of an index is typically minor. Table 3–5 shows that changes in dividends have the opposite effect on option values that changes in interest rates have. When the dividend yield is raised from 2 percent to 3 percent, the 800 Call decreases in value, an inverse effect, and the 800 Put increases, a direct effect. This impact occurs because an underlying security that pays a dividend is more attractive on a relative basis than a security that does not. Consequently, owning calls on that underlying is relatively less attractive while owning puts is relatively more attractive.

Changes in Volatility

The volatility factor in options is analogous to the risk factor in insurance. Since higher risk means higher insurance premiums, one would expect that higher volatility means higher option prices. Table 3–6 verifies this reasoning. When volatility increases from 15 percent to 16 percent, both the 800 Call and 800 Put increase in value. Changes in volatility have a direct effect on option values.

Note also that when call and put values change as a result of a change in volatility, the relationship of their time values does not change. In Table 3–6, the new time value of the 800 Call is 1.97 greater than the new time value of the 800 Put, just as it was before the change in volatility.

Table 3–5 Effect of Increase in Dividend Yield

	Initial	New	
Inputs			
Index level	800	800	
Strike price	800	800	
Dividend yield	2.0%	3.0%	← Increase in dividend yield only
Volatility	15.0%	15.0%	
Interest rates	5.0%	5.0%	
Days to expiration	30	30	
Outputs			
800 Call value	14.69	14.34	← Call value down
800 Put value	12.72	13.03	← Put value up

Table 3–6 Effect of Increase in Volatility

	Initial	New	
Inputs			
Index level	800	800	
Strike price	800	800	
Dividend yield	2.0%	2.0%	
Volatility	15.0%	16.0%	← Increase in volatility only
Interest rates	5.0%	5.0%	
Days to expiration	30	30	
Outputs			
800 Call value	14.69	15.60	← Call value up
800 Put value	12.72	13.63	← Put value up

The sensitivity of option value to change in volatility is known as *vega*, which is discussed in Chapter 5. Volatility, itself, is the topic of Chapter 6, and volatility and vega appear in discussions throughout this book. The comments beginning on page 55 are an introduction to this important subject.

Change in Interest Rates

A change in interest rates has a direct effect on call prices and an inverse effect on put prices. The 1 percent rise in interest rates illustrated in Table 3–7 caused an 0.44 rise in the 800 Call value and an 0.31 decrease in the 800 Put value. While it is possible that interest rates can change 1 percent in a short time frame, this is not a common occurrence. Consequently, traders of short-term index options should be aware of the impact of changes in interest rates,

Table 3–7 Effect of Increase in Interest Rates

	Initial	New	
Inputs			
Index level	800	800	
Strike price	800	800	
Dividend yield	2.0%	2.0%	
Volatility	15.0%	15.0%	
Interest rates	5.0%	6.0%	← Increase in interest rates only
Days to expiration	30	30	
Outputs			
800 Call value	14.69	15.03	← Call value up
800 Put value	12.72	12.41	← Put value down

but this need not be a primary concern. The impact of interest rates over longer periods of time can be significant, however, and traders of longer-term options must pay much closer attention to the impact of interest rates.

Change in Days to Expiration

Table 3–8 shows the direct effect on both the 800 Call and 800 Put when the number of days is increased from 30 to 45. The sensitivity of option value to change in time is known as *theta,* and it will be discussed in detail in Chapter 5. At this point, however, two observations should be made about the impact of time on option values.

First, even though the time to expiration was increased by 50 percent from 30 days to 45 days, while keeping other inputs constant, the call's value increased by only 24 percent from 14.69 to 18.25. Also, the put's value increased by only 20 percent from 12.72 to 15.30. This is known as "non-linear time decay" and refers to the phenomenon whereby changes in option values from changes in time do not equal, in percentage terms, the change in time. This topic will be explored in greater detail in Chapter 5.

The second observation is about the change in the relationship of the call time value and the put time value. The difference between the time value of the 800 Call and the time value of the 800 Put at 30 days is 1.97 (14.69 − 12.72). At 45 days, however, the difference is 2.95 (18.25 − 15.30). This is almost exactly a 50 percent increase, equal to the change in time in percentage terms. Without going into detail, the increase in call time value over put time value is explained by the interest rate, or cost of money, component introduced earlier. The time value of a call will be greater than the time value

Table 3–8 Effect of Increase in Days to Expiration

	Initial	New	
Inputs			
Index level	800	800	
Strike price	800	800	
Dividend yield	2.0%	2.0%	
Volatility	15.0%	15.0%	
Interest rates	5.0%	5.0%	
Days to expiration	30	45	← Increase in days only
Outputs			
800 Call value	14.69	18.25	← Call value up
800 Put value	12.72	15.30	← Put value up

of a put with the same underlying, same strike, and same expiration by an interest factor. The more or less the time to expiration, the more or less the difference between call and put time values.

THE CONCEPT OF VOLATILITY

Volatility is often said to be the most used and least understood word in options. Volatility simply means *movement,* but this concept is not easily grasped by stock and futures traders, who are accustomed to thinking in terms of direction, not movement. A 10 percent movement up and a 10 percent movement down, for example, are equal in volatility terms, but they are not equal to the owner of an underlying for whom a 10 percent movement up is "good" and the opposite is "bad."

Movement can be described conceptually or mathematically. "Big movement" and "small movement" are conceptual, while "35 percent volatility" and "25 percent volatility" are mathematical. Unfortunately, both types of descriptions leave something to be desired. "Big" and "small" are inexact, while "35 percent" and "25 percent" mean little or nothing to those who are mathematically challenged. Option traders need to develop a familiarity with the mathematical terms without worrying too much about the mathematics. To do this, traders should ask the following questions: What is a "normal" level of volatility for the index options I am trading? What is the recent level of volatility? What is the level now? And what is my forecast?

With a little experience, anyone can develop a comfort level with volatility numbers such as 25 percent and 35 percent without studying the mathematics. Consider for a moment that many investors already have a comfort

Table 3–9 Effect of Changes in Components on Option Values

Component	Call Value	Put Value
Price of underlying	Direct	Inverse
Strike price	Inverse	Direct
Dividends	Inverse	Direct
Volatility	Direct	Direct
Interest rate	Direct	Inverse
Time	Direct	Direct

Direct effect means that option values change in the same direction as the component; e.g., if the component increases, option values will also increase.
Inverse effect means that option values change in the opposite direction as the component; e.g., if the component increases, option values will decrease.

level with price-earnings ratios (p/e). When assessing a new stock, one of the first questions, is, typically, "What's the p/e?" The answer may seem exact—12, 17, or 33—but such numbers could be based on the last fiscal year's earnings, the current trailing 12-month earnings, or the estimated next year's earnings. Consequently, it is not the precise value of a p/e ratio that matters, but a subjective evaluation of that ratio. That subjective evaluation—along with subjective evaluations of other information, such as the company's historic p/e, the average p/e in the industry, and the average market p/e—are all part of the subjective decision to invest or not to invest. Option traders must develop a similar, conceptual understanding of volatility. In later chapters, this book will demonstrate how the OP-EVAL3™ program is used to estimate the current level of volatility of an option—known as the *implied volatility.* This will be an important step toward developing a subjective understanding of volatility.

Table 3–9 summarizes the effects of changes in individual components on call and put values. A *direct effect* means that option values change in the same direction as the change in the component. An *inverse effect* means that option values change in the opposite direction as the change in the component.

SUMMARY

Options have value, because they are similar to insurance. Puts insure owned assets against a market decline. Calls insure cash or liquid assets from missing a rally. The factors that actuaries consider in determining insurance premiums correspond to the components used by formulas such as the Black-Scholes option pricing model to calculate theoretical option values.

The asset value component of insurance premiums corresponds to the index level component of index option values. The deductible in insurance corresponds to the strike price in options. Time is the same for both, but interest rates in insurance correspond to interest rates and dividends in options. Finally, the risk factor in insurance is similar to volatility in options.

Volatility means movement, and the challenge for option traders is to develop a subjective understanding of numbers—20 percent, 30 percent, and so forth—that describe option volatility levels in mathematical terminology. The goal for traders is to gain perspective on certain questions: What is a "normal" volatility level for this index? What is the recent level? What is the current level? And what level is forecast?

Section 2

Option Price Behavior and Volatility

Four

Pricing and Graphing Strategies with OP-EVAL3™

INTRODUCTION

Computer programs are tools designed to perform calculations quickly and improve analysis. They are not designed to take over the decision-making process. Although the profit and loss diagrams presented in Chapter 2 can be drawn by hand, the calculations required to calculate theoretical values require a computer. OP-EVAL3™, the computer program that accompanies this text, can perform both of these tasks. This chapter will explain how to install and operate the program. Later chapters will show how the program can be used to analyze alternative strategies in trading situations.

INSTALLING AND STARTING OP-EVAL3™

Enclosed with this book is a 3½" computer disk labeled OP-EVAL3™ Setup Disk. This disk is designed to work on computers with either Windows 3.1 or Windows 95 operating systems. Although the installation procedures are straightforward, if you have little experience with computers, you may want the help of a more computer-knowledgeable friend. Once the program is installed, you will find it is easy to use.

The installation instructions are as follows:

WINDOWS 3.1

To install: 1. Turn on the computer and start Microsoft Windows. Insert Setup Disk in drive A (or drive B).

2. From Program Manager, select the File menu and choose Run.

    3. Type a:\setup (or b:\setup), press ENTER, and follow
       instructions.

To run: 1. Double-click on the OP-EVAL3™ icon in the Op-Eval
              Programs window.

WINDOWS 95

To install: 1. Turn on the computer and start Microsoft Windows.
                 Insert Setup Disk in drive A (or drive B).

           2. Click on Start, and then click on Run.

           3. Type a:\setup (or b:\setup), press ENTER, and follow
              instructions.

To run: 1. Click on Start. Move the arrow to Programs in the first
              menu column, and then to OP-EVAL™ Programs in
              the second menu column. Click on OP-EVAL3™ in
              the third menu column.

When you start the program, the first few pages you will see are Disclaimers
and Disclosures, which contain important information about the assumptions made by the program. You should read these pages carefully. Only with
a thorough understanding of the limitations of this (or any) program can
you make informed decisions. If you proceed on your own intuition and
uninformed perceptions, you are not likely to do well in any area of trading,
let alone option trading. After you have read all disclosures and disclaimers
carefully, you will be instructed to press Y if you accept the conditions. If you
have not read the Disclaimers and Disclosures pages, or if you would like to
study them again, or if you do not want to proceed for any other reason,
then press any other key and the program will terminate. To restart the program, follow the "To run" instructions above.

COMMONLY ASKED QUESTIONS

Familiarize yourself with the Help pages, which contain information on all
aspects of the program, including operational techniques and definitions
of terms.

    Most experienced computer users want to know about the graphing
capabilities of OP-EVAL3™. The graphing capability is available only from
the Four Option Analysis page. Click on the Four Option Analysis item on
the Menu bar, and simply enter the desired position according to the procedures presented in this chapter. Then click on the Graph item on the Menu

bar, and a graph of the position will appear. The Graph item on the Menu bar cannot be accessed from other pages in the program.

It is possible to graph a position in an underlying instrument, even though most underlying indexes on which options are traded do not have underlying instruments that can be traded. This feature was added to the program for educational purposes only. To graph a position in an underlying instrument, click on the Four Option Analysis page, set the strike of Option 1 to zero (0.000), and set the Option Type to Call. You will then observe that the words "Option 1" have changed to "Underlying." To graph a position in the underlying, key a non-zero number in the Quantity row of the Underlying column, and then click on the Graph item of the Menu bar.

A complete discussion of operating OP-EVAL3™ will now be presented. Even experienced computer users should read this section to learn the full range of capabilities of the program.

CALL/PUT PRICER PAGE

When you press Y in response to the question on the last page of the Disclaimers and Disclosures, you will see a screen that looks like Figure 4–1. This is the Call/Put Pricer page, the first of three calculation pages. This page provides theoretical values, delta, gamma, theta, vega, and rho for a call and put with the same strike, same expiration, and same underlying. Later chapters will explain how this information can be used to analyze option prices and

Figure 4–1 OpEval3™ Call/Put Pricer Page

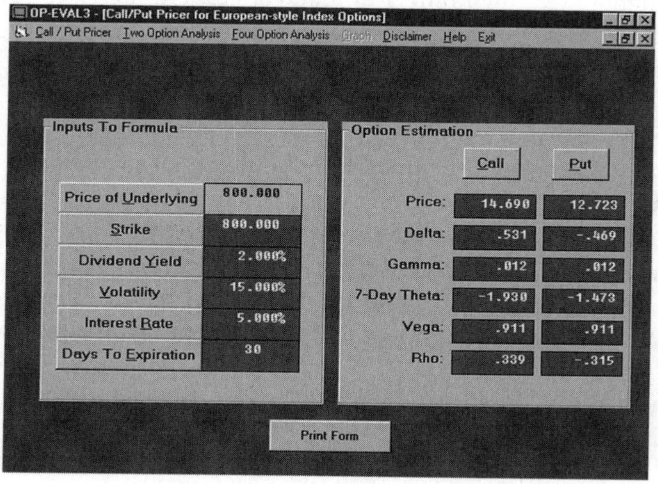

estimate how those prices might change given your forecast, but this chapter only describes how the Call/Put Pricer and other aspects of the program work.

Moving Around the Call/Put Pricer Page

The highlighted rectangle can be changed either by clicking on a desired rectangle or by pressing the arrow keys. The down arrow (↓) and right arrow (→) move the highlight effect down the Inputs to Formula column first, then over to the Call Price rectangle, then to the Put Price rectangle, and finally, back to the Price of Underlying rectangle. Except for the Call Price and Put Price rectangles, the rectangles below Call and Put cannot be highlighted, as they are output only. The up arrow (↑) and left arrow (←) move the highlight effect in the opposite direction.

After familiarizing yourself with movement around the calculation page, highlight the Price of Underlying rectangle, and make sure the default settings appear as in Figure 4–1: 800.000 for Price of Underlying, 800.000 for Strike, and so on. Given these inputs, OP-EVAL3™ has calculated the theoretical value of the 800 Call as 14.690. This information appears in the Call Price rectangle.

Changing Price of Underlying

With the Price of Underlying rectangle highlighted, you can input any price from 0.001 to 99,999.999. If a whole number, such as 805, is entered, OP-EVAL3™ assumes all three numbers to the right of the decimal point are zeros. When the ENTER key or an arrow key is pressed or when another rectangle is highlighted, the number 805.000 appears in the Price of Underlying rectangle and all output values are recalculated.

You can now practice with the different input rectangles and observe how OP-EVAL3™ calculates option theoretical values, given your inputs.

As will be explained in Chapter 7, "The Importance of Futures Prices," readers should be aware that much care should be taken when selecting the appropriate value for Price of Underlying. There are times when the current index level is not the appropriate number for Price of Underlying. And if supply and demand conditions in the stock index futures market cause those contracts to trade sufficiently above or below theoretical value, then index options are likely to trade at prices that do not appear to be consistent with prices generated by OP-EVAL3™. When these situations occur, index option traders must adjust the Price of Underlying as explained in Chapter 7, and the information from OP-EVAL3™ must be interpreted very carefully.

Changing Strike Price

In U.S. option markets, index option strike prices on most indexes are set at five-point intervals: 900, 905, 910, and so on. Options which are based on the Dow Jones Industrial Average, however, have strike prices every 1 index point such as 80.00, 81.00, and so on. OP-EVAL3™ has the flexibility to set the strike price at any number between 0 and 99,999.999. This feature allows OP-EVAL3™ to be used for options on a wide variety of underlying instruments.

Changing Dividend Yield

Although dividends are paid in discrete payments, the Black-Scholes option pricing formula used in OP-EVAL3™ assumes dividends are paid continuously and evenly throughout the year. This is one of the limitations described in the Disclaimers pages. Because securities valuation involves a process known as "discounting cash flows," this assumption can mean there will be a difference between the values calculated by OP-EVAL3™ and prices observed in the real marketplace. This assumption does not diminish the value of OP-EVAL3™ for educational purposes. Adapting the program to account for specific dividend payments and specific payment dates for all the stocks in a particular index would make the program cumbersome. Fortunately, the simplifying assumption made by the Black-Scholes formula is not, for all practical purposes, a significant problem.

To choose a number for Dividend Yield you may refer to index dividend yield numbers presented on Mondays in *The Wall Street Journal*, *Investor's Business Daily*, or *Barron's*.

Changing Volatility

Volatility, as discussed in Chapter 6, is a statistical measure of potential price changes in an option's underlying instrument. If other factors remain constant, a wider range of possible stock prices (that is, higher volatility) means options have a higher theoretical value. It is common practice to express volatility as a percentage, and this practice is used in OP-EVAL3™. The default setting for volatility is 15.000, or 15 percent. When the Volatility rectangle is highlighted, it is possible to enter any number from 0.000 to 999.999. If all inputs are at their default settings (as in Figure 4–1), then changing the volatility to 16 and pressing ENTER results in 16.000 appearing in the Volatility rectangle and the prices 15.601 and 13.634, respectively,

Figure 4–2 Call/Put Pricer with Volatility of 16%

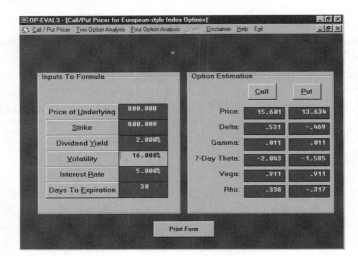

appearing under Call and Put, as illustrated in Figure 4–2. Experiment with the volatility input and develop a feel for how changes in volatility affect index option prices.

Changing the Interest Rate

Interest rates are a factor in the values of options on individual stocks because time and the cost of money directly affect purchasing decisions. Consequently, interest rates are also a factor in the value of index options. The default setting for interest rates is 5.000, or 5 percent. After experimenting with this input, observe that changes in interest rates have the smallest impact on index option prices of any of the inputs. This is consistent with the discussion in Chapter 3.

Changing Days to Expiration

The effect of time on option values was introduced in Chapter 3. Table 3–8 illustrates how the time value portion of option prices erodes as expiration approaches.

In OP-EVAL3™ the default setting for Days to Expiration is 30. When counting the calendar days to expiration for index options, include the current day if it is before or during market hours, but do not include the current day if it is after the market closes. Also, be sure to use the correct last day of trading as the expiration day. For American-style index options, such as OEX options, the correct day is the third Friday of the expiration month. For European-style index options, such as SPX, DJX, or XMI options, the correct last day is one day earlier, the Thursday preceding the third Friday of the expiration month. Even though expiration is technically on the Saturday following the last trading day, the last trading day is the last opportunity to exercise.

Although all in-the-money index options are subject to automatic exercise by the Options Clearing Corporation (OCC) at expiration, index option traders should be sure to know their brokerage firm's exact early exercise procedures and deadlines for American-style options. While you may think that you will never use the early exercise feature, it takes so little effort to learn these details. Not needing something and knowing it is not costly. Needing something and not knowing it, however, could be very costly!

Changing Call and Put Prices to Estimate Implied Volatility

Given the default input settings, the Call Price rectangle reads 14.690 (Figure 4–1). Highlight that rectangle, type in "16," and press ENTER. The number in the Call Price rectangle is now 16.000. But another change is far more important. Can you tell what it is?

Look at the Volatility rectangle. You will observe that the volatility number has been recalculated from 15.000 to 16.438 (Figure 4–3). As will be explained in Chapter 6, 16.438 is the implied volatility of this call if its market price is 16.

Figure 4–3 Call Price 16 and New Implied Volatility

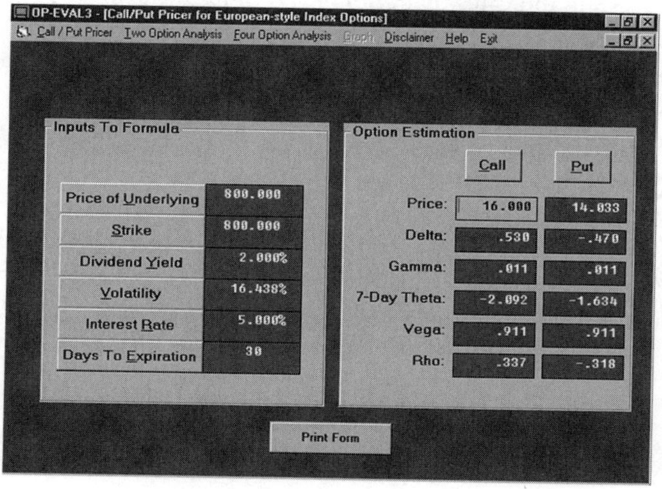

When the value in the Call rectangle is changed, OP-EVAL3™ not only recalculates the volatility, it also recalculates the Put value using the new volatility percentage, and all other outputs as well.

OP-EVAL3™ will also calculate an "implied volatility" percentage given a new put value. A new Call value is also calculated using the new volatility percentage, and all other outputs are also recalculated.

THE TWO OPTION ANALYSIS PAGE

The purpose of the Two Option Analysis page is to analyze two-option positions. Clicking on the Two Option Analysis item on the Menu bar at the top of the screen brings up a new screen that looks like Figure 4–4. The Two Option Analysis page operates in a similar way to the Call/Put Pricer page. Left-clicking highlights rectangles whose values can then be changed. Arrow keys can also be used to change the highlighted rectangle and recalculate outputs. Pressing the ENTER key recalculates the outputs while leaving the highlighted rectangle unchanged. The following features on this page do not appear on the Call/Put Pricer page.

A and I Settings

The A and I buttons make it possible to analyze two options with the same volatility or different volatilities, or two options with the same days to expiration or different days to expiration. They also make it possible to analyze spreads involving calls only, puts only, or both calls and puts.

The A setting indicates that *all numbers in that row are set alike* and that a change in the contents of one rectangle will change the contents of the other rectangles in that row. For example, if the Two Option Analysis page is set to the default settings, as in Figure 4–4, then a change in the underlying price of Option 1 will also change the underlying price of Option 2. Similarly, a change in the volatility of Option 2 will change the volatility of Option 1.

The I setting indicates that all numbers in that row are set *individually*. A change in the contents of one rectangle will not change the contents of the other rectangles in that row. Referring to Figure 4–4, if the strike price of Option 1 is changed, this will not affect the strike price of Option 2.

The user may change the A and I settings in two ways. Method one: First highlight the desired rectangle and then right-click the mouse to toggle to the desired setting. Method two: Highlight the desired rectangle and then type A or I, whichever is desired.

Figure 4–4 Two Option Analysis Page Default Settings

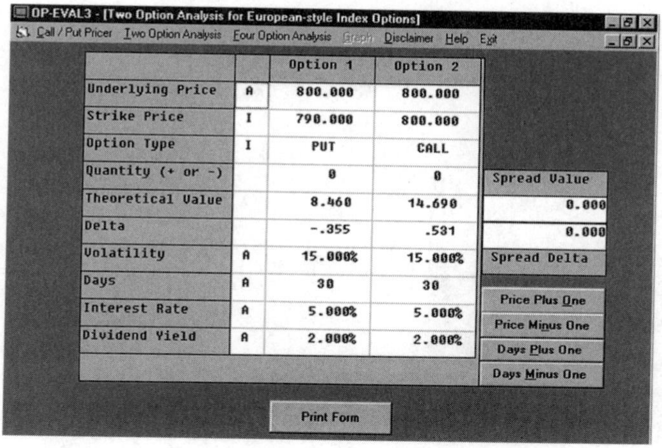

		Option 1	Option 2	
Underlying Price	A	800.000	800.000	
Strike Price	I	790.000	800.000	
Option Type	I	PUT	CALL	
Quantity (+ or -)		0	0	Spread Value
Theoretical Value		8.460	14.690	0.000
Delta		-.355	.531	0.000
Volatility	A	15.000%	15.000%	Spread Delta
Days	A	30	30	
Interest Rate	A	5.000%	5.000%	Price Plus One
Dividend Yield	A	2.000%	2.000%	Price Minus One
				Days Plus One
				Days Minus One

Print Form

Changing Call to Put

The right-click toggle feature of OP-EVAL3™ also works for changing Call to Put and vice versa. Simply highlight the desired rectangle containing Call or Put and right-click the mouse. If the row setting is A, then right-clicking on any Call or any Put will change the contents of every rectangle in that row to the new setting. If the row setting is I, then a right click will change only that rectangle.

ANALYZING A HYPOTHETICAL SPREAD

The Two Option Analysis page can be used to analyze ratio spreads and positions involving calls and puts, but the most common spread is a one-to-one vertical spread with only calls or only puts, for example, the simultaneous purchase of one 750 Call and sale of one 760 Call. Both calls are assumed to have the same expiration and same underlying instrument. A one-to-one vertical call spread is illustrated in Figure 2–9. Here is how a one-to-one 750–760 vertical Call spread might be analyzed.

Standard Inputs

The first step in estimating the value of a hypothetical 750–760 Call spread is entering all of the standard inputs: the underlying price, strike price, volatility, days to expiration, interest rate, and dividend yield, as shown in Figure 4–5.

Figure 4–5 Hypothetical 750–760 Call Spread

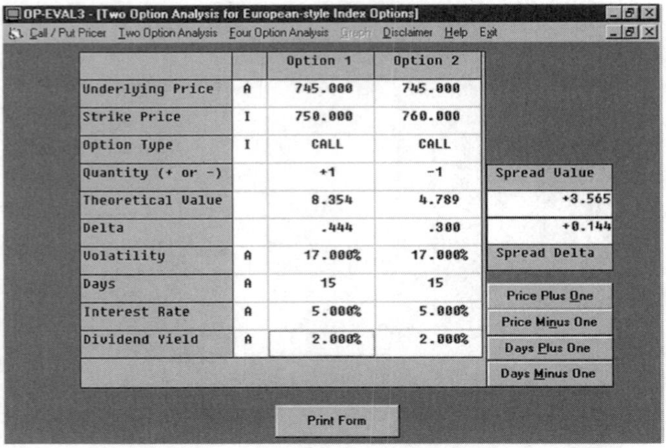

The Quantity Row

Next, enter a position, using the Quantity row. The +1 in the Option 1 column indicates that one of these options, the 750 Call, was purchased. The −1 in the Option 2 column indicates that one 760 Call was sold. The result is a position consisting of one long (or purchased) 750 Call at 8.354 and one short (or sold) 760 Call at 4.789.

Spread Value

For the simple 750–760 Call spread position shown in Figure 4–5, it is easy to calculate the net spread value of 3.565 by subtracting the 760 Call value of 4.789 from the 750 Call value of 8.354. But for more complicated positions, it is nice to have the help of the computer. The Spread Value rectangle, which appears at the right of the Two Option Analysis page, contains the result of this calculation. OP-EVAL3™ has done the work for us!

A positive number in the Spread Value rectangle indicates a debit; that is, the position is established for a net payment, or cost, not including transaction costs. In our example, the 750 Call is purchased for 8.354 and the 760 Call is sold for 4.789. The net cost, therefore, is 3.565; this is what the plus sign and number in the Spread Value rectangle indicates.

A negative number in the Spread Value rectangle indicates a credit; that is, the position is established for a net receipt of money as opposed to a net payment. Some traders speak of this as "selling a spread." Suppose, for example that the 750 Call had been sold for 8.354 and the 760 Call had been purchased for 4.789. In this case, a −1 would appear in the Quantity row under Option 1, indicating that this option was sold, and a +1 would appear under Option 2, indicating that this option was purchased. The Spread Value in this case would then be −3.565, indicating the net amount that was received.

Spread Delta

The Spread Delta rectangle presents the "position delta." A *position delta* is the sum of the deltas of Option 1 and Option 2. The *delta* of an individual option is an estimate of how much that option will change in price for a one-point change in the underlying instrument. The *spread delta* is an estimate of how much a multiple-part option position will change in price when the underlying changes by one point, assuming all other inputs remain constant. The Spread Delta of +0.144 in Figure 4–5 indicates that the value of the 750–760 Call spread will increase by 0.144 if the underlying price is raised by one point and the value will decrease by a like amount with a one-point decrease in the underlying.

Plus One and Minus One Buttons

In the lower right corner of the Two Option Analysis page are four command buttons. Click on one and see what happens. As you might expect, a click on the Price Plus One button raises all numbers in the Underlying Price row by one full point and recalculates the option values, their deltas, the spread value, and the spread delta. Similarly, clicking on the other three buttons will produce a one-unit change in either price of the underlying or days to expiration, as indicated, and all outputs will be recalculated.

These Plus One and Minus One buttons make it easy to estimate how a position will change in value given a change in the underlying (in whole points) and/or a change in a specific number of days to expiration. For example, a trader might want to know how much the 750–760 Call spread value illustrated in Figure 4–5 will change if the index rises five points in two days. To answer this question, just click on the Price Plus One button five times (raising the index from 745 to 750) and then click on the Days Minus One button two times (decreasing the days from 15 to 13). The result is that the spread value has increased to 4.246

Changing Theoretical Value to Estimate Implied Volatility

On the Two Option Analysis page, the rectangles in the Theoretical Value row are equivalent to the Call or Put rectangles on the Call/Put Pricer page. Theoretical values are normally a calculated output. However, it is possible to enter a price as an input. To do this, first highlight a rectangle in the Theoretical Value row. Then, type in the market price of the option and press ENTER. Volatility now becomes a calculated output, and this is the implied volatility of the option whose price was entered. Also, note that the setting in the Volatility row defaults to I. This means that calculating an implied volatility for one option in one column does not affect the value of the option in the other column even if the setting for Volatility is A.

THE FOUR OPTION ANALYSIS PAGE

Get ready for a shock! The Four Option Analysis page illustrated in Figure 4–6 may initially seem overwhelming, but it is just an expansion of the Two Option Analysis page. The Four Option Analysis page makes it possible to analyze and graph a position with one to four options or one underlying and zero to three options. The A, I, Call, and Put settings operate in the same way as they do on the Two Option Analysis page, as do the Plus One and Minus One buttons, the Spread Value, and Spread Delta.

Figure 4–6 The Four Option Analysis Page

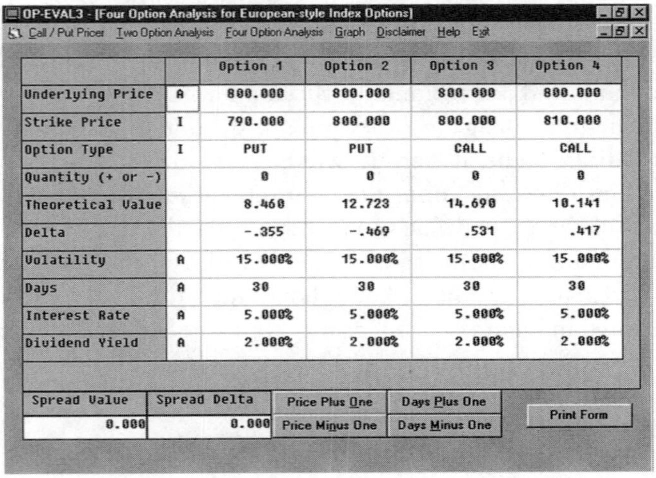
OP-EVAL3 - [Four Option Analysis for European-style Index Options]
Call / Put Pricer Two Option Analysis Four Option Analysis Graph Disclaimer Help Exit
Option 1 Option 2 Option 3 Option 4
Underlying Price A 800.000 800.000 800.000 800.000
Strike Price I 790.000 800.000 800.000 810.000
Option Type I PUT PUT CALL CALL
Quantity (+ or -) 0 0 0 0
Theoretical Value 8.460 12.723 14.690 10.141
Delta -.355 -.469 .531 .417
Volatility A 15.000% 15.000% 15.000% 15.000%
Days A 30 30 30 30
Interest Rate A 5.000% 5.000% 5.000% 5.000%
Dividend Yield A 2.000% 2.000% 2.000% 2.000%
Spread Value 0.000
Spread Delta 0.000
Price Plus One
Price Minus One
Days Plus One
Days Minus One
Print Form

Graphing Profit and Loss Diagrams

As explained earlier in this book, profit and loss diagrams are valuable for educational purposes and trading analysis. The graphing capability of OP-EVAL3™ makes it possible to quickly prepare and print diagrams such as the ones that appear throughout this book. The graphing capability is available only from the Four Option Analysis page.

Any position involving up to four options or one underlying instrument and three options can be graphed quickly and easily in three steps. As an example, the process of graphing a 780–790–800 Long Call butterfly spread will be illustrated. Commissions, other transaction costs, margin requirements, and risks associated with short American-style index options will not be included in this example. An index level of 790, a volatility of 17 percent, 10 days to expiration, interest rates of 5 percent, and a dividend yield of 2 percent are assumed.

Step 1: Value the options.   The first step is entering the standard inputs. On the Four Option Analysis page, the assumed index level of 790 must be entered in the Underlying Price row under Option 1. Notice that when the ENTER key is pressed, all rectangles in this row change to 790.000. This happens because of the A setting. Next, type 780, 790, and 800 in the Strike Price row under Options 1, 2, and 3, respectively. In the Option Type row, change the I to A, then highlight the rectangle under Option 1 in which Put appears, and right-click the mouse. All rectangles in the Option Type row now contain Call. Finally, under Option 1, enter the assumptions of 17 for Volatility, 10 for Days, 5 for Interest Rate, and 2 for Dividend Yield. Pressing the ENTER key after each of these entries changes the contents of all the rectangles in these rows because of the A settings. At this point, the Four Option Analysis page will look like Figure 4–7. All three options involved in the 780–790–800 Long Call butterfly spread have *values* in the Theoretical Value row. You can ignore the information in the Option 4 column, because this is not needed to create the desired butterfly spread. We are ready for the next step.

Step 2: Create the position using the Quantity row.   There must be a non-zero number in the Quantity row for a position to be graphed. A plus sign (+) before a number indicates a long, or purchased, option. A minus sign (−) indicates a short, or written, option. Therefore, step two is entering the appropriate numbers in the Quantity row.

A 780–790–800 Long Call butterfly spread is created by simultaneously purchasing one 780 Call, selling two 790 Calls, and purchasing one 800 Call.

Figure 4–7 Inputs for 780–790–800 Long Call Butterfly Spread

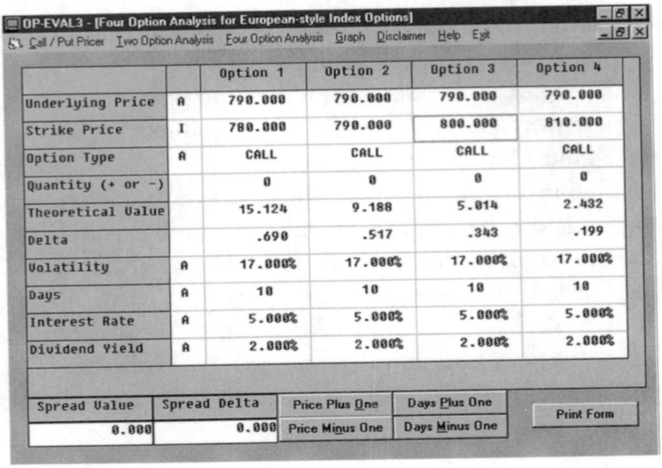

OP-EVAL3 - [Four Option Analysis for European-style Index Options]

Call / Put Pricer | Two Option Analysis | Four Option Analysis | Graph | Disclaimer | Help | Exit

		Option 1	Option 2	Option 3	Option 4
Underlying Price	A	790.000	790.000	790.000	790.000
Strike Price	I	780.000	790.000	800.000	810.000
Option Type	A	CALL	CALL	CALL	CALL
Quantity (+ or -)		0	0	0	0
Theoretical Value		15.124	9.188	5.014	2.432
Delta		.690	.517	.343	.199
Volatility	A	17.000%	17.000%	17.000%	17.000%
Days	A	10	10	10	10
Interest Rate	A	5.000%	5.000%	5.000%	5.000%
Dividend Yield	A	2.000%	2.000%	2.000%	2.000%

Spread Value	Spread Delta			
0.000	0.000	Price Plus One / Price Minus One	Days Plus One / Days Minus One	Print Form

Type +1 in the Quantity row under Option 1 and under Option 3 to indicate one 790 Call and one 800 Call are purchased. Then type −2 under Option 2 to indicate two 790 Calls are sold. Our Four Option Analysis page will now look like Figure 4–8, and we are ready for the final step.

Step 3: Creating the graph. Check Figure 4–8 to make sure all information is correct. Are the Volatility and other inputs correct? Is the Quantity under each option correct? Be careful, because it is easy to make mistakes until you become familiar with the layout of the Four Option Analysis page. When all the inputs are correct, you are ready to graph the butterfly spread.

Just click Graph on the Menu bar at the top of the screen, and the graph shown in Figure 4–9 will appear.

THE GRAPH PAGE

The Graph page shows three lines. The first line, with straight segments, is a graph of the strategy at expiration. The second, middle line (in red if you have a color monitor) is a graph of the strategy at half of the days to expiration indicated on the Four Option Analysis page in the Days row. The middle line may be recalculated by clicking on the up or down arrow on the middle box in the lower right corner of the Graph page. The third line (in blue) is a graph of the strategy at the number of days prior to expiration indicated on the Four Option Analysis page.

Figure 4–8 Four Option Analysis Page with Quantity Row Completed

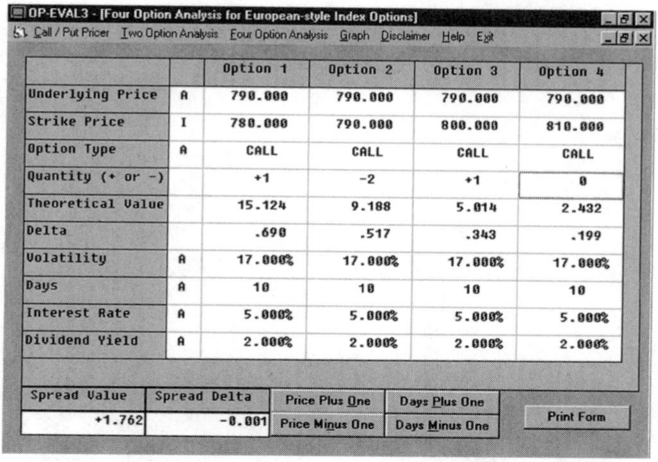

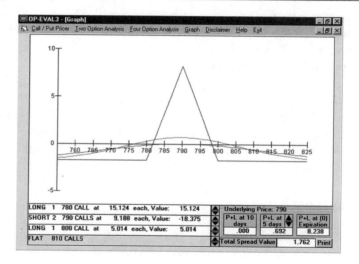

Figure 4–9 Graph of 780–790–800 Long Call Butterfly Spread

Quick-Change to Graph

In the lower left corner of the Graph page are four lines which describe the strike and quantity of Options 1, 2, 3, and 4 from the Four Option Analysis page. These lines also have up and down arrow buttons. A click on an up arrow will increase by one the quantity of that particular option. Changing

Figure 4–10 Changed Graph after Clicking on Up Arrow Next to 790 Calls

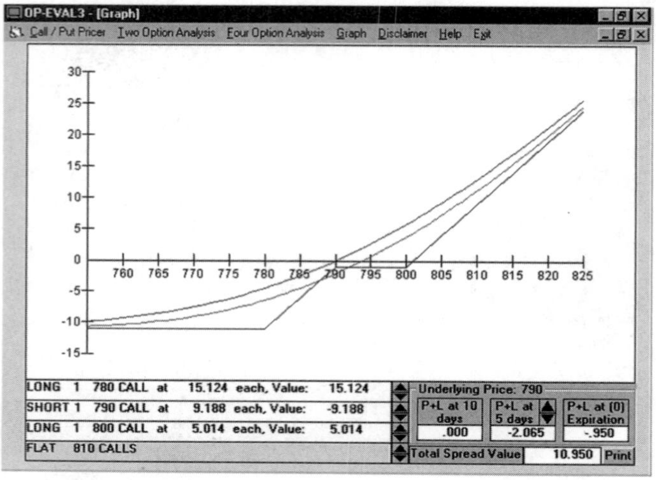

the quantity of a particular option in a position will, of course, change the total position; OP-EVAL3™ immediately graphs the new position. Clicking on a down arrow will decrease by one the quantity of a particular option, and the new position will be graphed.

Figure 4–10 shows how the graph of the 780–790–800 Long Call butterfly spread is changed by clicking on the up arrow next to the 790 Call position. Originally, the butterfly spread had two short 790 Calls, indicated by the –2 in Figure 4–8. After clicking on the up arrow next to the 790 Call, there is only one short 790 Call. The new position is long one 780 Call, short one 790 Call, and long one 800 Call. This position is graphed in Figure 4–10.

Graphing a Position in the Underlying

Most indexes on which options are traded do not have underlying instruments that can be traded. However, OP-EVAL3™ can graph a position in an underlying instrument. This feature was added to the program for educational purposes.

When the Option Type of Option 1 is set to Call and the Strike Price is set to 0.000, then the heading in that column becomes Underlying, and the Theoretical Value is equal to the underlying price. If +1 is in the Quantity row of the Underlying column and the other rectangles in the Quantity row are set to zero, then clicking on the Graph item in the Menu bar brings up a screen like Figure 4–11. This is a graph of a long position in an underlying instrument.

Figure 4–11 Graph of Long Underlying

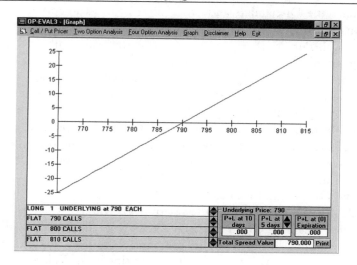

BEWARE THAT MULTIPLIERS ARE CONSISTENT

OP-EVAL3™ assumes a multiplier of 1 for all option types. This allows positions to be valued and graphs to drawn on a per-unit basis. For individual stocks and options on those stocks, this is referred to as a "per-share basis." As a result of this feature, however, care must be taken in setting a Quantity to be sure that the number of units—that is, the multiplier—is consistent between the options and the underlying instrument. If, for example, a position contained SPX index options, options on the Standard & Poor's 500 Index, which are traded at the Chicago Board Options Exchange, and SPDRS, Standard & Poor's Index Depository Receipts, which are traded at the American Stock Exchange, it would be not be possible to create a position that looks like an OP-EVAL3™ graph of one option and one underlying because SPX index options have a multiplier of 100, and SDPRS have a multiplier of 10. Consequently, creating a real position with a one-to-one relationship would involve 10 SPDRS for every 1 SPX index option.

SUMMARY

Computer programs such as OP-EVAL3™ are designed to perform calculations and draw diagrams quickly and to improve the analytic process. They are not designed to take over the decision-making process.

After installing the program, you must read carefully and thoroughly understand the Disclaimers and Disclosures before attempting to use the program to analyze individual or multiple-part option strategies.

The Call/Put Pricer page presents theoretical values of a call and put with the same strike, underlying, and expiration along with their respective deltas, gammas, thetas, vegas, and rhos, which will be explained in Chapter 5. Starting with the default settings, one or more of the six inputs may be changed by highlighting the desired rectangle and typing in the new information. When the ENTER key is pressed, OP-EVAL3™ recalculates all outputs and leaves the highlighted rectangle the same. Typing new information and pressing an up or down arrow or clicking on a different rectangle recalculates all outputs and changes the highlighted rectangle.

If the Call or Put or Theoretical Value rectangles are changed on any page, OP-EVAL3™ recalculates the volatility percentage, which is known as the implied volatility. On the Call/Put Pricer page, the Put or Call price is recalculated using the new volatility percentage. On the Two Option Analysis and Four Option Analysis pages, if an A setting in the Volatility row is set to I, the calculation of no other option value is affected.

The graphing feature is available only from the Four Option Analysis page. The line with straight segments on the Graph page is a graph of the strategy at expiration. The middle line (red) is a graph of the strategy at half of the days to expiration and may be recalculated by clicking on the up or down arrow on the middle box in the lower right corner of the Graph page. The third line (blue) is a graph of the strategy at the number of days prior to expiration indicated on the Four Option Analysis page.

A position in an underlying can be graphed by setting the Option Type of Option 1 to Call and the Strike Price to zero. The ability to graph a position in an underlying instrument was added for educational purposes, because most indexes on which options are traded do not have underlying instruments that can be traded. OP-EVAL3™ assumes that the multiplier is 1 in all cases.

It is important to practice with the many pages and features of OP-EVAL3™ because it is easy to make mistakes inputting information if you are not familiar with the layout of the various pages. However, once you get to know the many features of OP-EVAL3™, you will find that it is a valuable tool for trading index options.

Five

"The Greeks"

INTRODUCTION

The purpose of this chapter is to explain some specific tools that traders use to analyze, understand, and anticipate how option prices might change given a forecast for the underlying. While it is helpful to understand that call values increase and put values decrease when the underlying index rises and other factors remain constant, it is much more helpful to have a specific estimate of the change in value. Such an estimate makes it possible to choose between a number of strategies that are appropriate for a specific market forecast.

This chapter explains the five option "estimators," delta, gamma, theta, vega, and rho, which are frequently referred to as "the Greeks." Each is an estimate of the change in option value caused by a change in one of the inputs, assuming other factors remain constant. Used in conjunction with a specific market forecast, these tools are helpful in estimating the potential profit or loss of a particular strategy.

This chapter will first define each of the Greeks and explain why they are positively or negatively correlated to option values. Second, it will discuss how each of the Greeks changes with movement in an index level and time to expiration. Third, position Greeks will be explained. It is important to understand that position Greeks are different from Greeks of individual option values.

The discussion in this chapter gets fairly technical. Consequently, readers with less experience may want to skim this chapter, or skip it for now and come back to it after reading Section 3, "Trading Strategies." Reading Section 3 first will raise questions about how and why option prices behave the way they do. After you read through the examples in that section, some of the detailed information in this chapter may seem more relevant to the decision-making process.

DELTA

As discussed in Chapter 3, the price of the underlying instrument is an important factor in the determination of option values. Mathematically, the delta of an option is the first derivative of option value with respect to change in price of the underlying. While this technical definition may be helpful to some, it is undoubtedly confusing to others. It is not important to know the mathematics, but it is important to understand the concept of delta. *Delta is an estimate of the change in option value given a one-unit change in price of the underlying instrument, assuming other factors remain constant.* Delta answers this question: If the underlying index rises or falls by one point, how much should I make or lose?

As will be shown later, a one-unit change in price of the underlying causes relatively bigger changes in the values of in-the-money options, relatively smaller changes in the values of at-the-money options, and even smaller changes in values of out-of-the-money options.

Table 5–1 assumes the default parameters of OP-EVAL3™, an index level of 800, a strike of 800, a dividend yield of 2 percent, volatility of 15 percent, interest rates of 5 percent, and 30 days to expiration. Given these inputs, four of the outputs on the Call/Put Pricer page are an 800 Call value of 14.690, an 800 Call delta of +0.531, an 800 Put value of 12.723, and an 800 Put delta of −0.469.

In Table 5–1, the delta of the 800 Call estimates that, if the index rises by one point to 801 and other factors remain constant, then the 800 Call value will rise by 0.531 to 15.221. The delta of the 800 Put estimates that, under

Table 5–1 Illustration of Delta

	Initial		With Changed Index Level
Inputs			
Index level	800	→	801
Strike price	800		
Dividend yield	2.0%		
Volatility	15.0%		
Interest rates	5.0%		
Days to expiration	30		
Outputs			
800 Call price	14.690	→	15.227
800 Call delta	+0.531		
800 Put price	12.723	→	12.261
800 Put delta	−0.469		

the same circumstances, the 800 Put value will fall by 0.469 to 12.254. These deltas closely estimate the change in call and put values, but not exactly, as the values to the right of the arrows in Table 5–1 show. Raising the index level to 801, while leaving the other factors unchanged, causes the 800 Call value to increase to 15.227, a change of +0.537, slightly more than the delta. The 800 Put value decreases to 12.261, a change also slightly different from the put's delta. The differences between the estimated changes and the actual changes will be explained in the section entitled "Gamma." First, however, there are some observations to be made about delta.

> ## DELTA
> Estimated change in option value resulting from a change in the price of the underlying

Call Values Have Positive Deltas

The plus sign (+) associated with the delta of the 800 Call in Table 5–1 indicates a positive, or direct, relationship between the change in price of the underlying instrument and the change in theoretical value of the call. As Table 5–1 illustrates, when only the underlying index level rises, the theoretical value of the 800 Call also rises. It should be noted that a plus or minus sign associated with an *option value* may be different from the sign of an *option position*. The subject of position deltas will be discussed later.

Put Values Have Negative Deltas

The minus sign (–) associated with the delta of the 800 Put indicates a negative, or inverse, relationship between the change in price of the underlying instrument and the change in value of the put. In Table 5–1, a rise in the index level caused the put value to decline.

Finding Deltas in OP-EVAL3™

Delta appears in the OP-EVAL3™ program on three pages in two different forms. On the Call/Put Pricer page, deltas appear under the respective call and put values. On the Two Option Analysis and the Four Option Analysis pages deltas appear in two places. Deltas of individual options appear in the Delta row, and a spread delta appears in the rectangle labeled as such. The *spread delta* is the sum of the deltas of individual options in a position. How traders might use a spread delta is explained in Chapter 10, "Vertical Spreads."

GAMMA

Refer back to Table 5–1 and note that the delta of +0.531 does not exactly predict the 800 Call value after a one-point increase in the underlying index. Why? This difference between the estimated change in value and the actual change in value occurs because the delta changes when the price of the

> ### GAMMA
> Estimated change in option delta resulting from a change in the price of the underlying

underlying changes. *Gamma is an estimate of the change in delta for a one-unit change in price of the underlying instrument, assuming other factors remain constant.* Mathematically, gamma is the second derivative of the option pricing formula with respect to change in price of the underlying. Gamma answers this question: How much does my exposure to the market, that is, my delta, change when the underlying index changes? Gamma makes it possible to estimate more accurately the change in option value when the underlying index changes.

Table 5–2 illustrates the concept of gamma by starting with the information in Table 5–1 and adding the new call and put deltas and the call and put gammas before and after the change in the index level. When the index

Table 5–2 Illustration of Gamma (1)

	Initial		With Changed Index Level
Inputs			
Index level	800	→	801
Strike price	800		
Dividend yield	2.0%		
Volatility	15.0%		
Interest rates	5.0%		
Days to expiration	30		
Outputs			
800 Call price	14.690	→	15.227
800 Call delta	+0.531		+0.543
800 Call gamma	+0.012		+0.011
800 Put price	12.723	→	12.261
800 Put delta	−0.469		−0.457
800 Put gamma	+0.012		+0.011

rises from 800 to 801, the delta of the 800 Call increases from +0.531 to +0.543, a rise of 0.012, a change exactly equal to the gamma.

Similarly, the delta of the 800 Put increases by 0.012 from −0.469 to −0.457. That's right! This is an *increase* in the put delta. For readers comfortable with math, this may seem obvious. Others should take note: it is important to keep track of plus and minus signs and increases and decreases in value.

While the change in call and put deltas exactly equals the gamma in Table 5–2, there will frequently be small differences due to rounding and changing gammas. In Table 5–2 the gammas of both the 800 Call and the 800 Put decline from 0.012 to 0.011 when the index rises. Nothing is constant in the options business!

Gammas of option values are positive. Plus signs (+) are associated with gammas of both calls and puts, because change in delta is positively correlated to change in price of the underlying. Table 5–2 illustrates that an increase in the index causes an increase in the deltas of both the 800 Call and the 800 Put. Table 5–3 shows that a decrease in the index causes a decrease in the deltas of both options. As the index decreases and other factors remain constant, the 800 Call delta decreases from +0.531 to +0.520. The 800 Put delta also decreases, from −0.469 to −0.480. This is a positive correlation: index up, delta up; index down, delta down.

Table 5–3 Illustration of Gamma (2)

	Initial		With Changed Index Level
Inputs			
Index level	800	→	799
Strike price	800		
Dividend yield	2.0%		
Volatility	15.0%		
Interest rates	5.0%		
Days to expiration	30		
Outputs			
800 Call price	14.690	→	14.166
800 Call delta	+0.531		+0.520
800 Call gamma	+0.012		+0.012
800 Put price	12.723	→	13.197
800 Put delta	−0.469		−0.480
800 Put gamma	+0.012		+0.012

Gammas of calls and puts with the same underlying, same strike, and same expiration are equal. This is always true because of a very technical concept. According to a concept known as call-put parity, the sum of the absolute values of the call delta and put delta equals +1.00 if the call and put have the same underlying, same strike, and same expiration. In other words, if the absolute value of the delta of the call increases, then the absolute value of the put delta must decrease by an equal amount. Otherwise, the sum of the absolute values of the deltas would no longer equal +1.00. Consequently, since the deltas of the call and put change by the same amount, their gammas must be equal, because gamma is the change in delta. An in-depth discussion of call-put parity is beyond the scope of this book, but readers interested in this topic can refer to the book by Sheldon Natenberg, *Option Volatility and Pricing* (revised edition, McGraw-Hill, 1995).

VEGA

Volatility will be discussed in depth in the next chapter, but vega will be defined here. *Vega is the change in option value that results from a 1 percent change in volatility, assuming other factors remain constant.* Mathematically, vega is the first derivative of option price with respect to change in volatility. Since first derivatives are theoretically "instantaneous rates of change," and since vega estimates the impact of a 1 percent change, there will frequently be rounding errors. Vega answers this question: If volatility changes by 1 percent, how much do I make or lose?

> ## VEGA
> Estimated change in option value resulting from a 1 percent change in volatility

Table 5–4 illustrates how the 800 Call and 800 Put values change from 14.690 to 15.601 and from 12.723 to 13.634, respectively, when the volatility assumption is increased from 15 percent to 16 percent. The slight difference between the vega of the 800 Call and the change in theoretical value is due to rounding.

Vegas of Option Values Are Positive

Vegas of both call values and put values are positive, because changes in option value are positively correlated to changes in volatility: volatility up, option value up; volatility down, option value down.

Table 5–4 Illustration of Vega

	Initial		With Changed Volatility
Inputs			
Index level	800		
Strike price	800		
Dividend yield	2.0%		
Volatility	15.0%	→	16.0%
Interest rates	5.0%		
Days to expiration	30		
Outputs			
800 Call price	14.690	→	15.601
800 Call vega	+0.911		
800 Put price	12.723	→	13.634
800 Put vega	+0.911		

Another result of the call-put parity concept mentioned above is that vegas of calls and puts with the same underlying, strike, and expiration are equal. According to call-put parity, there is a quantifiable relationship between the price of the underlying instrument and the prices of calls and puts with the same strike and same expiration. In order for the call-put parity relationship to be maintained, when the call or put value increases, the put or call must rise by an identical amount. Thus, vegas of calls and puts with the same underlying, strike, and expiration must be equal.

Readers familiar with the Greek alphabet may note that "vega" is not a Greek letter. It is not clear how the use of this term evolved, but it is common in the options industry. One theory is that option traders wanted a short word beginning with a V and sounding like delta, gamma, and theta. But exactly who coined the term and when it was first used is not known. Some mathematicians and writers use another Greek letter, such as kappa or lambda, instead of vega. Why there is no uniform terminology about such a widely discussed topic as volatility is one of the quirks of the options business. It is just another indication of how flexible options traders must be!

THETA

Theta is an estimate of the change in option value given a one-unit change in time to expiration, assuming other factors remain constant. Theta answers this question: If time passes, how much do I make or lose? Table 5–5 illustrates what happens to call and put values when days to expiration decreases from 30 to

Table 5–5 Illustration of Theta (7-day)

	Initial	With Changed Days to Expiration	
Inputs			
Index level	800		
Strike price	800		
Dividend yield	2.0%		
Volatility	15.0%		
Interest rates	5.0%		
Days to expiration	30	→	23
Outputs			
800 Call price	14.690	→	12.760
800 Call theta	−1.930		
800 Put price	12.723	→	11.251
800 Put theta	−1.473		

23. The call value decreases from 14.690 to 12.760, a change equal to the theta of −1.930. The put value decreases from 12.723 to 11.251, a change nearly equal to the theta of −1.473. The difference of 0.001 is due to rounding.

The definition of theta raises an important question: What is "one unit of time"? Mathematically, theta is the first derivative of option value with respect to change in time to expiration. This means, theoretically, that "one unit of time" is instantaneous. Such a concept, however, is not helpful to traders who need a tool they can use to estimate the impact of time decay on a strategy. While many professional floor traders use a "1-day theta," off-floor traders generally have a different time frame, perhaps 2 to 3 days or 2 to 3 weeks or some other time frame. Consequently, there is no single definition for "one unit of time."

> **THETA**
> Estimated change in option value resulting from a "one unit" change in the time to expiration

OP-EVAL3™ calculates a 7-day theta when days to expiration is greater than 10 and a 1-day theta when days to expiration is 10 or less. These theta calculations are the result of subtracting the value in 7 days (or 1 day) from the current value and were chosen because they are thought to be typical time frames for individual, nonprofessional traders. Different programs, of course, define the term "unit of time" differently, so it is important to know how a theta is defined before attempting to use any program to estimate option price behavior.

An important observation to be made from Table 5–5 is that the theta of the 800 Call and the theta of the 800 Put are not equal. Generally speaking, calls and puts with the same underlying, same strike, and same expiration have different thetas, because they have different time values. Different time values decaying to zero over the same time period means different rates of decay—hence, different thetas. Although the call-put parity concept can be used to explain why calls and puts have different time values, suffice it to say that call values contain an interest component that is not in put values.

Thetas of option values are negative. The minus sign (–) associated with thetas is sometimes a source of confusion to new option traders. Option values themselves are directly correlated to changes in the days to expiration: the more time to expiration, the higher an option's value and the less time, the lower the value, assuming other factors are constant. Consequently, one might think that thetas should be preceded by plus signs. But they are preceded by minus signs! Why?

It is standard practice to have a minus sign in front of thetas because options decrease in value the longer they are held, other factors remaining constant. The minus sign associated with thetas assumes that the option is owned and that it decays, or loses money, as expiration approaches.

Experienced option traders may be aware that there is one exception to this rule. Although an in-depth discussion of this topic is beyond the scope of this book, it is possible for the theoretical value of a deep in-the-money European-style option to be less than intrinsic value. This can occur because European-style options cannot be exercised early. When such a situation exists, the option has a positive theta, which indicates that the theoretical option value increases to intrinsic value as expiration approaches.

> **RHO**
> Estimated change in option value resulting from a 1 percent change in interest rates

RHO

Rho is an estimate of the change in option value given a 1 percent change in interest rates, assuming other factors remain constant. Rho answers this question: If interest rates change by 1 percent, how much do I make or lose? Table 5–6 illustrates how the 800 Call and 800 Put values change when the interest rate is increased from 5 percent to 6 percent. The 800 Call value increases from 14.690 to 15.029, a change equal to the call's rho of +0.339. The value of the 800 Put decreases from 12.723 to 12.408, a change equal to the put's rho of –0.315.

Table 5–6 Illustration of Rho

	Initial		With Changed Interest Rates
Inputs			
Index level	800		
Strike price	800		
Dividend yield	2.0%		
Volatility	15.0%		
Interest rates	5.0%	→	6.0%
Days to expiration	30		
Outputs			
800 Call price	14.690	→	15.029
800 Call rho	+0.339		
800 Put price	12.723	→	12.408
800 Put rho	−0.315		

Why rhos of call values are positive and rhos of put values are negative is another consequence of the call-put parity relationship, and a detailed discussion is beyond the scope of this book. Fortunately, the impact of changes in interest rates on short-term option values is small. Traders of short-term index options, therefore, need not be as concerned with rho as they should be with the other Greeks. Consequently, the impact of interest rates and rho will not be discussed in this book.

HOW THE GREEKS CHANGE

It is difficult to measure something when the measure itself changes, and the task of estimating changes in option values is complicated by the fact that the Greeks themselves change when market conditions change. To illustrate this concept, Table 5–7 presents a grid of 800 Call values, 800 Put values, and corresponding Greeks at various index levels and days to expiration. A study of this table reveals how delta, gamma, vega, and theta change as market conditions change. The concepts in Table 5–7 are important for option traders who must consider the impact of changing market conditions on their strategies.

Table 5–7 Delta, Gamma, Vega, and Theta for In-the-Money, At-the-Money, and Out-of-the-Money Options

Row	Call/ Put	Col. 1: 35 Days	Col. 2: 28 Days	Col. 3: 21 Days	Col. 4: 14 Days	Col. 5: 7 Days	Col. 6: Exp.
				Index Level 820			
A 800 Call		**28.646**	**27.021**	**25.274**	**23.380**	**21.364**	**20.000**
Delta		0.731	0.749	0.774	0.814	0.890	1.000
Gamma		0.009	0.009	0.010	0.011	0.011	0.000
Vega		0.845	0.732	0.601	0.440	0.224	0.000
Theta(7-day)		−1.624	−1.747	−1.894	−2.016	−1.364	0.000
B 800 Put		**6.390**	**5.216**	**3.919**	**2.476**	**0.912**	**0.000**
Delta		−0.269	−0.251	−0.226	−0.186	−0.110	0.000
Gamma		0.009	0.009	0.010	0.011	0.011	0.000
Vega		0.845	0.732	0.601	0.440	0.224	0.000
Theta(7-day)		−1.174	−1.299	−1.443	−1.564	−0.912	0.000
				Index Level 800			
C 800 Call		**15.949**	**14.161**	**12.161**	**9.830**	**6.858**	**0.000**
Delta		0.534	0.530	0.526	0.521	0.515	0.000
Gamma		0.011	0.012	0.014	0.017	0.024	0.000
Vega		0.983	0.880	0.763	0.624	0.442	0.000
Theta(7-day)		−1.787	−2.000	−2.332	−2.972	−6.858	0.000
D 800 Put		**13.655**	**12.325**	**10.783**	**8.910**	**6.398**	**0.000**
Delta		−0.466	−0.470	−0.474	−0.479	−0.485	0.000
Gamma		0.011	0.012	0.014	0.017	0.024	0.000
Vega		0.983	0.880	0.763	0.624	0.442	0.000
Theta(7-day)		−1.330	−1.542	−1.873	−2.513	−6.398	0.000
				Index Level 780			
E 800 Call		**7.424**	**5.945**	**4.365**	**2.676**	**0.937**	**0.000**
Delta		0.323	0.297	0.262	0.210	0.119	0.000
Gamma		0.010	0.011	0.012	0.013	0.013	0.000
Vega		0.872	0.754	0.617	0.449	0.224	0.000
Theta(7-day)		−1.480	−1.579	−1.689	−1.739	−0.937	0.000
F 800 Put		**25.092**	**24.078**	**22.964**	**21.741**	**20.469**	**20.000**
Delta		−0.677	−0.703	−0.738	−0.790	−0.881	0.000
Gamma		0.010	0.011	0.012	0.013	0.013	0.000
Vega		0.872	0.754	0.617	0.449	0.224	0.000
Theta(7-day)		−1.015	−1.114	−1.223	−1.272	−0.469	0.000

How Deltas Change

Delta estimates how much an option value changes when the underlying index changes and other factors remain constant. There are four general rules about how deltas change. Because calls have positive deltas and puts have negative deltas, the four rules will be stated by using the absolute values of the deltas.

The first rule relates to deltas of in-the-money, at-the-money, and out-of-the-money options. In-the-money options have deltas with absolute values greater than +0.500. At-the-money options have deltas with absolute values of approximately +0.500; and out-of-the-money options have deltas with absolute values less than +0.500.

Table 5–7 verifies these rules. Rows A and B show an index level of 820, where the 800 Call is in-the-money and the 800 Put is out-of-the-money. Row A shows that the absolute value of the delta of the 800 Call is always above +0.500, and Row B shows that the absolute value of the delta of the 800 Put is always below +0.500. With an index level of 780 (Rows E and F), the situation is reversed. The 800 Call is out-of-the-money, and its delta is always below +0.500. The 800 Put is in-the-money, and the absolute value of its delta is always above +0.500.

With the index at 800 (Rows C and D), both the 800 Call and the 800 Put are at-the-money, and the absolute values of their deltas are +0.534 and +0.466, respectively, both of which are approximately +0.500.

The second general rule relates to how deltas change as expiration approaches. The absolute values of deltas of in-the-money options increase toward +1.00 as expiration approaches. The absolute values of deltas of at-the-money options remain near +0.500, and absolute values of deltas of out-of-the-money options decrease toward zero as expiration approaches.

The third rule relates to how deltas change as the underlying index changes in price. Both call and put deltas increase as the underlying instrument rises in price and decrease as the underlying falls in price. Column 1 in Table 5–7 shows that, as the index level rises, the 800 Call delta rises from +0.323 (Row E) to +0.534 (Row C) to +0.731 (Row A) and the 800 Put delta rises from −0.677 (Row F) to −0.466 (Row D) to −0.269 (Row B). Remember to keep increases and decreases straight when minus signs are involved! The same concept, deltas rising with a rising price and falling with a falling price, holds true for any column in Table 5–7.

The fourth general rule is that the sum of the absolute values of the call delta and put delta is +1.00. With the index at 780 at 35 days to expiration, for example, the delta of the 800 Call is +0.323, and the delta of the 800 Put is −0.677. The sum of the absolute values of these numbers, +0.323

and +0.677, is +1.00. This is another result of the call-put relationship, and is true at any point in Table 5–7.

How Gammas Change

Table 5–7 shows that gammas are biggest when options are at-the-money and they increase as expiration approaches. This concept is significant to option traders, because it explains the way option prices behave as an underlying index changes and an option changes from being out-of-the-money to at-the-money and then in-the-money. Out-of-the-money options, with low deltas and smaller gammas, do not respond dramatically to small price changes in the underlying index. However, as the index approaches the strike price, the newly at-the-money option seems to "explode," moving noticeably more than its delta. Such price behavior brings tears of joy to option owners and screams of horror to option writers.

Consider the case of Debra, who bought an 800 Call for 7⅜, or approximately 7.424, when the OEX index was 780 at 35 days to expiration (Table 5–7, column 1, row E). If the index rises to 820 at 14 days to expiration and Debra's call rises to 23⅜, or approximately 23.380 (column 4, row A), then she will have an unrealized profit of 16, or $1,600 per option on the 40-point rise in the index in 28 days. However, if the index then falls 20 points in the next week, her call will decline to 6⅞, or 6.858 (column 5, row C). Thus, in only one-quarter of the time and with 50 percent of the index change, Debra's entire profit is lost. It is the delta of 0.814, up from 0.323 initially, that explains the potential for loss. If Debra is aware of the new sensitivities to market changes, she may be inclined to take her profit more quickly if the market starts to move down.

How Vegas Change

Table 5–7 shows that vegas, the change in option value from a 1 percent change in volatility, are biggest when options are at-the-money, and that they decrease as expiration approaches. In any column, vegas are biggest in rows C and D, when the 800 Call and 800 Put are at-the-money. Vegas are biggest for at-the-money options because movement of any size in the underlying has the biggest impact on at-the-money options.

Across any row from column 1 to column 6, the vegas get smaller. Vegas decrease as expiration approaches because the potential for movement is less when there is less time to expiration.

How Thetas Change

It is important to understand how thetas change, because the impact of time erosion on option prices is frequently misunderstood or oversimplified or both. A word of warning: theta, the estimate of the impact of time on option values, is preceded by a minus sign, which can be confusing when discussing "biggest" and "smallest" values. Read this section carefully!

Option thetas are smallest (the highest absolute value) when options are at-the-money. In any column in Table 5–7, the thetas have the highest absolute values in Rows C and D, when the 800 Call and 800 Put are at-the-money. At-the-money options have larger time values than in-the-money or out-of-the-money options, and it is the time value portion of an option's price that erodes. Given the same amount of time to expiration, at-the-money options lose more value per unit of time than in-the-money or out-of-the-money options.

Thetas of at-the-money options decrease (increase in absolute value) as expiration approaches, and they are smallest (largest absolute value) during the last unit of time prior to expiration. In column 5, rows C and D, the index is 800, there are 7 days to expiration, and both the 800 Call and 800 Put have the smallest thetas (largest absolute value): –6.858 and –6.398, respectively.

Thetas of in-the-money and out-of-the-money options behave differently than thetas of at-the-money options. They get smaller (absolute value increases) for a while, but then they get larger (absolute value decreases) as expiration approaches. In row A, with an index level of 820, the 800 Call is in-the-money and its theta decreases from –1.624 in column 1 to –2.016 in column 4. It then increases to –1.364 in column 5. With an index level of 820, the 800 Put is out-of-the-money, and row B illustrates that its theta changes in a similar fashion, decreasing from column 1 to column 4 and then increasing in column 5. The point to remember is that traders must be careful about making generalizations about the impact of time decay on option values.

How does a trader use theta? Since theta estimates how time decay will affect a position, a trader buying options can estimate how much the underlying must move in a specific time period in order for the delta effect (price movement of the underlying) to make more than the theta effect (time decay). A trader selling options can estimate the price range an index must stay within in order for the short option position to break even or make a profit.

POSITION GREEKS

The term *position* refers to whether an option is purchased (long) or written (short). For example, if Bob buys 10 OEX 800 Calls, his position is "long

10." If Sally buys 15 TXX 230 Puts and sells 15 220 TXX Puts, her position is "long 15 230 Puts and short 15 220 Puts."

What Bob and Sally and all traders need is a method of estimating how their position will perform if market conditions change, that is, if one or more of the inputs to the option pricing formula changes. *Position Greeks indicate whether a position will profit or lose when a particular input to the option pricing formula is changed.*

How position Greeks are calculated and interpreted will be explained after the following discussion about the use of positive and negative signs.

Three Different Meanings of Plus and Minus Signs

Plus and minus signs can have three different meanings. When associated with a *quantity of options* in a position, as in "+3 NDX January 950 Puts at 12½" or "−15 XMI November 775 Calls at 9⅛," the plus sign means "long," and the minus sign means "short." These positions should be read as "long 3 NDX 950-strike Puts at 12½ each" and "short 15 XMI November 775-strike Calls at 9⅛ each."

When associated with a *Greek of an option value,* a plus sign means that the option value is positively correlated to changes in the indicated component, and a minus sign means that the option value is inversely correlated. For delta, the indicated component is underlying price. Consequently, the statement "the call has a delta of +0.50" means that, as the underlying price rises, the call value rises, and, as the underlying price falls, the call value also falls. Put values have negative deltas. So the statement "the put has a delta of −0.32" means that, as the underlying price rises, the put value falls and, as the underlying price falls, the put value rises. For vega, the indicated component is volatility. "The call has a vega of +0.22" mean that, as volatility rises, the call value rises, and, as volatility falls, the call value also falls.

Finally, when associated with a *Greek of an option position,* plus and minus signs, with one exception, indicate whether a position will profit or lose from an increase in the indicated component. For example, in the statement "the vega of Felecia's three long calls is +2.733," the plus sign means that Felecia's position will profit by 2.733 points if volatility rises 1 percent and other factors remain constant. In the statement "the theta of Dione's four long puts is −3.644," the minus sign means Dione's position will lose 3.644 points if time changes by one unit and other factors remain constant.

The three different meanings may be hard to remember without some practice. During the following discussion of position Greeks, keep in mind that plus and minus signs can mean any of these depending on usage: (1) long or short, (2) positively or inversely correlated, and (3) profit or loss.

Position Deltas

A position with a positive delta will profit if the price of the underlying rises and will lose if it declines, assuming other factors remain constant. Long call positions and short put positions have positive deltas (see Table 5–8).

Position 1 is long 4 OEX 870 Calls at 9⅛ each. These are options on the S&P 100 Stock Index traded at the CBOE. The position delta of +1.032 is the product of the quantity of long calls (+4) and the option delta (+0.258). The position delta estimates that if the underlying index, the OEX in this case, rises by one point and other factors remain constant, then the position of these four long calls will profit by 1.032, or $103.20, not including transaction costs. The position delta also estimates that this amount will be lost if the OEX index falls by one point and other factors remain constant.

Position 2 is short 6 NDX 940 Puts at 12½ each. These are options on the NASDAQ 100 Stock Index traded at the CBOE. The position delta of +2.742 estimates that this position will make a profit of $274.20 if the NDX index rises by one point or will lose this amount if the index falls by one point, other factors remaining constant.

Table 5–9 shows that short call positions and long put positions have negative deltas. A position with a negative delta will lose if the price of the underlying rises and profit if it declines, assuming other factors remain constant. Position 1 is short 9 TXX 210 Calls at 12⅛ each. These are options on the CBOE Technology Index. The position has a delta of −3.033, which means that it will lose 3.033, or $303.30, if the index rises by one point, and profit by the same amount if the index falls by one point.

Table 5–8 Positive Delta Positions

Position	Option Position	×	Option Delta	=	Position Delta
1. Long 4 OEX 870 Calls at 9⅛ each	+4	×	+0.258	=	+1.032
2. Short 6 NDX 940 Puts at 12½ each	−6	×	−0.457	=	+2.742

Table 5–9 Negative Delta Positions

Position	Option Position	×	Option Delta	=	Position Delta
1. Short 9 TXX 210 Calls at 12⅛ each	−9	×	+0.337	=	−3.033
2. Long 3 DRG 450 Puts at 7⅞ each	+3	×	−0.652	=	−1.956

Position 2 is long 3 DRG 450 Puts at 7⅞ each. These are options on the Pharmaceutical Index which are traded at the AMEX. The position delta is −1.956. These are obviously in-the-money puts, because the delta of each option is −0.652.

Position Gammas

Gammas of positions do not indicate profit or loss. They indicate how the position delta will change when the price of the underlying changes. A positive position gamma indicates that the position delta will change in the same direction as the change in price of the underlying. A negative position gamma indicates the position delta will change in the opposite direction as the change in price of the underlying.

Positive gamma. Table 5–10 shows that long call positions and long put positions have positive gammas. Position 1, for example, is long 15 AUX 220 Calls at 4⅛ each. These are options on the Automotive Index traded at the CBOE. This call position has a gamma of +0.210, which means that as the AUX Index rises one point, and other factors remain constant, the position delta will rise by +0.210. If the AUX Index falls by one point, the position delta will fall by this amount. Positive gamma means this: index up, position delta up; index down, position delta down.

With a positive gamma, the change in delta works to the advantage of the position. Referring back to Table 5–2, as the underlying index increases from 800 to 801, the delta of the 800 Call increases from +0.531 to +0.543. Underlying price up, delta up! This benefits the call owner, because the market exposure (delta) is changing in the call owner's favor. Initially, the call owner's exposure to the market was a delta of +0.531, which means that for every one point increase in the underlying, with other factors constant, the call owner participates by approximately 53 percent. After a one-point price rise in the index, however, the call owner's exposure has increased to approximately 54 percent. And as the market continues to rise, the call owner makes more and more per unit of price change, because the delta of the position is increasing toward +1.00.

Table 5–10 Positive Gamma Positions

Position	Option Position	×	Option Gamma	=	Position Gamma
1. Long 15 AUX 220 Calls at 4⅛ each	+15	×	+0.014	=	+0.210
2. Long 10 SPX 840 Puts at 7½ each	+10	×	+0.012	=	+0.120

What about a price decline? Look back at Table 5–3. As the price of the underlying declines, and other factors remain constant, the call owner loses less than the amount estimated by the initial delta. This happens because the delta decreases from +0.531 to +0.520. With an index decline to 799, the 800 Call declines from 14.690 to 14.166, a decline of 0.524, which is less than the initial delta of +0.531. Losing less than the amount estimated by the original delta is a benefit to the call owner.

Now consider a long put position. Position 2 in Table 5–10 is long 10 SPX 840 Puts at 7½ each. These are options on the S&P 500 Stock Index which are traded at the CBOE. The position gamma of +0.120 means that as the index declines by one point, the delta of this position will decrease by 0.120. Index down, delta down! When the market declines, a trader wants as low a delta as possible (or a negative delta with a high absolute value). It is important to remember that a delta of −5.120 is lower and "more short" than a delta of −5.000.

A decrease in the position delta as the market declines is the result of the position's positive gamma, and it is a beneficial change in market exposure for a put owner. As the market continues to fall, the put owner's exposure decreases toward −1.00 per long put, or −10.00 in the case of 10 long puts.

A positive position gamma also has a beneficial impact on a long put position when the market rises. A positive position gamma means that the delta of the long put increases as the index rises. Consequently, less is lost than estimated by the original delta.

Negative gamma.   Table 5–11 shows that short call positions and short put positions have negative gammas. A negative position gamma indicates that the position delta will change in the opposite direction as the change in price of the underlying: index up, position delta down; index down, position delta up.

Position 1 is short 2 XCI 390 Calls at 8¼ each. These are options on the American Stock Exchange's Computer Technology Index. The position gamma of −0.018 indicates that, as the XCI Index rises and other factors remain constant, the position delta will decrease by 0.018. Also, if the XCI Index falls by one point, the position delta will rise by this amount.

Position 2 is short 11 PSE 260 Puts at 4⅜ each. These are options on the Pacific Exchange's Technology Index. The position gamma of −0.110 estimates that the position delta will decrease by this amount if the index rises one point and increase by this amount if the index falls by one point, other factors remaining constant.

When a position has a negative gamma, the change in delta works to the disadvantage of the position. Assume the 800 Call in Table 5–2 is sold, so the initial delta of the short call position is −0.531 and the position gamma

Table 5–11 Negative Gamma Positions

Position	Option Position	×	Option Gamma	=	Position Gamma
1. Short 2 XCI 390 Calls at 8¼ each	− 2	×	+0.009	=	−0.018
2. Short 11 PSE 260 Puts at 4⅜ each	−11	×	+0.010	=	−1.110

is −0.012. This position gamma estimates that an increase in the index from 800 to 801 causes the position delta to decrease by 0.012 from −0.531 to −0.543. Underlying price up, delta down! This hurts the short call position, because the loss of −0.537 as the short call rises in price from 14.690 to 15.227 is greater than the loss that was estimated by the initial delta. As the market continues to rise, the position loses more and more per unit of price rise as the exposure to the market of the short call position continues to decline toward −1.00 per short call.

Table 5–3 shows that, when the index declines, the change in delta of a position with a negative gamma also works to the disadvantage of a short call position. Assuming the 800 Call in Table 5–3 is sold, the initial position delta is −0.531. As the index declines from 800 to 799, the short call position profits less than the amount estimated by the initial delta of −0.531. The profit is less, because the delta of the short call position is increasing from −0.531 to −0.520. Making less than the amount estimated by the initial delta is a disadvantage for the call writer.

Now consider a short put position. Assuming the 800 Put in Table 5–3 is sold, a decrease in the index from 800 to 799 causes the put to rise in price from 12.723 to 13.197, a change in value of 0.474, which is a loss for the put seller. The loss for the put seller is greater than that estimated by the initial delta of −0.469, because the delta of the short put position increased from +0.469 to +0.480. This change in market exposure is a disadvantage for the put seller, because more is lost than estimated by the initial delta. As the market continues to fall, the put seller's market exposure increases toward +1.00 per short put.

When an index rises, the delta of a short put position decreases. This works to the disadvantage of put sellers, because less is made than estimated by the initial delta.

Position Vegas

A position with a positive vega will profit if volatility rises and other factors remain constant. Table 5–12 shows that long option positions have positive vegas. The vega of +1.375 of position 1 means that if volatility rises by 1

Table 5–12 Positive Vega Positions

Position	Option Position	×	Option Vega	=	Position Vega
1. Long 5 SOX 300 Calls at 6⅛ each	+ 5	×	+0.275	=	+1.375
2. Long 20 MSH 410 Puts at 6½ each	+20	×	+0.194	=	+3.880

Table 5–13 Negative Vega Positions

Position	Option Position	×	Option Vega	=	Position Vega
1. Short 20 JPN 205 Calls at 4⅝ each	−20	×	+0.223	=	−4.460
2. Short 6 NWX 290 Puts at 6½ each	− 6	×	+0.293	=	−1.758

percent and other factors remain constant, then the position of long 5 SOX 300 Calls, options on the Semiconductor Index at the Philadelphia Stock Exchange, will profit by 1.375, or $137.50.

A position with a negative vega will lose if volatility rises and profit if volatility declines, assuming other factors remain constant. Table 5–13 shows that short option positions have negative vegas. Position 1 is short 20 JPN 205 Calls at 4⅝ each. These are options on the Japan Index which are traded at the American Stock Exchange. The position vega of −4.460 means that if volatility rises by 1 percent and other factors are the same, then this position will lose 4.460, or $440.60. However, the vega also estimates that if volatility falls by 1 percent, then the position will profit by $440.60.

Position Thetas

The theta of a position estimates whether that position will profit or lose as expiration approaches and other factors remain constant. Since option values decay over time, short option positions profit if factors other than time are unchanged, so those positions have positive thetas. Position 1 in Table 5–14 is short 5 SML 170 Calls at 3 each. These are options on the S&P Small Cap 600 Stock Index which are traded at the CBOE. The position theta of +6.555 estimates that the position will profit by $655.50 if time to expiration is reduced by "one unit" and other factors remain constant. The OP-EVAL3™ program assumes "one unit" of time is 7 calendar days, or one week.

Position 2 is short 50 XII 990 Puts at 16⅜ each, options on the Institutional Index which are traded at the American Stock Exchange. This position

Table 5–14 Positive Theta Positions

Position	Option Position	×	Option Theta	=	Position Theta
1. Short 5 SML 170 Calls at 3 each	− 5	×	−1.311	=	+ 6.555
2. Short 50 XII 990 Puts at 16⅜ each	−50	×	−1.127	=	+56.350

Table 5–15 Negative Theta Positions

Position	Option Position	×	Option Theta	=	Position Theta
1. Long 15 VLE 770 Calls at 9¼ each	+15	×	−1.432	=	−21.480
2. Long 8 BIX 550 Puts at 8½ each	+ 8	×	−1.091	=	− 8.728

has a positive theta of +56.350, which estimates that the position will profit by $5,635 if "one unit of time" passes and other factors are unchanged.

A position with a negative theta will incur a loss if only the time factor changes, and long option positions have negative thetas. Table 5–15 shows two long option positions, long 15 VLE 770 Calls at 9¼ each and long 8 BIX 550 Puts at 8½ each. These are options on the Value Line Stock Index which are traded at the Philadelphia Stock Exchange and the S&P Bank Stock Index which are traded at the CBOE, respectively. The theta of position 1 of −21.480 means that if only time to expiration is reduced by "one unit," then the position will lose 21.480, or $2,148.00. The theta of −8.728 of position 2 means that this amount will be lost if "one unit of time" passes and other factors remain constant.

Position Greeks Summarized

Table 5–16 matches long and short options with positive and negative position Greeks. Long calls have positive deltas, positive gammas, positive vegas, and negative thetas. Short calls have negative deltas, negative gammas, negative vegas, and positive thetas. Long puts have negative deltas and thetas and positive gammas and vegas. Short puts have positive deltas and thetas and negative gammas and vegas. No two rows in Table 5–16 are the same. Each option position has its own unique sensitivities to changes in price of the underlying, volatility, and time to expiration. Although it is confusing at first, with a little practice an understanding of position Greeks can help option traders select appropriate strategies for particular market forecasts.

Table 5–16 Summary of Position Greeks

Position	Delta Change in Price of Underlying	Gamma Change in Delta	Vega Change in Volatility	Theta Change in Time to Expiration
Long call	+	+	+	−
Short call	−	−	−	+
Long put	−	+	+	−
Short put	+	−	−	+

+ indicates a position will profit, or benefit, from an increase in an input and incur a loss from, or be hurt by, a decrease, assuming other inputs remain constant.

− indicates a position will incur a loss from, or be hurt by, an increase in an input and profit, or benefit, from a decrease, assuming other inputs remain constant.

SUMMARY

The Greeks are tools used by option traders to estimate the profit or loss impact of changes in market conditions on option positions. Delta is an estimate of the change in option value given a one-point change in price of the underlying instrument. Gamma is an estimate of change in delta for a one-point change in price of the underlying. Vega is an estimate of the change in option value resulting from a 1 percent change in volatility. Theta is an estimate of the change in option value resulting from a one-unit change in time to expiration. Traders who use computer programs should be sure to know the definition of "unit of time" used by the program.

The Greeks change as market conditions change, and this complicates the job of estimating how option prices will behave as market conditions change. The absolute values of deltas of in-the-money options are greater than +0.500 initially and increase toward +1.00 as expiration approaches. The absolute values of deltas of at-the-money options remain near +0.500 as expiration approaches. The absolute values of deltas of out-of-the-money options are initially less than +0.500 and decrease toward zero as expiration approaches. Gammas are biggest for at-the-money options and tend to increase as expiration approaches. Vegas are biggest for at-the-money options and decrease as expiration approaches. Thetas are smallest (largest absolute value) for at-the-money options. The behavior of thetas as expiration approaches differs for at-the-money options, in-the-money options, and out-of-the-money options.

Depending on usage, plus and minus signs have three different meanings. They indicate "long" or "short" when used in conjunction with a quantity of options in a position. They indicate positive or negative correlation when used in conjunction with option values. They indicate profit or loss when used in conjunction with option positions.

Positions with positive deltas are long calls and short puts. If other factors remain constant, these positions profit with a rise in price of the underlying instrument and lose with a decline. Short calls and long puts are positions with negative deltas.

When a position has a positive gamma, its delta changes in the same direction as the change in price of the underlying: index up, delta up; index down, delta down. Long calls and long puts are positions with positive gammas. Negative gamma means that the delta of a position changes in the opposite direction as the change in price of the underlying: index up, delta down; index down, delta up. Short calls and short puts are positions that have negative gammas.

A position with a positive vega will profit if volatility rises and lose if volatility declines, assuming other factors remain constant. Long calls and long puts are positions with positive vegas. Positions with negative vegas will lose if volatility rises and profit if volatility declines. Short calls and short puts have negative vegas.

Long calls and long puts are positions with a negative theta, because they lose money as time passes toward expiration and other factors remain constant. Short calls and short puts are positions with a positive theta. They profit as time passes toward expiration and other factors remain constant.

With a little practice, any trader can learn to interpret the Greeks. Such a skill is valuable in anticipating how strategies will perform with changes in market conditions.

INTRODUCTION

O ption traders need a conceptual understanding of volatility and how it affects trading decisions. A detailed knowledge of mathematical formulas is not required. While volatility simply means movement, there are four ways of describing movement, and this can be confusing. Nevertheless, spending the time necessary to understand volatility is a worthwhile endeavor, because the goal is to make more informed trading decisions.

In this chapter historic volatility will be defined and two methods of calculating relative historic volatility will be presented. Future volatility, expected volatility, and implied volatility will be defined, and an example of how two traders might evaluate the implied volatility level of an option will be presented. CBOE's innovation, the Volatility Index (VIX), will be introduced, and its usefulness for index option traders will be explained. Finally, the concept of volatility skews will be introduced.

VOLATILITY DEFINED

With regard to stock prices and stock index levels, *volatility* is a measure of changes in price expressed in percentage terms without regard to direction. This means that a rise from 200 to 202 in one index is equal in volatility terms to a rise from 100 to 101 in another index, because both changes are 1 percent. Also, a 1 percent price rise is equal in volatility terms to a 1 percent price decline.

One difficulty in grasping the concept of volatility is that traders tend to think in terms of direction and in terms of "good" or "bad." A trader with a bullish position, for example, thinks of a price rise as good and a price decline as bad. A trader with a bearish position thinks the opposite. If one has always thought this way, it can be hard to think in terms of movement rather than direction.

VOLATILITY I: HISTORIC VOLATILITY

Historic volatility is a measure of actual price changes in the past. Mathe-matically, historic volatility is the annualized standard deviation of daily returns during a specific period. Do not let this definition intimidate you, because the following discussion is conceptual, not mathematical.

Price observations can be made over 30 days, 90 days, or some other defined period. Also, the exact time when prices are observed must be specified. Daily closing prices are typically used, but daily opening prices or weekly clos-ing prices or some other consistent method of observation could also be used.

While it seems simple to compare one specific price change to another, it is more difficult to compare two series of price changes. Figure 6–1, for example, contains graphs of daily closing prices of two indexes. The question is: Which index is more volatile? Take a moment to reflect on this question and then compare your answer, which is based on your own subjective, visual evaluation, to the technical answer that is presented below.

The historic volatility of index 1 is calculated from the information in Table 6–1. The first column simply assigns a number to each closing price; in the real world this would be a date. The middle column contains the 23 closing prices that are plotted in Figure 6–1. The third column, Daily Returns, contains percentage changes in price from the previous day's price. The daily return is calculated by subtracting the closing price of the previ-ous day from the closing price of the current day and then dividing the dif-ference by the closing price of the previous day. For example, the daily return for Day 1 is −1.0 percent. This is arrived at by subtracting the closing price on Day 0, 250, from the closing price on Day 1, 247½, to yield a difference of −2.5. This difference is then divided by the closing price on Day 0, 250, and the result is −0.01, or −1.0 percent. There is no daily return for Day 0, because this is the first price observation, so the previous price is unknown.

Historic volatility is the annualized standardized deviation of the daily returns in the third column, and the result, 24.8 percent, appears at the bot-tom of Table 6–1. Although the mathematics of standard deviations is beyond the scope of this book, this calculation is a standard spreadsheet function, so it is relatively easy for the mathematically inclined to do their own research. But if you are not mathematically inclined, do not worry. OP-EVAL3™ performs the most important volatility calculations.

While it is not necessary to learn advanced calculus to trade options, it is important to know what 24.8 percent volatility means and what a stan-dard deviation is. These can best be explained by comparing the price action of index 1 to the price action of index 2.

Figure 6–1 Which Index Is More Volatile?

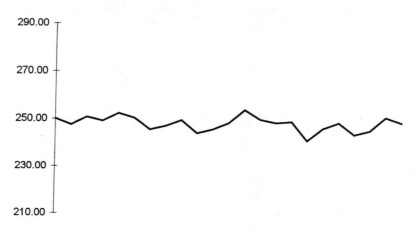

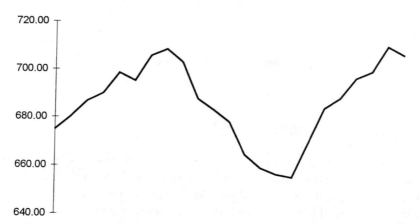

Table 6–1 Index 1: Calculation of Volatility

Day	Closing Price	Daily Return (Day 2 – Day 1)/Day 1
0	250	—
1	247½	−1.0%
2	250¾	+1.3%
3	249¼	−0.6%
4	252½	+1.3%
5	250½	−0.8%
6	245¾	−0.2%
7	247¼	+0.6%
8	249¾	+1.0%
9	244¼	−2.2%
10	246	+0.7%
11	248¾	+1.1%
12	254¼	+2.2%
13	250¼	−1.6%
14	249	−0.5%
15	249½	+0.2%
16	241½	−3.3%
17	246¾	+0.2%
18	249¼	+1.0%
19	244¼	−2.0%
20	246	+0.7%
21	251¾	+2.3%
22	249½	−0.9%

Annualized standard deviation of daily returns = 24.8%.

Comparing Historic Volatility: Method 1

Table 6–2 shows one method of comparison. Table 6–2 lists daily closing prices and daily returns for both indexes. As you look down the daily returns column for each index, you will observe that the absolute value of every percentage change of Index 1 is larger than the corresponding percentage change of index 2. This is the first indication that the volatility of Index 1 is higher than the volatility of Index 2. The second indication appears at the bottom of Table 6–2. The standard deviation for Index 2 is 18.9 percent, which is lower than that of Index 1. This is conclusive: Index 1 is more volatile than Index 2!

Some may find this result surprising since Index 2 rose 30 points, fell 50 points, and then rose 50 points, while Index 1 traded within a 10-point

Table 6–2 Comparing Historic Volatility: Method 1

	Index 1		Index 2	
Day	Closing Price	Daily Return	Closing Price	Daily Return
0	250	—	675	—
1	247½	−1.0%	680¼	+0.8
2	250¾	+1.3%	686¾	+0.9
3	249¼	−0.6%	690	+0.5
4	252½	+1.3%	698½	+1.2
5	250½	−0.8%	695¼	−0.5
6	245¾	−0.2%	705¾	+0.1
7	247¼	+0.6%	708½	+0.4
8	249¾	+1.0%	703	−0.8
9	244¼	−2.2%	687¾	−0.2
10	246	+0.7%	683¼	−0.6
11	248¾	+1.1%	678¼	−0.7
12	254¼	+2.2%	664¾	−2.0
13	250¼	−1.6%	659¼	−0.8
14	249	−0.5%	656¾	−0.4
15	249½	+0.2%	655½	−0.2
16	241½	−3.3%	670	+2.2
17	246¾	+2.2%	684¼	+2.1
18	249¼	+1.0%	688½	+0.6
19	244¼	−2.0%	697	+1.2
20	246	+0.7%	699¾	+0.4
21	251¾	+2.3%	710¼	+1.5
22	249½	−0.9%	706¾	−0.5

Annualized standard deviation of daily returns: Index 1 = 24.8%; Index 2 = 18.9%.

range. But remember, volatility is a measure of *movement,* not absolute size of price change or direction. Index 2 had several smaller percentage changes in the same direction relative to Index 1. When discussing volatility, "several smaller percentage changes" is the operative term.

Method 2: Ranking Percentage Price Changes

In the real world, of course, it is unlikely that every percentage change in one index will be larger or smaller than every corresponding percentage change in another index. Table 6–3 presents another method of comparing the volatilities: ranking the absolute values of the percentage changes (daily returns) from smallest to largest.

Table 6–3 Comparing Historic Volatility: Method 2

	Index 1			Index 2	
Day	Change Percentage	Breakdown	Day	Change Percentage	Breakdown
15	0.2		15	0.2	
14	0.5		14	0.4	
3	0.6		7	0.4	
7	0.6		20	0.4	
10	0.7		5	0.5	
20	0.7		3	0.5	
5	0.8		22	0.5	
22	0.9		18	0.6	
1	1.0		10	0.7	
8	1.0		11	0.7	
18	1.0		1	0.8	
11	1.1		8	0.8	
4	1.3		13	0.8	
2	1.3		2	1.0	
13	1.6		4	1.2	
6	1.9		19	1.2	
19	2.0		21	1.5	
17	2.2		6	1.5	
12	2.2		12	2.0	
9	2.2		17	2.1	
21	2.3		16	2.2	
16	3.2		9	2.2	

Index 1 breakdown annotations: 68% less than 1.6%, avg. 0.9%; 95% less than 2.3%, avg. 1.3%

Index 2 breakdown annotations: 68% less than 1.2%, avg. 0.6%; 95% less than 2.2%, avg. 1.0%

Table 6–3 compares a sample of the total observations: 15 observations, which is approximately two-thirds (68 percent) of the 22 price-change observations. The smallest 15 percentage price changes for Index 2 are less than 1.2 percent and average 0.6 percent. In contrast, the smallest 15 percentage price changes for Index 1 are less than 1.6 percent and average 0.9 percent. The comparison of this subgroup indicates that Index 1 has a higher volatility than Index 2.

Table 6–3 also compares the smallest 21 observations, or approximately 95 percent of the total observations; again, the measures for Index 1 are greater than those for Index 2. The absolute values of 21 percentage changes were less than 2.3 percent for Index 1, but less than 2.2 percent for Index 2. Also, the average of these changes was 1.3 percent for Index 1 and 1.0 percent for Index 2. Statistically, Index 1 was more volatile than Index 2 during the historic period observed.

VOLATILITY 2: FUTURE VOLATILITY

Future volatility means the annualized standard deviation of daily returns during some future period, typically between now and an option expiration. And it is future volatility that option pricing formulas need as an input in order to calculate the theoretical value of an option. Unfortunately, future volatility is only known when it has become historic volatility. Consequently, the volatility numbers used in option pricing formulas are only *estimates* of future volatility. This might be a shock to those who place their faith in theoretical values, because it raises questions about those values. If the volatility number in a formula is only an estimate of future volatility, then the calculated value must only be an estimate of theoretical value. And that is correct! So-called theoretical values are only estimates, and as with any estimate, they must be interpreted very carefully.

VOLATILITY 3: EXPECTED VOLATILITY

Many option traders study market conditions and historic price action to forecast volatility just as stock analysts research industry trends, company earnings, and the like to make stock price predictions. *Expected volatility* is an estimate of future volatility used by a trader in an option pricing formula to estimate an option's theoretical value. Since forecasts vary, there is no specific number that everyone can agree on for expected volatility.

Consider a situation in which two experienced option traders, Erin and Michael, disagree on their estimates of the future volatility of a hypothetical index. Assume that 10 weeks ago the most recent 30 closing levels of the index indicated a historic volatility of 22 percent. Assume also that 6 weeks ago, 3 weeks ago, and yesterday, the same calculation using the then most-recent 30 closing index levels indicated volatilities of 21 percent, 19 percent, and 18 percent, respectively. Michael and Erin cannot dispute these historic volatility percentages because they are the results of mathematical calculations.

They can make different forecasts, however. Michael may believe that the downward trend in volatility will continue. He may expect that in 1 week, the 30-day historic volatility will be 17 percent. Consequently, he may use 17 percent volatility in his option pricing formula. Erin may believe that the downward trend is about to reverse and that historic volatility will be higher in 1 week. She may predict, therefore, that in 7 days, the 30-day historic volatility will be 20 percent. Consequently, she may use 20 percent in her option pricing formula. Stock analysts have differing opinions on the outlook for individual stocks, and option traders differ on their expected volatilities.

VOLATILITY 4: IMPLIED VOLATILITY

Implied volatility is the volatility percentage that explains the current market price of an option. This concept is best illustrated with an example. Consider a situation in which Terry, an experienced NDX option trader, uses OP-EVAL3™ to estimate the theoretical value of the NDX November 1120 Call.

Figure 6–2 shows the Call/Put Pricer page with Terry's inputs: the current index level of 1105, the strike of 1120, a dividend yield of 0.20 percent, interest rates of 5 percent, and days to expiration of 50. Terry chose a volatility of 25 percent because this was the historic volatility based on the 30 most recent daily closing index levels. Given Terry's inputs, OP-EVAL3™ calculates a value of 37.190 for the NDX November 1120 Call.

Terry now calls his broker and discovers that the NDX November 1120 Call is trading at 43!! What is going on? Did Terry do something wrong? Or could the market be assuming something different than Terry? For Instance, could the market be assuming a different index level? No. The index is known to be 1105. A different strike price or time to expiration? A different interest rate or dividend yield? Again the answer is no; a slight difference in interest rates or dividend yield may produce a change in option value of a few pennies, but not 6 dollars!

What, then, can account for the difference? The only remaining factor is volatility. What volatility, then, is the market assuming? Figure 6–3 shows the Call/Put Pricer page with the price of 43 entered in the Call rectangle. When

Figure 6–2 Terry's Estimate of the 50-Day 1120 Call

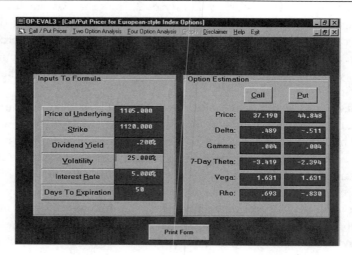

Figure 6–3 Calculating the Implied Volatility of the 1120 Call

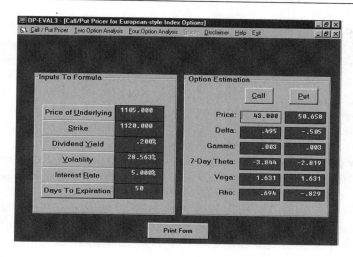

the ENTER key is pressed, OP-EVAL3™ calculates a volatility of 28.563 percent. This is the volatility percentage that explains the market price of this NDX November 1105 Call. It is the implied volatility of this option.

The Role of Supply and Demand

Option prices, like all prices in free markets, are determined by the forces of supply and demand. Since future volatility is the one variable in an option pricing formula that cannot be observed, the volatility percentage must be adjusted to explain the market price of an option. The volatility percentage that produces the option's market price as the theoretical value is the implied volatility. In Terry's NDX call, 28.563 percent is the volatility that made the formula's calculated value equal the option's market price.

The concept of implied volatility facilitates the tracking of information about market conditions. It is common parlance to describe Terry's NDX call as "trading at 28.653 percent volatility," and such information makes comparisons possible. This call, for example, at some previous time, may have been trading at a higher or lower implied volatility. If all other factors are equal, then an option trading at a lower implied volatility is a relatively good purchase and an option trading at a higher implied volatility is a relatively better sale. But rarely, if ever, are all other factors equal, so the level of implied volatility is not, in and of itself, an indication to buy or sell an option. Implied volatility is, however, important information for a trader to incorporate into the subjective decision-making process.

Changes in Implied Volatility

The implied volatility level of index options is important information because implied volatility changes frequently and these changes can have a dramatic effect on the results of trading strategies. It is, therefore, important to understand why implied volatility changes and how it affects trading decisions.

One explanation of why implied volatility changes is based on the analogy between options and insurance presented in Chapter 3. In that analogy volatility is comparable to the risk factor in insurance, and the level of insurance premiums depends on the level of risk.

For example, if an insurance company had records that showed that 1 out of 100 homes is destroyed by fire, then, in theory, fire insurance would cost 1 percent of the value of a home plus a profit margin. But if the insurance company perceives that fire will destroy a greater percentage of homes in the future than in the past, then it will raise its premiums. Similarly, if the company perceives that fire will destroy fewer homes, then premiums are lowered. However, insurance companies live in a competitive environment, and some premiums are set to "meet the competition." This means that premiums are sometimes raised above the calculated level and sometimes they are lowered below that level.

Historic volatility is like the insurance company's records of actual experience, expected volatility is like a particular insurance company's perception of future risk, and implied volatility is like the competitive premium level in the market. In options as in insurance, many market participants compete. It is the perception of the marketplace, through the forces of supply and demand, that determines implied volatility. Since perceptions change, implied volatility also changes.

Implied volatility may rise, for example, when a company issues a statement that it will make a "major announcement next week." Before the statement, it may have been reasonable to believe that the future volatility of the stock price would be the same as the historic volatility. Consequently, the implied volatility of option prices may have been close to historic volatility. The statement, however, is likely to change expectations.

After the statement there is reason to believe that the stock price could rise or fall dramatically depending on whether the news is good or bad. Such a change in expectations would mean that buyers of options would be willing to pay a higher price and sellers of options would want to receive a higher price. This change in consensus means that implied volatility has increased.

Implied volatility may decline after the major announcement. If the announcement causes a reduction of anxiety about future stock price changes, then option sellers will be willing to receive lower prices and option buyers will only be willing to pay lower prices. Consequently, implied volatility will decrease.

Much as stock traders use price-to-earnings (p/e) ratios to make judgments about a stock's relative value, option traders use the implied volatility of an option to make a subjective judgment about an option's relative value. This concept is important and will be explained next.

P/E Ratios Compared to Implied Volatility

The p/e ratio is a common denominator that allows comparison across a range of variables such as the number of shares outstanding, the value of company assets, and total sales, just to name a few. If the p/e ratio of Company A is 15, then it is trading at a relatively lower value per share than Company B, whose p/e ratio is 20. This is true even if Company A has $6 billion in sales and a stock price of $100 and Company B has $1 billion in sales and a stock price of $50. Other common denominators are book value per share, sales per share, and percentage growth of earnings. The per-share amount of these variables provides insight for making subjective judgments about the value of a particular stock.

Implied volatility does the same thing for option prices that p/e ratios do for stock prices. Implied volatility is a common denominator that makes it possible to compare options. Prices of options on two different stocks can be compared, and prices of the same option at different times can be compared.

Consider a Company C 90-day $40 Call trading at 3, or $300. Without knowing the implied volatility of this call, it is impossible to compare it to a Company D 45-day $65 Call trading at 4¼, or $425. However, if it is known that the implied volatility of the call on Company C is 30 percent and the implied volatility of the call on Company D is 40 percent, then there is a basis for describing the relative values of the two options.

Implied volatility also makes it possible to compare the same option at two different times when the price of the underlying has changed. Assume Day 1 is 85 days to expiration, Index E is 448, the 450 Call is trading at 4¾ with a 35 percent implied volatility. If, on Day 2, which is 65 days to expiration, the index level is 452, the 450 Call is 5½, and the implied volatility is 25 percent, then it can be said that on Day 2 this option is a "better relative value in volatility terms" for the purchaser than on Day 1. It can also be said that its total price is higher and that it has less time to expiration. These are three variables that describe an option.

Implied volatility, like a p/e ratio, is information that can be used as part of the subjective decision-making process, but neither the implied volatility level nor the p/e ratio gives a specific recommendation to purchase or sell.

Is 34 percent implied volatility high? Is 12 percent low? There is no absolute answer to such questions. There are only relative answers. By keeping track of implied volatility, a trader can gain historical perspective. As a result, more informed predictions can be made. This does not guarantee that the predictions will be accurate, but generally speaking, predictions based on more information are better.

THE CONCEPT OF THEORETICAL VALUE

Although the mathematics of the Black-Scholes option pricing formula involves derivative calculus, the concept of an option's theoretical value is similar to the concept of "expected value," which is calculated in two steps. First, given a range of possible outcomes, an "expected value of each outcome" is calculated by multiplying the probability of each outcome by the value of each outcome. Second, the individual expected outcomes are added together to arrive at the "total expected value" or "theoretical value."

Consider a simplified scenario in which an index, currently at 100, has a 50 percent chance of rising to 110 and a 50 percent chance of falling to 90: no other outcomes are possible in this example. Also, assume interest rates to be zero so that time is unimportant. The "expected value," or theoretical value, of the 100 Call is calculated as follows: If the index rises to 110, the 100 Call will have a value of 10. Since this event has a 50 percent chance of happening, the expected value of this outcome is 0.50 times 10, or 5. If the index falls to 90, the 100 Call will have a value of zero and expire worthless. The expected value of this outcome is 0.50 times 0, or 0. Consequently, the "expected value" or "theoretical value" of the 100 Call, in this example, is 5 (0.50 × 10 + 0.50 × 0). This situation is depicted Figure 6–4.

Now that a "theoretical value" has been calculated, it is reasonable to ask what the assumptions are and if they apply to the real world. The first assumption is that the process can be repeated an infinite number of times, that is, the index can start at 100 an infinite number of times and finish at 110 half of the time and at 90 half of the time. As a result of this process, the 100 Call will have a value of 10 half of the time and of 5 half of the time. While the average, or theoretical, value is 5, any specific outcome will be either 10 or zero.

Figure 6–4 "Theoretical Value" of 100 Call (simplified range of outcomes)

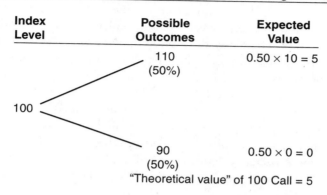

Index Level	Possible Outcomes	Expected Value
	110 (50%)	0.50 × 10 = 5
100		
	90 (50%)	0.50 × 0 = 0

"Theoretical value" of 100 Call = 5

Do these assumptions apply to trading in the real world? Can traders repeat the same trade an infinite number of times under identical circumstances? No, they cannot. Nothing is ever the same in the real world. The conclusion is that for traders, the concept of theoretical value is just that, a concept!

Rather than focus on the notion of theoretical value as an absolute value, traders should think about relative value. Since implied volatility is the common denominator of option prices, it is often used as a guide to relative value.

There is, perhaps, no greater misconception in the options business than about the meaning of the terms "overvalued" and "undervalued." Novice traders misconstrue these terms to mean that "easy money" can be made by purchasing options "below theoretical value" or by selling them "above theoretical value." Nothing could be further from reality!

An option will appear "overvalued" or "undervalued" at one particular moment only because an option pricing formula, at the moment, calculates a different "value" than the market price. If a "value" of 7 is calculated but the option is trading at 6, for example, then that option appears undervalued. A trader who purchases this option would profit only if the option returns to "theoretical value" and *all other factors remain constant*. But this means that the stock price and the time to expiration would remain constant and only the volatility would change. Is such a scenario likely—or even possible? Definitely not.

Reflect for a moment on the difference between the calculated theoretical value of 7 and the market price of 6 in the previous paragraph. What is the *conceptual difference* between 6 and 7? Is it the underlying index level? No. Is it the strike price or time to expiration or interest rates or dividends?

Again, no. The difference is the volatility percentage. The volatility percentage used in the formula that produced a value of 7 is the trader's expected volatility, and the volatility percentage that explains the market price of 6 is implied volatility. Therefore, this option appears undervalued because the trader's expected volatility is higher than the implied volatility. When an option appears overvalued, it is because the trader's expected volatility is lower than the implied volatility.

This is an important concept to grasp. "Undervalued" and "overvalued" depend on the relationship of expected volatility to implied volatility. Implied volatility can be objectively observed, because market prices can be observed, but expected volatility depends on the judgment of a trader. Therefore "overvalued" and "undervalued" depend on the same judgment.

The subjective nature of the terms "overvalued" and "undervalued" raises questions about the concept of theoretical value. The term "theoretical value" sounds so impressive and so authoritative, but theoretical value depends on future volatility—and future volatility is unknown. This means that any price presented as the theoretical value of an option is actually only an estimate, an educated guess. This may be a startling notion to new option traders, but everything depends on judgment in trading, including the determination of value.

Two Traders, Two Opinions about Value

Consider two experienced OEX option traders and how they might arrive at different conclusions about the "value" of a particular OEX call. Tony is a salesman in San Antonio who "day-trades" OEX options when he is not traveling for business. Sandy, is an aerospace engineer in Los Angeles with a different trading style. She charts the OEX and looks for patterns, which, in her opinion, predict a 5- to 10-day move of 10 to 20 OEX points.

On the day in question, the OEX is trading at 868, it is 37 days to August expiration, and the OEX August 880 Call is trading at 15½. In this example we assume that the dividend yield is 1.7 percent and interest rates are 4.5 percent. Tony predicts that the OEX Index will rise five points to 873 today, and he is considering the purchase of the August 880 Call at 15½.

Tony has observed that both OEX historic volatility and implied volatility have been declining. He calculates a 15 percent 30-day historic volatility of the OEX Index and an implied volatility of 18 percent for the August 880 Call. He believes that the implied volatility of this call will drop to 15 percent by the end of today, and he creates Table 6–4 to estimate how the August 880 Call will change in price if his forecast is realized.

Table 6–4 Tony's Analysis of the OEX 880 Call

Row	Index	Col. 1: 15% Volatility	Col. 2: 18% Volatility
1	866	11½	14¾
2	867	11⅞	15⅛
3	868	12⅜	15½
4	869	12¾	15⅞
5	870	13⅛	16⅜
6	871	13½	16⅞
7	872	14	17⅜
8	873	14½	17⅞
9	874	15	18⅜

Dividend yield, 1.7%; interest rates, 4.5%; days to expiration, 37.

As Table 6–4 indicates, if the OEX rises to 873 today (row 8) and implied volatility falls to 15 percent (column 1), then the 880 Call will decline from 15½ (row 3, column 2) to 14½ (row 8, column 1), for a loss of 1. Table 6–4 also shows that if implied volatility remains at 18 percent, then the 880 Call will rise from 15½ to 17⅞ (row 8, column 2). If Tony's forecast called for implied volatility to remain constant or increase, then he might be inclined to purchase the August 880 Call to attempt to profit from his forecast. However, his forecast predicts a decrease in implied volatility to 15 percent; therefore, to Tony, this call appears overvalued. Tony does not purchase the August 880 Call and looks for another trade.

The second trader, Sandy, analyzes the same situation and arrives at a different conclusion. Sandy is considering buying the August 880 Call, because she forecasts a 20-point rise in the OEX in 7 days and a rise in implied volatility to 20 percent. Sandy creates Table 6–5 to estimate the results of her forecast.

Table 6–5 Sandy's Analysis of the OEX 880 Call

Row	Index	Col. 1: 18% Volatility	Col. 2: 20% Volatility
1	863	11⅜	13⅜
2	868	13⅜	15⅜
3	873	15⅝	17⅜
4	878	18	20
5	883	20¾	22¾
6	888	23⅝	25⅝

Dividend yield, 1.7%; interest rates, 4.5%; days to expiration, 30.

If Sandy's forecast is realized, then the OEX will be 888 at 30 days to expiration, and Table 6–5 estimates that the price of the August 880 Call will be 25⅝ (row 6, column 2). Purchasing the 880 Call for 15½ and selling it at 25⅝ results in a profit of 10⅛, not including commissions. Table 6–5 also estimates that if implied volatility remains constant at 18 percent, then the price of the 880 Call will be 23⅝ (row 6, column 1). Purchasing the 880 Call at 15½ and selling it a 23⅝ yields a profit of 8⅛, not including commissions. The rise in implied volatility accounts for two points of Sandy's estimated 10⅛ profit with the index at 888 in 7 days and implied volatility at 20 percent, but she still estimates a profit if implied volatility is unchanged at 18 percent.

If the OEX declines to 863, then Sandy's forecast for the index level will be wrong. If, however, her forecasts for time and implied volatility are correct, then Table 6–5 estimates that the price of the 880 Call will be 13⅜ (row 1, column 2), a loss of 2⅛, not including commissions, from a purchase price of 15½. Of course, if the implied volatility remains unchanged at 18 percent, then Table 6–5 indicates that the price of the 880 Call will be 11⅜ (row 1, column 1), a loss of 4⅛.

To Sandy, this analysis indicates that the August 880 Call appears undervalued, because she profits if all three parts of her forecast are accurate. She also profits if her index level and time forecasts are accurate but implied volatility is unchanged, and she nearly breaks even before commissions if her time and volatility forecasts are accurate but the index declines five points. Confident of her forecast and willing to assume a loss if all three parts of her forecast are wrong, Sandy instructs her broker to purchase the OEX August 880 Call at 15½.

To summarize, Sandy and Tony agreed that the 880 Call is trading at an implied volatility of 18 percent. They disagreed, however, on whether it was overvalued or undervalued because they have different trading styles and, in this case, different expected volatilities. The general conclusion is that value, like beauty, is in the eye of the beholder. The only variable in the market price of an option is implied volatility, and the only variable in the calculation of an option's theoretical value is expected volatility. Consequently, a judgment that the market price of an option is above or below theoretical value is actually a judgment about the relationship of implied volatility to expected volatility.

CBOE'S VOLATILITY INDEX: THE VIX

One measure of the level of implied volatility in index options is CBOE's Volatility Index (VIX). This index is calculated by taking a weighted average of the implied volatilities of eight OEX calls and puts. The chosen options have an average time to maturity of 30 days. Consequently, the VIX is intended to indicate the implied volatility of 30-day index options. It is used by some traders as a general indication of index option implied volatility. Implied volatility levels in index options change frequently and substantially. Consequently, when trading short-term index options, traders should forecast the index level, the time period, and the volatility level. Traders of long-term index options should also include a forecast of interest rates.

VOLATILITY SKEWS

Volatility skew is a market condition in which options with the same underlying and the same expiration but different strike prices trade at different implied volatilities. This is a common occurrence in markets for options on stock indexes and futures contracts.

Table 6–6 contains prices and the implied volatilities of calls and puts with 11 strike prices. The index level is 900, the dividend yield is 1.60 percent, interest rates are 4.50 percent, and it is 35 days to expiration. Note that the implied volatility of the at-the-money 900 Call and 900 Put is 18.0 percent and that the implied volatilities of the other options increase as strike prices increase or decrease. The implied volatility of the 910 Call and 910 Put, for example, is 18.45 percent.

Figure 6–5 presents the information in Table 6–6 in graphical form. Note that the line above 900 is not symmetrical with the line below 900. Also note that neither line is perfectly straight. Although this information is not real data on a real index, Table 6–6 and Figure 6–5 are illustrative of the levels of implied volatilities of options on numerous indexes that exist from time to

Table 6–6 Volatility Skews

Call	Strike	Put	Implied Volatility
58¾	850	6½	22.40%
50¼	860	7⅞	21.40%
42¼	870	9⅞	20.60%
34⅝	880	12¼	19.70%
27⅝	890	15¼	18.90%
21¼	900	18¾	18.00%
17	910	24½	18.45%
13⅞	920	31¼	19.10%
11	930	38⅜	19.60%
9	940	46⅜	20.30%
7¼	950	54½	20.80%

Index level, 900; dividend yield, 1.6%; interest rates, 4.5%; days to expiration, 35.

Figure 6–5 Graph of Volatility Skew

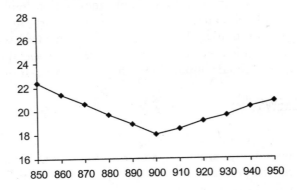

time. In dynamic markets such as index option markets, the overall level of implied volatility and the slopes of implied volatility skews as depicted by the lines in Figure 6–5 change frequently. Option traders must beware of this potential market condition and prepare themselves accordingly.

Why Skews Exist

It seems illogical that one underlying instrument could have more than one volatility, and, to date, no theoretical reason for the existence of volatility skews has been presented. One practical explanation, however, has been suggested. Since option prices are determined by supply and demand, it is possible that there are different forces of supply and demand for different options. Since options are analogous to insurance policies and strike prices are analogous to deductibles, it is possible that there are different elements of supply and demand for the different protection, or insurance, offered by options with different strike prices. It is possible that there is more demand for "cheap insurance policies"—policies with a low absolute price.

   In order to meet this increased demand, the logic goes, sellers of low-cost insurance policies require a "high-risk premium." In options, this means a high implied volatility, not a high absolute price.

How Volatility Skews Affect Trading Decisions

Traders must consider the existence of volatility skews when making forecasts. If out-of-the-money option, Strike O, is trading at a higher implied volatility than at-the-money option, Strike A, for example, then, as the index moves from Strike A to Strike O, there may be a tendency for the implied volatility of the call and put with Strike O to decrease and for the implied volatility of the call and put with Strike A to increase.

Consider the forecasting problem being addressed by Floyd, an experienced OEX option trader. Floyd is studying the purchase of an OEX 880 Put. Assuming an OEX level of 900 and the option prices and market conditions in Table 6–6, Floyd must first state his three-part forecast for the OEX level, the time to expiration, and the implied volatility of the 880 Put. Floyd is bearish, predicting that the OEX will decline to 880 in two weeks; he also believes that implied volatility will remain constant. Floyd's volatility forecast, however, raises a question.

What does "implied volatility will remain constant" mean when there is a volatility skew? What implied volatility level should Floyd use when estimating the value of the 880 Put? If the OEX declines to 880 in 10 days, as Floyd predicts, the 880 Put will have moved from 20 points out-of-the-money to at-the-money. If the "implied volatility level remains constant" as Floyd predicts, then the implied volatility of the 880 Put will decline from 19.75 percent to 18 percent. Table 6–7 shows the implications of this change.

Column 1 shows the initial market conditions: the index level is 900, there are 35 days to expiration, the implied volatility is 19.7 percent, and the 880 Put is 12¼. Column 2 estimates a price of 17¼ for the 880 Put, assuming an index level of 880, 25 days to expiration, and the implied volatility of the 880 Put unchanged at 19.7 percent. Column 3 estimates a price of 15⅝ for the 880 Put, assuming the same conditions as Column 2 but with an implied volatility decline to 18 percent. This difference means that Floyd will

Table 6–7 Floyd Analyzes the Impact of the Volatility Skew

	Col. 1: Initial Inputs		Col. 2: Index and Days Changed; Volatility Unchanged		Col. 3: Index, Days, and Volatility Changed
Inputs					
Index level	900	→	880	→	880
Strike price	880				
Dividend yield	1.6%				
Volatility	19.7%	→	19.7%	→	18.0%
Interest rates	4.5%				
Days to expiration	35	→	25	→	25
Outputs					
880 Put price	12¼	→	17¼	→	15⅝
Estimated profit			5		3⅜

make 3⅜ per option instead of 5 per option. Whether this difference is sufficient to dissuade Floyd from making this trade is a subjective decision that only he can make. Nevertheless, even if Floyd is confident of his forecasts for the index level and time, the existence of the volatility skew has an impact on his decision.

The conclusion from Floyd's example is that if other factors remain constant, then the existence of implied volatility skews tends to be a disadvantage for buyers of out-of-the-money options. Other factors, of course, are rarely equal. There could be change in the overall level of implied volatility, or there could be a change in the slope of the volatility skew. Changes in either or both of these market conditions could change in favor of or against a particular option strategy. Consequently, volatility skews and the overall level of implied volatility must be considered by option traders.

SUMMARY

Volatility is a measure of price change without regard to direction. Historic volatility is a measure of actual price changes during a specific time period in the past. Expected volatility is a trader's forecast of volatility used in an option pricing formula to estimate the theoretical value of an option. Implied volatility is the volatility percentage that explains the current market price of an option.

Implied volatility is the common denominator of option prices. Just as p/e ratios allow comparisons of stock prices over a range of variables such as total earnings and number of shares outstanding, implied volatility enables comparison of options on different underlying instruments and comparison of the same option at different times.

Theoretical value of an option is a statistical concept, and traders should focus on relative value, not absolute value. The terms "overvalued" and "undervalued" describe a relationship between implied volatility and expected volatility. Two traders could differ in their opinion of the relative value of the same option if they have different market forecasts and trading styles.

CBOE's innovation, the Volatility Index, VIX, is an index of implied volatility of OEX options. It is used by some traders as a general indication of index option implied volatility. Volatility skews describe a market condition in which options with the same underlying and same expiration but with different strike prices trade at different implied volatilities. Traders must consider both volatility skews and the overall level of implied volatility when making forecasts.

Seven

The Importance of Futures Prices

INTRODUCTION

This chapter focuses on stock index futures contracts, their mechanics, their valuation, and their pricing relationships to stocks and stock index options. First, futures contracts will be defined and their advantages and disadvantages will be summarized. Second, the mechanics of these contracts and of margin accounts will be reviewed. Third, the relationship of futures prices to underlying prices will be explained. This explanation will involve a brief discussion of arbitrage. Finally, why index option traders need to know about futures prices will be discussed.

Equity markets have three components: stocks, options, and futures. They are related by price, because investors will choose one over the others if its price is sufficiently advantageous.

Conceptually, stocks, options, and futures provide investors with the service of risk transfer, but each has unique mechanics and trade-offs, in other words, different advantages and disadvantages. The stock market provides total risk transfer for individual stocks. Stock buyers assume risk in return for profit potential, and stock sellers eliminate risk but give up profit potential. Stock index futures provide total risk transfer for broad market exposure. Buyers of these futures gain market exposure with the associated risks, and sellers who own portfolios that match the underlying index eliminate market risk. Options offer insurance-like risk transfer. Stock index option buyers can reduce the market risk of a portfolio that matches the index and, at the same time, benefit if the index rises. Option sellers receive the premium in return for assuming market risk beyond the break-even point.

FUTURES CONTRACTS DEFINED

A *futures contract* is an agreement between two parties, a buyer and a seller, to exchange a standardized good, the commodity, for an agreed-upon price at a standardized date in the future, the expiration date. The agreement is made through representatives of the parties, commodities brokers, on the floor of an organized futures exchange, and the exchange guarantees the performance of both parties. The specifications and delivery procedures of the standardized good are detailed in the futures contract. Also, each party must deposit funds in an account with their broker to demonstrate that they are financially capable of fulfilling the terms of the futures contract. The deposit is known as a margin deposit. The actual risk born by the parties is usually substantially larger than the margin deposit.

The standardized nature of a futures contract and the exchange guarantee distinguishes it from a *forward contract,* which is a unique, negotiated agreement between two parties: for example, Party A agrees to buy 22,500 gallons of a specific grade of heating oil from Party B on September 23. The advantage of a negotiated forward contract is that the buyer gets exactly what is needed when it is needed, and the seller gets a desired price and a desired delivery schedule. One disadvantage is that both parties assume performance risk. In this example, Party A assumes the risk that Party B will deliver heating oil of the specified grade on the specified date, and Party B assumes the risk that Party A will accept delivery and pay. Another disadvantage of forward contracts is that neither party can get out of the contract, not even at a loss, without the permission of the other party. If Party A wants to cancel the contract but Party B refuses, then Party A has to search for a third party to buy exactly 22,500 gallons of the specific grade of heating oil on September 23. This is known as an "illiquid" contract.

Futures contracts, however, are very liquid. Unless extraordinary market conditions exist in which a futures contract has reached its upper or lower price limit for a particular trading session, then futures contracts can be traded freely. Also, futures contracts involve neither the expenses of negotiation nor performance risk. Futures contracts are generally far less costly than forward contracts.

Standardization is the disadvantage of futures contracts. If a contract covers 1,000 gallons of heating oil, for example, it is impossible to get 22,500 gallons delivered through the exchange's delivery mechanism. A buyer must purchase either 21 or 22 contracts. Nevertheless, the growth of futures markets indicates that many market participants find that the advantages outweigh the disadvantages.

MARGIN ACCOUNT BALANCES ADJUSTED DAILY

Marking to the market is a mechanism by which the margin account balances of both the buyer and seller are adjusted daily to reflect changes in price of the futures contract. Marking to the market insures that each party is in compliance with the minimum margin requirements established by the exchange.

Assume, for example, that on day 1 Richard buys one corn futures contract from Vicki. Assume also that this contract covers 5,000 bushels of corn, the price is $5.00 per bushel, and the margin requirement is $2,000. This means that both Richard and Vicki must deposit $2,000 in accounts with their brokers.

Now consider the risk that each party is assuming. Richard has agreed to buy 5,000 bushels at $5.00 each for a total commitment of $25,000. In theory, if the price of corn were to drop to zero, then Richard would be obligated to pay $23,000 in addition to the $2,000 already in his account, and his total loss would be $25,000.

Vicki's risk is different. If Vicki has 5,000 bushels of corn ready to deliver, then she has no risk other than opportunity risk, the risk that the price of corn could rise and a higher price could have been received. In this case, Vicki simply waits to the delivery date and then delivers her corn in accordance with exchange procedures. Upon delivery she receives $25,000. If Vicki does not have any corn, however, then she is assuming an unlimited risk, because the price of corn could rise indefinitely.

Now consider how a change in price of the futures contract and "marking to the market" affect Richard's and Vicki's account balances. If, on day 2, the price of corn rises 10 cents to $5.10, then the value of 5,000 bushels rises to $25,500. Ignoring that Richard will feel good and Vicki will feel bad, the price rise has increased Richard's credit worthiness and decreased Vicki's. Richard's commitment to purchase corn at $5.00 is now backed by his $2,000 deposit plus the $500 increase in value of the futures contract. Vicki, in this example, however, has only $1,500 of "free and clear" margin, because $500 of her $2,000 deposit is an unrealized loss.

Something now happens in the futures business that does not happen in a normal purchase and sale transaction in the securities business. Given the 10-cent price rise indicated above, the exchange will instruct Vicki's broker to transfer $500 cash from her account to Richard's broker for deposit to his account. Such cash transfers occur every day in the futures business. When prices rise, cash is transferred from holders of short positions to holders of long positions. When prices fall, the opposite happens.

These daily cash transfers are an important element of the creditworthiness of the futures system. First, they assure that every futures position is backed by the exchange-required minimum deposit of cash or cash equivalents. Second, they provide assurance to every trader with an unrealized profit, by covering that unrealized profit with cash.

In the example above in which $500 is transferred out of Vicki's account, her margin account balance is reduced to $1,500. As long as her balance is above the exchange's minimum requirement, no action needs to be taken. If an account balance drops below the minimum, however, then the broker will notify the customer that additional funds must be deposited or the position must be closed. This notification is known as a *margin call.* If the customer does not deposit the required funds and does not close the position, then the broker has the authority to close the position without the customer's permission.

The important point about the workings of futures markets is that every open futures position is backed by at least the exchange's minimum margin requirement. If a trader who receives a margin call deposits sufficient additional funds, then the exchange minimum is met. If the trader closes the position either by selling a contract to close a long position or by purchasing a contract to close a short position, then another party will make the required deposit. In either case, all open futures contracts are backed by at least the minimum margin balance required by the exchange.

STOCK INDEX FUTURES CONTRACTS

A *stock index futures contract* is a participation in the value of the underlying stock index. In theory, the purchaser of a stock index futures contract is agreeing to buy a portfolio of stocks that matches the index, and, in theory, the seller is agreeing to sell this portfolio. The task, however, of purchasing and delivering many individual stocks in exact proportion to an index is difficult and expensive. For this reason cash-settled stock index futures were developed. *Cash-settled stock index futures* contracts require the transfer of cash on the delivery day rather than the transfer of a portfolio of stocks.

Stock index futures contracts work in much the same way as the corn futures contract described above. Margin deposits are required, and there are daily marking-to-the-market cash transfers. Stock index futures, however, have two features that distinguish them from traditional commodity futures. First, they are settled in cash at expiration, and second, the expiration settlement value is determined by a.m. settlement, identical to the settlement process of a.m.-settled stock index options described in Chapter 1.

Stock index futures contracts are available on several broad-based market indexes. Each contract is based on a stock market average, but contract size and margin requirements vary, so it is important for traders of these contracts to understand the contract specifications.

Stock index futures based on the Dow Jones Industrial Average (DJIA) are traded at the Chicago Board of Trade (CBOT) and have a value equal to $10 times the current index level. If the DJIA is trading at 8,000, for example, the buyer of a CBOT DJIA futures contract is agreeing to buy $10 times the index on the expiration date of the contract. The seller of a DJIA futures contract is agreeing to sell $10 times the index. The root ticker symbol for CBOT DJIA futures contract is DJ, and contracts are traded with March, June, September, and December expirations. Dow Jones and Dow Jones Industrial Average are trademarks of Dow Jones & Company, Inc., and have been licensed for use for certain purposes by the Chicago Board of Trade. The CBOT's futures and futures options contracts based on the Dow Jones Industrial Average are not sponsored, endorsed, sold, or promoted by Dow Jones & Company, and Dow Jones & Company makes no representation regarding the advisability of trading in such products.

The Chicago Mercantile Exchange has stock index futures contracts based on 12 market indexes. Two of the most popular contracts are based on the Standard and Poor's 500 Index. One contract is $250 times the index, and its root ticker symbol is SP. The other contract, the E-Mini, is $50 times the index, and its root ticker symbol is ES. Both SP and ES futures are traded with March, June, September, and December expirations.

Stock index futures contracts based on the NASDAQ 100 Index and the NIKKEI 225 Stock Average are also traded at the Chicago Mercantile Exchange. The root ticker symbol for futures contracts based on the NASDAQ 100 Index is ND and these contracts are $100 times the index. The root ticker symbol for futures contracts based on the NIKKEI 225 Stock Average is NK and these contracts are $5 times the index. Contracts based on both of these indexes are available with March, June, September, and December expirations.

Complete contract specifications are available from the exchanges on which the contracts are traded. The phone number of the Chicago Board of Trade is 312-435-3500; its home page is www.cbot.com. The phone number of the Chicago Mercantile Exchange is 312-930-1000; its home page is www.cme.com.

PRICING COMMODITY FUTURES CONTRACTS

Traditional commodity futures contracts, such as corn and wheat futures, are deliverable contracts. *Deliverable* means that settlement occurs at expiration by exchanging physical goods and cash. Essentially, a traditional commodity futures contract becomes the physical commodity on a known date.

Consequently, given a price at which the commodity can be purchased today, the *spot price,* an exact price for the futures contract can be calculated. Conceptually, the price of a futures contract is determined by the following formula:

$$\text{Theoretical value of futures contract} =$$
$$\text{spot price of underlying} + \text{cost of carry}$$

Cost of carry consists of storage, insurance, and transportation costs required to deliver a commodity in accordance with the specifications of a futures contract.

Assume, for example, 1 year to delivery, carrying costs of 10 percent of the spot price, and a spot market price of corn of $5.00 per bushel. Given these factors, then the theoretical value of a 1-year corn futures contract is $5.50, as calculated below:

$$\text{Theoretical value of 1-year futures} =$$
$$\text{spot price of corn} + (10\% \text{ carry cost} \times 1 \text{ year}) =$$
$$5.00 + (5.00 \times 0.10) \times 1 =$$
$$= 5.50$$

How the spot and futures markets interact is illustrated by the following examples. In the first example, the futures price is above the theoretical futures value, and, in the second, it is below. For these examples, assume the spot price of corn is $5.00 per bushel, and the cost of carry is 10 percent per year or 50 cents for 1 year, so the theoretical 1-year futures price is $5.50 as calculated above.

If futures were trading above the theoretical value of $5.50, at $6.00 for example, then it would be profitable to sell the 1-year futures contract at 6.00 and purchase corn for $5.00 per bushel in the spot market, hold it until expiration in 1 year, deliver it, and pay the carrying costs of $0.50. The result would be a profit of 50 cents per bushel.

Profit-seeking participants in a competitive market would not let such a situation exist! There would be buying pressure in the spot market and selling pressure in the futures market, and the two prices would be pushed toward each other until the spot price and the futures price were "in line" with each other as determined by the carrying costs. Market participants who engage in this profit-oriented endeavor are known as *arbitrageurs.* While the personal goal of every arbitrageur is to make a profit, the economic function that arbitrage serves is to keep prices of related instruments in the proper relationship with each other. This creates competition in the supply of products to all market participants, and this, from an overall perspective, lowers costs.

In the second example, assume futures are trading below theoretical value, at $5.00 for example. In this case, it would be advantageous for a user of corn in 1 year to buy a 1-year futures contract today at $5.00, rather than buy spot corn for $5.00 and incur carrying costs. The total cost of spot corn plus carrying costs is $5.50, so, in this example, buying a one-year futures contract would reduce costs by 50 cents per bushel. Such a futures price would be so enticing that holders of corn for use in 1 year would sell their corn and purchase 1-year futures. Consequently, if this pricing relationship existed between spot market corn and corn futures contracts, there would be selling in the spot market and buying in the futures market. The prices would be pushed apart until the price relationship was in line with the carrying costs.

In either case, whether futures prices are above or below theoretical value, there is market pressure that tends to push those prices back toward theoretical value.

PRICING STOCK INDEX FUTURES

A similar pricing relationship exists between stock index futures and the underlying stocks in the index. Even though the stocks themselves are not delivered, the settlement value of the futures contract at expiration, by definition, equals the value of the index as determined by prices of the individual stocks in the index. This means that, given an index level, it is possible to calculate a theoretical price for a stock index futures contract. Since some stocks pay dividends, however, an adjustment must be made to the futures pricing formula as it applies to traditional commodity futures. Dividends are a form of income that reduces the cost of carry. As a result, the general pricing formula for stock index futures is as follows:

Theoretical stock index futures price =
spot index level + cost of carry − dividends

The calculation of the theoretical value of a September DJ futures is shown in Table 7–1. Note that this calculation assumes that dividends are received at an even and continuous rate during the life of the futures contract. Real stocks, however, pay discrete dividends at specific, announced dates. Therefore, this calculation is only a rough approximation of the theoretical futures price. Actual futures prices will vary from the price calculated by this formula.

Table 7–1 Calculating the Theoretical Value of a September DJ Futures

Assumptions: Current market level of DJIA index: 7,893
              Dividend yield: 1.7%
              Days to expiration: 65
              Interest rates: 5.0%

Cost of carry = index level × interest rate × time factor
                 (days to expiration/days per year)
               = 7,893 × 0.05 × (65/365)
               = 70

Dividends received = index level × dividend yield × time factor
                      (days to expiration/days per year)
                    = 7,893 × 0.017 × (65/365)
                    = 24

Theoretical value = spot index level + cost of carry – dividends
                   = 7,893 + 70 – 24
                   = 7,939

WHAT STOCK INDEX OPTION TRADERS NEED TO KNOW ABOUT FUTURES

The price of the underlying is an essential input to an option pricing formula. Traders of options on individual stocks can observe the current stock
price and use it in their formulas, but there is no equivalent security for stock
index option traders. The closest thing to such a security is a stock index
futures contract, if one exists.

   If a futures contract is trading at its theoretical value, then the spot level
of the underlying index can be used in option pricing formulas as the price
of the underlying. If this is the case, then the at-the-money call should be
greater than the at-the-money put by approximately the same amount as the
futures is over the spot index. This difference is approximately the cost of
carry as calculated above.

Hectic Market Conditions

Although the procedure for valuing index option prices described above
works in theory, there are some complications in the real marketplace. There
are occasions when futures contracts trade at a significant premium or dis-
count to theoretical value. On these occasions, market conditions are usually
described as hectic. *Hectic market conditions* mean erratic price fluctuations
and possible delays in order processing due to an extremely heavy volume of
orders. Consequently, without constantly updated information it may be

difficult for a trader to know exactly at what price stock index futures contracts are trading or exactly where the underlying spot index level is, because both are changing rapidly and erratically. While such a situation is theoretically impossible, there are occasions when such hectic trading activity occurs and, as a result, stock index futures contracts and stock index options trade at prices significantly different from those implied by the theory of futures and options pricing. Index option traders must be aware of the risks of such market action and prepare themselves accordingly.

Consequently, if a stock index futures contract is not trading near its theoretical price, then the price of the underlying used in an option pricing formula must be adjusted. If, for example, an index futures contract is trading above its theoretical price by two points, then, the price of the underlying in an option pricing formula should be raised by two points. Such an adjustment should, in theory, result in option price calculations that are consistent with the pricing relationship that links prices of stock index futures to prices of stock index options. There are no guarantees, however, that such an adjustment will produce meaningful option values.

Inability to Profit from Price Discrepancies

Even if price discrepancies between stock index futures and stock index options are detected, it is virtually impossible for nonprofessional traders to take advantage of such a situation. The only "riskless" method of profiting from a price discrepancy is to create an arbitrage. But this is impossible for nonprofessional traders for a least two reasons. First, commissions and other transaction costs for a nonprofessional trader are, almost certainly, greater than any profit potential from observed price discrepancies. Second, entering orders and getting trade executions at the observed prices is highly unlikely in periods of hectic market activity.

SUMMARY

Futures contracts obligate both the buyer and the seller. Margin deposits are required, but the risk of trading futures contracts is typically substantially greater than the margin deposit. A process known as marking to the market involves daily cash transfers and adjustment of margin account balances. Traditional commodity futures are deliverable contracts, but stock index futures are subject to cash settlement.

There is an exact, theoretical pricing relationship between futures contracts and the underlying instrument. Cost of carry and time to expiration determine the relationship. If futures prices are trading at their theoretical price, then the current level of the underlying index can be used in an option pricing formula to calculate stock index option prices. There are a number of stock index futures contracts available. Since contract specifications vary, traders should be fully informed before trading these instruments.

Section 3

Trading Strategies

Eight

Buying Options

INTRODUCTION

 ne of the most popular strategies is buying index options. It seems simple enough: buying index options is generally low in cost, the risk is limited, the commissions are not much different from buying stocks, and, as an added benefit, profits are leveraged if the forecast is right.

Is it really this simple?

Unfortunately, no. Like most activities, trading index options involves a number of risks that balance the apparent advantages. The purpose of this section on trading strategies is to discuss many of the nuances involved with trading options. This chapter focuses specifically on the decision-making process for buying index options.

Typically, the first question option buyers ask is: How does a trader find "the right option"? There are, after all, many options to choose from, and one option is undoubtedly better suited to a particular forecast than others. In the process of looking for "the right option," other questions come up: How are results measured? How should trading capital be managed? And what must a trader know about volatility?

This chapter will go through the steps of taking a market forecast, analyzing several potential options, and using the results of the analysis to select a particular option. OP-EVAL3™ will be used, first, to illustrate how implied volatility is calculated and second, to track how implied volatility changes so that a volatility forecast can be made with greater confidence. The program will then be used to estimate the results of various specific forecasts. Capital management will be discussed, and the chapter will conclude with a description of a three-part market forecasting technique that helps traders focus on the important elements of option trading decisions.

Commissions and other transaction costs are not included in the examples in this chapter, but these are important factors to be considered when analyzing real trading decisions.

STARTING THE ANALYSIS

The trader in this example is a training manager in Philadelphia named Pat. He traded stocks for several years before starting with options, which he has been trading for five years. Pat subscribes to a weekly stock market charting service, and he spends from 1 to 3 hours each week analyzing the charts and planning trades. He typically makes one to four trades per month. His preferred trading strategy is buying index options because of the limited-risk feature.

Right now it is 42 days before September expiration, the S&P 100 Index (OEX) is trading at 795, and Pat believes the index is ready for a rally to 820, but he is not exactly sure when. He is considering whether to buy some OEX September 800 Calls for 15 ($1,500) or some OEX September 820 Calls for 7½ ($750). We will follow Pat as he examines the issues in making this decision.

Step one is making a market forecast, and Pat has made one: he is forecasting a rise in the OEX from its current level of 795 to 820. Because the topic of market forecasting is beyond the scope of this book, Pat's forecast will be taken as presented and the justification for the forecast will not be addressed. However, the biggest risk of any trading decision is a wrong forecast, which can lead to a loss. Pat is well aware of this primary risk. He is financially capable of bearing it and ready to move forward.

Step two is creating profit and loss diagrams of the two alternative strategies. Experienced traders may be able to do this quickly in their heads, but for the sake of this example, Pat uses OP-EVAL3™ to create Figure 8–1, which illustrates the purchase of one 800 Call at 15, and Figure 8–2, which illustrates the purchase of one 820 Call at 7½. These graphs show that the strategies have different maximum risks and different break-even points. Although these diagrams may be unnecessary for experienced traders when basic strategies are being considered, this step should not be overlooked when complex strategies are being studied.

Step three is estimating the implied volatility of the options under consideration. As explained in Chapter 6, implied volatility is the volatility percentage, which, if used in an option pricing formula with known inputs, will produce the current market price of an option as the theoretical value. The current level of implied volatility will be the basis for creating theoretical value tables that are used to estimate strategy results. The current level of

Figure 8–1 Long 1 800 Call at 15

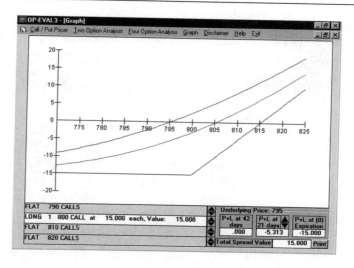

Figure 8–2 Long 1 820 Call at 7½

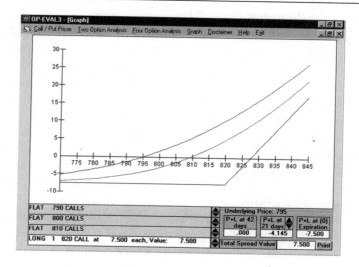

implied volatility will also be compared to historic levels so that a volatility forecast can be included in estimating strategy results.

To estimate the implied volatility of the 800 Call, Pat uses the Call/Put Pricer page in OP-EVAL3™. He creates Figure 8–3 by entering the inputs based on his knowledge of current market conditions. The OEX Index is

Figure 8–3 Estimating Implied Volatility of the 800 Call

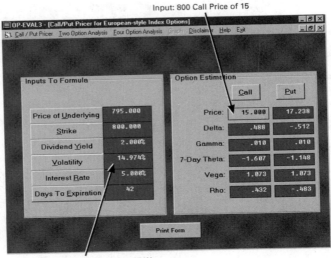

Input: 800 Call Price of 15

Output: Implied Volatility of 14.974%

795, and the strike is 800. According to a well-known business newspaper, the 90-day Treasury Bill interest rate is 5 percent, and the dividend yield of the OEX is 2 percent. As mentioned earlier, the days to expiration of the September options is 42 calendar days. When these inputs are entered along with the market price of the 800 Call of 15, OP-EVAL3™ calculates an implied volatility of 14.974 percent. Pat will round this number to 15 percent when creating a theoretical value table for the 800 Call.

Repeating this process to estimate the implied volatility of the 820 Call, Pat creates Figure 8–4 by changing the strike to 820, entering a call price of 7.500, and then pressing ENTER. This produces an implied volatility for the 820 Call of 14.904 percent. Pat will also round this number to 15 percent when creating a theoretical value table for the 820 Call.

Step four is creating theoretical value tables, which will be used to estimate the results of different strategies over a range of index levels and different times to expiration. Pat might create Tables 8–1 and 8–2 for the 800 and 820 Calls, respectively. The rows in these tables represent five-point increments in the OEX Index level, and the columns represent 7-day time intervals. Although OP-EVAL3™ generates theoretical values in numbers with three decimal places, the numbers in Tables 8–1 and 8–2 have been rounded to the nearest eighth to simulate real market prices.

Pat's current situation in both tables is row 8, column 1: the OEX is 795, it is 42 days to expiration, the 800 Call is 15 (Table 8–1), and the 820

Figure 8–4 Estimating Implied Volatility of the 820 Call

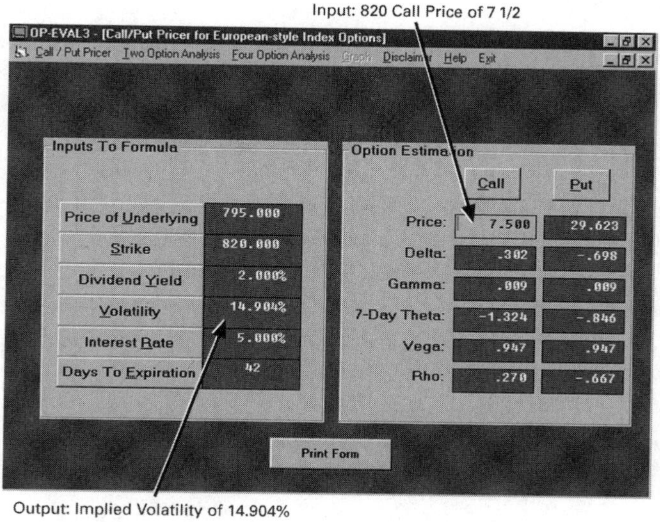

Input: 820 Call Price of 7 1/2

Output: Implied Volatility of 14.904%

Table 8–1 Theoretical Values of 800 Call at Various Index Levels and Days to Expiration

Row	Index Level	Col. 1: 42 Days	Col. 2: 35 Days	Col. 3: 28 Days	Col. 4: 21 Days	Col. 5: 14 Days	Col. 6: 7 Days	Col. 7: Exp.
1	830	37¾	36⅜	34⅞	33½	32	30¾	30
2	825	33⅜	32⅜	30⅞	29¼	27⅝	26⅞	25
3	820	30⅛	28⅝	27	25¼	23⅜	21⅜	20
4	815	26⅝	25⅛	23⅜	21½	19½	17	15
5	810	23⅜	21¾	20	18⅛	15⅞	13⅛	10
6	805	20⅜	18¾	17	15	12⅝	9¼	5
7	800	17½	16	14⅛	12⅛	9⅞	6⅞	0
8	795	15	13⅜	11⅝	9¾	7⅜	4½	0
9	790	12¾	11⅛	9½	7⅝	5½	2⅞	0

Dividend yield, 2%; volatility, 15%; interest rates, 5%.

Call is 7½ (Table 8–2). These tables assume a dividend yield of 2 percent, interest rates of 5 percent, and volatility of 15 percent. The issue of changing volatility will be discussed later. Pat now has two tools to help him make a trading decision.

Table 8–2 Theoretical Values of 820 Call at Various Index Levels and Days to Expiration

Row	Index Level	Col. 1: 42 Days	Col. 2: 35 Days	Col. 3: 28 Days	Col. 4: 21 Days	Col. 5: 14 Days	Col. 6: 7 Days	Col. 7: Exp.
1	830	23⅞	22⅛	20⅜	18⅜	16⅛	13¼	10
2	825	20⅞	19⅛	17¼	15¼	12⅞	9⅞	5
3	820	18	16⅜	14½	12½	10⅛	7	0
4	815	15½	13¾	12	10	7⅝	4¾	0
5	810	13⅛	11½	9¾	7⅞	5⅝	3	0
6	805	11⅝	9½	7⅞	6⅛	4⅛	1¾	0
7	800	9¼	7¾	6¼	4⅝	2⅞	1	0
8	795	7½	6¼	4⅞	3⅜	1⅞	½	0
9	790	6⅛	5	3¾	2½	1¼	¼	0

Dividend yield, 2%; volatility, 15%; interest rates, 5%.

So how does Pat use these tools? He starts with his forecast and uses the tables to estimate how the 800 Call and the 820 Call will perform. Pat believes the OEX will rise to 820, but he is not exactly sure when. Although he typically buys three or more options, to keep the analysis simple, Pat will start by comparing the purchase of one 800 Call to the purchase of one 820 Call. Later, Pat will examine purchasing more than one 800 Call and more than one 820 Call.

First, consider a 1-week time frame. If the OEX rises from 795 at 42 days to 820 at 35 days, Table 8–1 estimates that the 800 Call will rise from 15 to 28⅜ (row 3, column 2) for a profit of 13⅜, or $1,362.50, before transaction costs. Table 8–2 estimates that the 820 Call will rise from 7½ to 16⅜ for a profit of 8⅞, or$887.50, before transaction costs.

Now consider 2-week and 3-week time frames. Table 8–1 estimates that, with the OEX at 820, the 800 Call will be trading at 27 at 28 days to expiration (row 3, column 3) and 25¼ at 21 days (row 3, column 4), for profits of 12 ($1,200) and 10¼ ($1,025), respectively. Table 8–2 estimates that, with the index at 820 in 2 weeks and 3 weeks, the 820 Call will be trading at 14½ and 12½, respectively, for profits of 7 ($700) and 5 ($500), respectively.

Of course, Pat's bullish forecast might not be realized, and a loss could result. Table 8–1 estimates that if the index declines to 790, the 800 Call will fall to 9½ in 2 weeks (row 9, column 3) and to 7⅝ in 3 weeks (row 9, column 4), for losses of 5½ ($550) and 7⅜ ($737.50), respectively. Table 8–2 estimates that the 820 Call will fall to 3¾ and to 2½ in 2 and 3 weeks, respectively, for losses of 3¾ ($375) and 5 ($500), respectively.

What conclusion can be drawn from Pat's initial analysis? Simply stated, if results are measured in dollars, the two strategies are not equal!

The purchase of one 800 Call has a higher profit potential, in dollars, in all of the positive outcomes than the purchase of one 820 Call. However, the 800 Call also has higher risk potential, in dollars, in all of the negative outcomes. Conclusion: The choice between buying a quantity of calls at one strike and buying an equal quantity of calls at a different strike is not a choice between equal alternatives; it is a choice between trade-offs. Lower-strike call options have higher profit potential and higher risk potential when results are measured in dollars.

If results are measured in percentage terms, however, a different conclusion can be drawn.

MEASURING RESULTS IN PERCENTAGE TERMS

Table 8–3 summarizes, in both dollar terms and percentage terms, the information in rows 3 and 9 in Tables 8–1 and 8–2. The upper half of Table 8–3 assumes the OEX Index rises from 795 to 820 in 1-week intervals up to 6 weeks (row 3 in both tables). The lower half of Table 8–3 assumes a decline to 790 in similar time periods (row 9 in both tables).

Looking at the percentage results in Table 8–3, the choice between the 800 and 820 Calls depends on something other than index movement or amount at risk. Can you tell what it is?

Time is the critical variable when comparing the percentage results of the 800 Call and the 820 Call. If, for example, the index rises from 795 to 820 in 1 week, the profit from the 820 Call is 118 percent, versus 91 percent from the 800 Call. If the rise in the index to 820 takes 3 weeks, then buying one 800 Call is about equal in percentage terms to buying one 820 Call; both make approximately the same percentage profit in the 3-week time frame.

If the forecasted rise in the index from 795 to 820 takes 5 or 6 weeks, however, the percentage profits of the 800 Call surpass the results of the 820 Call. The 800 Call earns profits of 42 percent and 25 percent in 5 and 6 weeks, respectively. But the 820 Call has a 7 percent loss in 5 weeks and a 100 percent loss in 6 weeks. Remember, the options expire in 6 weeks, and with the index at 820 at expiration, the 820 Call expires worthless.

Table 8–3 800 Call versus 820 Call: Dollar and Percent Change

| | OEX 795 → 820 | | | | | |
| | 800 Call Purchased for 15 | | | 820 Call Purchased for 7½ | | |
Time Frame	800 Call Price OEX at 820	Dollar Change	Percent Change	800 Call Price OEX at 820	Dollar Change	Percent Change
1 week	28⅝	+$1,362	+91%	16⅜	+$887	+118%
2 weeks	27	+$1,200	+80%	14½	+$700	+ 93%
3 weeks	25¼	+$1,025	+68%	12½	+$500	+ 67%
4 weeks	23⅜	+$ 837	+56%	10⅛	+$262	+ 35%
5 weeks	21⅜	+$ 637	+42%	7	($ 50)	(7%)
6 weeks	20	+$ 500	+25%	0	($750)	(100%)

| | OEX 795 → 790 | | | | | |
| | 800 Call Purchased for 15 | | | 820 Call Purchased for 7½ | | |
Time Frame	800 Call Price OEX at 790	Dollar Change	Percent Change	800 Call Price OEX at 790	Dollar Change	Percent Change
1 week	11⅛	($ 387)	(26%)	5	($250)	(29%)
2 weeks	9½	($ 550)	(37%)	3¾	($375)	(50%)
3 weeks	7⅝	($ 737)	(51%)	2½	($500)	(66%)
4 weeks	5½	($ 950)	(66%)	1¼	($625)	(83%)
5 weeks	2⅞	($1,212)	(81%)	¼	($725)	(97%)
6 weeks	0	($1,500)	(100%)	0	($750)	(100%)

It is interesting to observe that if Pat's forecast is incorrect and the index drops to 790, then the percentage losses of the two strategies are not as dramatically different as the results of the positive outcomes. Both strategies, of course, risk total loss of the price paid for the call in the worst possible outcome. If the index declines to 790 in 1 week, the 800 Call loses 26 percent and the 820 Call loses 29 percent. This 3 percent difference in losses is small in comparison to the 27 percent difference in profits if the index rises to Pat's target of 820 in 1 week.

So what has Pat learned? First, comparing an equal quantity of 800 Calls and 820 Calls is not a comparison of equals. Second, when examining percentage results, time is the critical variable. Consequently, the question becomes, How does Pat find trading alternatives that are more equal in terms of risk?

This is an important question. But, first, we will discuss a method for getting information more quickly and efficiently. Tables 8–1 and 8–2 have given Pat much information about the performance of these two options, but they are time-consuming to create. Is there an easier, more efficient way to get the same information? The answer is a resounding yes!

USING THE GREEKS: METHOD 1

Position Greeks, as explained in Chapter 5, offer a quick and easy way of estimating how strategies will perform, and understanding them reduces the need for theoretical value tables. That is why experienced traders learn to interpret the delta, gamma, vega, and theta of a position—it saves time!

Using the Call/Put Pricer page in OP-EVAL3™ to create Table 8–4, Pat can evaluate the purchase of one 800 Call and one 820 Call. Table 8–4 compares the position Greeks of the two strategies. First, the long 800 Call has a position delta of +0.488 versus +0.302 for the long 820 Call. This difference in delta explains the short-term higher profit potential in dollars of the 800 Call relative to the 820 Call. This potential advantage of the 800 Call, however, is balanced by its higher premium, 15 versus 7½. The buyer of the 800 Call, therefore, is assuming a greater risk than the purchaser of the 820 Call.

Both positions have positive vegas, so both will benefit from a rise in volatility and be hurt by a decline. The 800 Call, however, with its larger vega, is more sensitive to volatility. Thus, if Pat has a strong belief that volatility will increase, he would be more inclined to buy the 800 Call than the 820 Call.

The position thetas indicate that the 800 Call will lose more per unit of time than the 820 Call. Table 8-4 indicates the 800 Call will lose 1.607 over 7 days if the index level, volatility, dividends, and interest rates are unchanged. Under these circumstances, the 820 Call will lose 1.324, almost 20 percent less. This is another indication of the higher risk of the 800 Call.

The position gammas are nearly equal and indicate that the position deltas will increase if the index rises and fall if the index declines.

Table 8–4 Position Greeks: Long 1 800 Call versus Long 1 820 Call

	Long 1 800 Call	Long 1 820 Call
Price	15.000	7.500
Delta	+0.488	+0.302
Gamma	+0.010	+0.009
Vega	+1.073	+0.947
Theta	−1.607	−1.324

Index level, 795; dividend yield, 2%; volatility, 15%; interest rates, 5%; days to expiration, 42.

The position Greeks confirm what was learned from Tables 8–1 and 8–2. Choosing between buying one 800 Call and buying one 820 Call is not a choice between equal alternatives. The higher delta and lower theta of the 800 Call indicates that it has a larger profit potential and a greater risk potential. The higher delta of the 800 Call says that this call has a higher market participation than the 820 Call; in other words, it will make more in dollars if the underlying price rises and lose more in dollars if it declines. The lower theta indicates that the 800 Call will decay more in dollars per week than the 820 Call if the index level, volatility, dividends, and interest rates remain constant. These two factors, delta and theta, present a quick picture of the profit and risk potentials of these two strategies. At this point, the position vegas and gammas may not seem to be significantly different. However, when multiple-option positions are analyzed, the importance of gamma and vega will become evident.

Now we can go back to looking for strategy alternatives that are "more equal."

CAPITAL MANAGEMENT

What makes two limited-risk strategies equal? The amount of the risk is certainly one factor. If the maximum theoretical risk is equal, then, at least in some basic sense, the two strategies are comparable. There may still be some trade-offs—relative advantages and disadvantages—but at least they have the same maximum theoretical risk.

Pat can make alternative strategies equal from a risk standpoint by deciding on the amount of capital he is willing to invest and risk. From that figure, he can then determine the number of calls of each strike that can be purchased. He will then be comparing alternatives that do not exceed his risk limit.

If Pat is willing to invest and risk $6,000, for example, he can purchase four September 800 Calls at 15 each (4 × $1,500 = $6,000) or eight September 820 Calls at 7½ each (8 × $750 = $6,000). To compare these two new strategies, Pat creates Figure 8–5, which illustrates a long 4 800 Call position, and Figure 8–6, which illustrates the alternative long 8 820 Call position. Both alternatives risk a maximum of 60 index points, or $6,000, but they have different break-even points. Above the respective strike prices, the lines in the diagram at expiration also have different slopes. The upward-sloping line of the 800 Call position, at expiration, has a slope of positive 4, because each of the calls has a delta of +1.00 if they are in-the-money at expiration. The upward-sloping line of the 820 Call position, at expiration, however, has a slope of positive 8, because this position has twice as many calls, each of which has a delta of +1.00 if they are in-the-money at expiration. Even though these

Figure 8–5 Long 4 800 Calls at 15 each

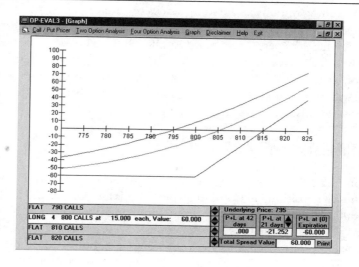

Figure 8–6 Long 8 820 Calls at 7½ each

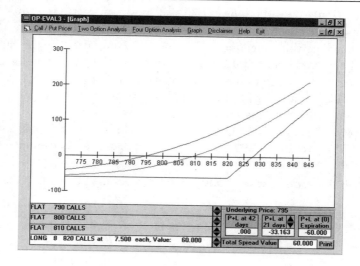

positions have the same maximum risk potential, they have different results at expiration if the index is above 800.

Since the capital at risk is the same for these two strategies, the analysis of profits in percentage terms, as shown in Table 8–3, is appropriate. The conclusion from that analysis was that time is the critical factor.

Pat must add time to the forecast! This is the first major difference between trading options and trading stocks or futures contracts.

Regarding time and the observations made from Table 8–3, 3 weeks is the point where the percentage profits of the 820 Call no longer exceed those of the 800 Call. Does Pat believe that the index will rise to 820 before 3 weeks or later? This is a subjective question that only Pat can answer, but his answer will be an important consideration in choosing between the purchase of four 800 Calls and the purchase of eight 820 Calls.

USING THE GREEKS: METHOD 2

Position Greeks can also help Pat evaluate his new alternatives. Table 8–5 compares the position Greeks of long 4 800 Calls and long 8 820 Calls. Buying 4 800 Calls and 8 820 Calls results in very different Greeks. Four 800 Calls have a position delta of +1.952 versus +2.416 for the 8 820 Calls. The difference in position gammas may not seem large, but the position gamma of the 8 820 Calls, +0.072, is nearly twice the position gamma of the 4 800 Calls, 0.040. This means that as the index rises and other factors remain constant, the delta of the 8 820 Calls increases faster than the delta of 4 800 Calls. Not only does the long 8 820 Call position start out with a higher delta; its higher gamma means that its delta also increases more rapidly. "Longer, and getting longer faster" is how one would describe the eight 820 Calls relative to the four 800 Calls. Judging from the position delta and the position gamma, the eight 820 Calls appear to be a better purchase than the four 800 Calls. Pat must, however, look at the position vegas and position thetas to see what information they provide.

Table 8–5 shows that eight 820 Calls have a bigger vega than four 800 Calls, +7.576 versus +4.292. Is this an advantage or a disadvantage for the

Table 8–5 Position Greeks: Long 4 800 Calls versus Long 8 820 Calls

	Long 4 800 Calls	Long 8 820 Calls
Price	60.000	60.000
Delta	+ 1.952	+ 2.416
Gamma	+ 0.040	+ 0.072
Vega	+ 4.292	+ 7.576
Theta	− 6.428	−10.592

Index level, 795; dividend yield, 2%; volatility, 15%;
interest rates, 5%; days to expiration, 42.

820 Call position? Unfortunately, there is no definitive answer to this question, because the answer depends on whether volatility increases or decreases. If volatility increases, a larger position vega is an advantage. But if volatility decreases, it is a disadvantage. What are the implications of this observation?

Pat must add a third component to the forecast: volatility. We will see how Pat might gather information for forecasting volatility later in this chapter.

The position thetas point out a clear advantage of the four 800 Calls. Table 8–5 shows that long 8 820 Calls have a position theta of −10.592, versus −6.428 for long 4 800 Calls. A lower theta means that a position has greater time risk. If other factors remain constant, eight 820 Calls will lose 10.64 points, or $1,064, per week, and four 800 Calls will lose 6.428 points, or $642.80.

SUMMARIZING THE TWO POSITIONS

At this point the Greeks tell Pat that the long 8 820 Calls are "longer and getting longer faster" than the long 4 800 Calls. The Greeks also indicate that the 820 Call position has more exposure to changes in volatility and greater time decay than the 800 Call position. Can it be said that one position is "better" than the other? Again, the answer is no.

Conceptually, in an efficient market, there is no such thing as "better." If there were a "better" strategy, the market would find that strategy and increase its price and, thereby, eliminate its advantage.

The trade-off between Pat's alternatives is that the 820 Calls have the advantage of a higher delta and the disadvantage of a lower theta. In short, the greater profit potential from a bullish move in the underlying index comes at the greater risk from time decay if the forecast move does not occur soon.

If there is no "better," then what is the conclusion? The main point is that trading options is different from trading stocks or futures contracts. "Being bullish" is not enough when trading options! Stocks and futures contracts do not have the time erosion that options have, but stocks involve substantially more investment and stocks and futures contracts have more risk. So how do traders conceptualize the differences?

A THREE-PART FORECAST

Pat needs to forecast market direction, just as stock and futures traders do, but the message of Table 8–3 is that Pat needs to have a different emphasis on time. The effect of volatility on option values also has implications for the way

Pat thinks. Having decided how much to invest and risk, in this case $6,000, Pat must concentrate on all three aspects: index level, time, and volatility.

The missing element in the analysis up to now is volatility. In Tables 8–1 through 8–3, volatility was assumed to remain constant. However, volatility is likely to change, and Pat must factor this into his decision. The following discussion will show how Pat might gather information about volatility that can be included in the forecast, and ultimately into his trading decision.

VOLATILITY

How does a trader forecast volatility? There is no proven method, but one can gain insights by tracking the history of implied volatility. When forecasting anything, a starting point is to gather historical information. There is, of course, absolutely no guaranty that this information, or any information, will lead to an accurate forecast, but it is the nature of trading to make forecasts and act on those forecasts.

In order to gather information on implied volatility, Pat starts with readily observable information, such as closing index levels and option prices. Columns 1 through 5 in Table 8–6 show information that Pat has gathered. The information is not actual data taken from any actual trading period; it is simulated for the purpose of making a realistic example.

To create such a table Pat would start with observable information from a period of time. Table 8–6 uses 15 consecutive days, but the time period could be different. Furthermore, the observations need not be consecutive, because the information will be used in a subjective decision-making process. Generally, the longer the period, the better, because more information may offer more clues.

Column 1 contains figures for closing index level. These figures are available in many daily newspapers, in *Barron's*, or from a broker. Column 2 contains the end-of-day Volatility Index. As explained in Chapter 6, the VIX is calculated by the CBOE as an index of implied volatility in OEX options. Although the specific implied volatility level of individual options varies due to supply and demand for different options, the VIX is designed to be a guide to the overall level of implied volatility in OEX options. An index option trader might choose to include the VIX because it is one more source of information about implied volatility levels.

Column 3 identifies the at-the-money strike price on each day. Since the index changes daily, the at-the-money strike price will also change. Column 4 lists the number of days to expiration of the option being studied. Over time, as monthly expirations come and go, the number of days in this column

Table 8–6 Pat's Implied Volatility Tracker

Day	Col. 1: OEX	Col. 2: VIX	Col. 3: Expiration/ ATM Strike	Col. 4: Days to Expiration	Col. 5: Call Price	Col. 6: Implied Volatility
1	787.63	18.88	Aug 790	34	16¾	17.55%
2	785.89	21.14	Aug 785	33	22¼	22.01%
3	786.36	17.93	Sep 785	58	25¾	18.56%
4	784.10	16.79	Sep 785	57	22¾	17.30%
5	783.94	16.66	Sep 785	56	21½	16.52%
6	780.99	16.64	Sep 780	55	22	16.31%
7	784.72	16.67	Sep 785	54	21½	16.22%
8	790.90	16.06	Sep 790	51	20¾	15.79%
9	794.27	16.38	Sep 795	50	20	15.98%
10	794.06	16.49	Sep 795	49	20	16.26%
11	793.44	16.87	Sep 795	48	19⅜	16.20%
12	794.49	16.85	Sep 795	47	19¾	16.24%
13	799.39	16.20	Sep 800	44	18⅜	15.56%
14	798.18	17.22	Sep 800	43	17¼	15.32%
15	795.12	16.67	Sep 795	42	17¾	15.15%

Dividend yield, 1.9%; interest rates, 5%.

gradually declines and then increases by approximately 28 or 35 as options with a new expiration in 4 or 5 weeks are added to the table. From Day 2 to Day 3, for example, the number of days increases from 33 to 58. This is because the 785 Call being analyzed in Day 2 has a different expiration date than the 785 Call in Day 3. Column 5 contains closing prices of the options being analyzed. These prices come from daily newspapers or from other market sources, such as brokers or quotation services on the World Wide Web. One such quotation service is offered free of charge on the CBOE's home page at http://www.cboe.com where intra-day quotes are delayed 20 minutes and end-of-day prices are available 20 minutes after the close of trading.

The implied volatility numbers in Column 6 were calculated with the OP-EVAL3™ program in exactly the same way as the implied volatility of the 800 and 820 Calls was calculated in Figures 8–1 and 8–2, respectively. Known information, such as the strike, dividend yield, interest rates, and days to expiration, is entered along with the market price of the option. When the ENTER key is pressed, OP-EVAL3™ calculates the implied volatility of that option.

How is the information in Table 8–6 helpful? Columns 2 and 6 provide historical information about implied volatility. While there is no assured method of using this information to forecast implied volatility, it may be possible to identify a trend that might be forecast to continue. Alternatively, if implied volatility has been in a range, a trader might forecast that it would stay in that range or break out of that range. Let's see how Pat uses this information.

The first observation is that the implied volatility of the 800 Call, 15 percent, as calculated in Figure 8–3, is lower than any observation in Table 8–6. This information might be the basis for a forecast that implied volatility is "low." Alternatively, it might be the basis for a forecast that implied volatility is in a "down trend" and likely to head lower. Because forecasting techniques are not within the scope of this book, Pat's forecast that implied volatility is low will be accepted. Pat, of course, must be willing to assume the risk if his forecast is wrong and a loss results.

The next step in Pat's analysis is to make a range of forecasts and evaluate the results. In this example, Pat will make an "optimistic" forecast, a "most likely" forecast, and a "pessimistic" forecast. In each case, Pat will forecast the amount the index level will change, the time it will take for that change to occur, and the implied volatility level after the change has occurred.

Pat's optimistic forecast predicts that the index will rise to his target level of 820 in 10 days and implied volatility will rise to 18 percent (Table 8–7). Given these assumptions, the 800 Call will rise to 30⅜ and the 820 Call will rise to 18⅜. Also, the purchase of four 800 Calls at 15 and sale at 30⅜ results in a profit of 61½ points, or $6,150. The purchase and sale of eight 820 Calls results in a profit of 87 points, or $8,700. In this optimistic forecast, the eight 820 Calls are the preferred choice.

In the most likely forecast, in Table 8–8, Pat believes the index will rise to 815 in 2 weeks and implied volatility will remain at 15 percent. Given these assumptions, the 800 Call will rise to 23⅜ and the 820 Call will rise to 12. Also, the purchase of four 800 Calls at 15 and sale at 23⅜ results in a profit of 33½ points, or $3,350. The purchase and sale of eight 820 Calls results in a profit of 36 points, or $3,600. In this most likely forecast, the 820 Calls are again the preferred choice.

Table 8–9 shows the results of Pat's pessimistic forecast; the index falls to 790 in 2 weeks and the implied volatility falls to 14 percent. Under these assumptions, OP-EVAL3™ calculates that the 800 Call will fall to 8 and the 820 Call will fall to 3⅛. The purchase of four 800 Calls at 15 and sale at 8 results in a loss of 28 points, or $2,800. The purchase of eight 820 Calls at 7½ and sale at 3⅛ results in a loss of 35 points, or $3,500. In this forecast, the 800 Calls are the preferred choice because they lose less than the 820

Table 8–7 Pat's Optimistic Forecast

	Initial		Optimistic Forecast
Inputs			
Index level	795	→	820
Strike price	800/820		
Dividend yield	2%		
Volatility	15%	→	18%
Interest rates	5%		
Days to expiration	42	→	32
Outputs			
800 Call price	15	→	30⅜
820 Call price	7½	→	18⅜

Strategy Results

Long 4 800 Calls at 15.00		Long 8 820 Calls at 7.50	
Sale price	30⅜	Sale price	18⅜
Purchase price	– 15	Purchase price	– 7½
Profit/loss per option	15⅜	Profit/loss per option	10⅞
Quantity	× 4	Quantity	× 8
Strategy profit/loss	61½	Strategy profit/loss	87
Profit/loss in dollars	$6,150	Profit/loss in dollars	$8,700

Table 8–8 Pat's Most Likely Forecast

	Initial		Most Likely Forecast
Inputs			
Index level	795	→	815
Strike price	800/820		
Dividend yield	2%		
Volatility	15%	→	15%
Interest rates	5%		
Days to expiration	42	→	28
Outputs			
800 Call price	15	→	23⅜
820 Call price	7½	→	12

Strategy Results

Long 4 800 Calls at 15.00		Long 8 820 Calls at 7.50	
Sale price	23⅜	Sale price	12
Purchase price	– 15	Purchase price	– 7½
Profit/loss per option	8⅜	Profit/loss per option	4½
Quantity	× 4	Quantity	× 8
Strategy profit/loss	33½	Strategy profit/loss	36
Profit/loss in dollars	$3,350	Profit/loss in dollars	$3,600

Table 8–9 Pat's Pessimistic Forecast

	Initial		Pessimistic Forecast
Inputs			
Index level	795	→	790
Strike price	800/820		
Dividend yield	2%		
Volatility	15%	→	14%
Interest rates	5%		
Days to expiration	42	→	28
Outputs			
800 Call price	15	→	8
820 Call price	7½	→	3⅛

Strategy Results

Long 4 800 Calls at 15.00		Long 8 820 Calls at 7.50	
Sale price	8	Sale price	3⅛
Purchase price	– 15	Purchase price	– 7½
Profit/loss per option	(7)	Profit/loss per option	(4⅜)
Quantity	× 4	Quantity	× 8
Strategy profit/loss	(28)	Strategy profit/loss	35
Profit/loss in dollars	($2,800)	Profit/loss in dollars	($3,500)

Calls. It should be noted that Pat's pessimistic forecast is not the worst case. It is possible for Pat to lose his entire investment in either the 800 or 820 Calls if those options expire worthless.

PAT'S DECISION

Pat has done a lot of work to arrive at the point of making a decision. To summarize the results of his forecasts, Pat creates Table 8–10, which summarizes the results of the two strategies in dollars under various market outcomes. This table is not intended to provide an answer to Pat's strategy-selection decision. It simply shows that if either Pat's optimistic or most likely scenarios are correct, buying eight 820 Calls will yield a higher profit than buying four 800 Calls. Regarding risk, the 820 Call position is also forecast to lose more than the 800 Call position. But compare the results. If the optimistic or most likely forecast is correct, then Pat makes $2,550 or $250 more, respectively, than buying four 800 Calls. If the pessimistic forecast occurs, then the 820 Call position loses $700 more than the 800 Call position. To Pat, the possibility of earning $2,550 more if he is right is worth the risk of losing $700 more if he is wrong, so Pat decides to buy the eight 820 Calls.

Table 8–10 Comparison of Strategy Results

Index Level/ Time/Volatility	Purchasing 4 800 Calls	Purchasing 8 820 Calls
Optimistic forecast 820 / 10 days / 18%	$6,150	$8,700
Most Likely forecast 815 / 14 days / 15%	$3,350	$3,600
Pessimistic forecast 790 / 14 days / 14%	($2,800)	($3,500)

Not all traders, of course, would interpret this information the same way or make the same decision as Pat. But that is not the point. The point is to demonstrate the analysis and decision-making process that Pat used.

OPTIONS ON DOW JONES AVERAGES

Traders interested in listed options on the Dow Jones Industrial Average (DJX), the Dow Jones Transportation Average (DTX), and the Dow Jones Utility Average (DUX) should be pleased to know that, despite the differences in contract construction, all of the concepts presented in this and other chapters apply equally to these index options.

Tables 8–11 and 8–12 illustrate how options on the Dow Jones Industrial Average might be analyzed. Table 8–11 contains theoretical values for a

Table 8–11 Theoretical Values of DJX 75.00 Call at Various Index Levels and Days to Expiration

Row	Index Level	Col. 1: 60 Days	Col. 2: 50 Days	Col. 3: 40 Days	Col. 4: 30 Days	Col. 5: 20 Days	Col. 6: 10 Days	Col. 7: Exp.
1	78.00	3.91	3.82	3.65	3.47	3.28	3.10	3.00
2	77.50	3.61	6.44	3.25	3.06	2.85	2.64	2.50
3	77.00	3.25	3.07	2.88	2.67	2.44	2.19	2.00
4	76.50	2.91	2.72	2.52	2.31	2.06	1.78	1.50
5	76.00	2.58	2.40	2.19	1.97	1.71	1.39	1.00
6	75.50	2.28	2.09	1.89	1.66	1.39	1.06	0.50
7	75.00	2.00	1.81	1.61	1.38	1.11	0.77	0.00
8	74.50	1.74	1.55	1.35	1.13	0.87	0.54	0.00
9	74.00	1.50	1.32	1.12	0.91	0.66	0.36	0.00

Dividend yield, 2%; volatility, 15%; interest rates, 5%.

Table 8–12 Theoretical Values of DJX 77.00 Call at Various Index Levels and Days to Expiration

Row	Index Level	Col. 1: 60 Days	Col. 2: 50 Days	Col. 3: 40 Days	Col. 4: 30 Days	Col. 5: 20 Days	Col. 6: 10 Days	Col. 7: Exp.
1	78.00	2.64	2.44	2.24	2.00	1.74	1.41	1.00
2	77.50	2.33	2.14	1.93	1.69	1.42	1.08	0.50
3	77.00	2.05	1.86	1.65	1.41	1.14	0.79	0.00
4	76.50	1.79	1.60	1.39	1.16	0.90	0.56	0.00
5	76.00	1.55	1.37	1.67	0.94	0.69	0.38	0.00
6	75.50	1.33	1.13	0.96	0.75	0.52	0.24	0.00
7	75.00	1.14	0.97	0.79	0.59	0.38	0.15	0.00
8	74.50	0.96	0.80	0.63	0.46	0.27	0.09	0.00
9	74.00	0.81	0.66	0.50	0.34	0.19	0.05	0.00

Dividend yield, 2%; volatility, 15%; interest rates, 5%.

DJX 75.00 Call and Table 8–12 contains theoretical values for a DJX 77.00 Call. These tables were created in the same way that Tables 8–1 and 8–2 were created but the prices are presented in decimals, not eighths. For each cell, a theoretical value was calculated by entering the inputs in the Call/Put Pricer page of OP-EVAL3™.

Table 8–13 compares the Greeks of the DJX 75.00 and 77.00 Calls, just as Table 8–4 compared the Greeks of the OEX 800 and 820 Calls. The information in Table 8–13 was taken from the Call/Put Pricer page in OP-EVAL3™ in the same manner as Figures 8–3 and 8–4, but it is not shown here.

If Julia, a trader who is bullish on the Dow Jones Industrial Average, has $2,000 to invest and risk, she could consider the purchase of 10 DJX 75.00 Calls at 2 each or the purchase of 17 DJX 77.00 Calls at 1⅛ each. To decide which position better suits her forecast, she would follow the same steps as Pat followed in choosing between the OEX 800 and 820 Calls. Like Pat, Julia would find that similar trade-offs exist. She would, ultimately, base her decision on her subjective evaluation of her three-part forecast for the amount of change in the DJX, the time for the change to occur, and the implied volatility after the change occurred.

Table 8–13 Position Greeks Long 1 75.00 Call versus Long 1 77.00 Call

	Long 1 75.00 Call	Long 1 77.00 Call
Price	1.999	1.137
Delta	+ 0.544	+ 0.374
Gamma	+ 0.085	+ 0.085
Vega	+ 0.120	+ 0.115
Theta	− 0.130	− 0.118

Index level, 75.00; dividend yield, 2%; volatility, 15%; interest rates, 5%; days to expiration, 60.

SUMMARY

Buying options is different from buying stocks or futures contracts because option prices behave differently than stock and futures prices and the forecasting process is different. For options, a three-part forecast is essential. Option traders should start with a specific forecast for the underlying. Second, a specific forecast for time is required, and the third element is a forecast for the level of implied volatility after the move occurs.

It is not a comparison of equal alternatives to compare equal numbers of options of the same type and expiration but with different strike prices. Such a comparison involves trade-offs.

The process for analyzing alternatives and choosing a strategy involves five steps. First, draw a profit and loss diagram at expiration of each strategy being considered. Profit and loss diagrams illustrate the maximum profit and risk potential and break-even points at expiration. Second, estimate the implied volatility of all options under consideration. Knowing the implied volatility is necessary to create theoretical value tables which estimate how option prices will behave under certain market conditions. Third, make a capital management decision by deciding on the amount of capital to invest and risk. Capital management is one method of making several alternatives "more equal." After an amount is chosen, determine the number of options of a particular strike that can be purchased. Fourth, create theoretical value tables or use the position Greeks to evaluate the trade-offs of the various alternatives. Fifth, make a range of forecasts that include three parts: the amount of the index level change, the time for the change to occur, and the implied volatility level after the change. Regarding volatility, it may be helpful to track the history of implied volatility over a recent period of time so that more information can be used to make a forecast. However, no method of forecasting volatility, time, or price is guaranteed to succeed, and traders must be prepared and able to withstand the risk of their forecast being wrong. When these five steps have been completed, making a logical strategy selection is possible.

Nine

Selling Options

INTRODUCTION

Selling, or writing, options is *not* the opposite of buying options! Traders who use strategies that involve short option positions must think differently about capital management, risk, and profit potential than they do when using strategies involving only long options.

Selling uncovered index options involves substantial or unlimited risk and is only suitable for experienced traders who can meet specific financial requirements such as a minimum net worth, a minimum annual income, and specific investment objectives. Also, a substantial minimum account equity will be required in the form of cash and/or securities on deposit as a pledge toward the performance of contract obligations. Traders who cannot meet these requirements will find this chapter useful for the analysis of trading decisions and tracking of positions, but they will not be able to implement these strategies.

This chapter presents a disciplined thinking process for planning trades and tracking the performance of positions that involve uncovered short options. After the basics of risk, profit potential, and sensitivities to changes in market conditions have been reviewed, margin requirements and capital management will be discussed. A consistent method of measuring profit potential will be explained next, and the chapter will conclude with a trading example in which a short option position is initiated and then followed through three possible outcomes. Criteria will be suggested as to when to close a short option position at either a profit or loss. The option positions used in the examples are hypothetical and are intended for educational purposes only.

THE BASICS OF SHORT OPTIONS

Short option positions have limited profit potential and substantial or unlimited risk potential. Figure 9–1 illustrates a short PNX 250 Call sold at 8. (PNX is the Phone Sector Index on which European-style options are traded at the Philadelphia Stock Exchange.) If the index is below 250 at expiration, the call expires worthless and the maximum potential profit of $800 is realized. If the index is above 250 at expiration, the 250 Call has value. The short call sold for 8 realizes a profit at expiration if the index level is below 258, the break-even point in this example, but a loss is incurred if the index is above this level at expiration. Potential risk of a short call position is unlimited, because losses increase as the price of the underlying rises.

A short call position has a negative delta, a negative gamma, a negative vega, and a positive theta. Table 9–1 shows that the short 250 Call has a delta of −0.488, which means that losses occur as the price of the underlying rises, assuming other factors remain constant. The gamma of −0.018 means that the delta changes in the opposite direction of the change in price of the underlying. The vega of −0.398 means that losses occur if volatility increases or profits occur if volatility decreases and other factors remain constant. The theta of +0.595 means that time erosion benefits the position. To summarize Table 9–1, a short call benefits from a decrease in the price of the underlying, a decrease in volatility, and the passage of time.

Figure 9–1 Short 1 250 Call at 8

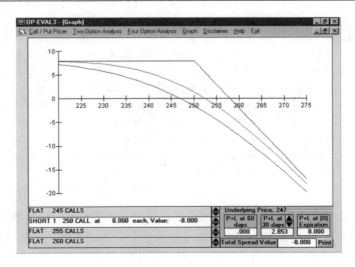

Table 9–1 Position Greeks: Short 1 250 Call

	Short 1 250 Call
Price	8.000
Delta	–0.488
Gamma	–0.018
Vega	–0.398
Theta	+0.595

Index level, 247; dividend yield, 1.7%; volatility,
22%; interest rates, 5%; days to expiration, 60.

MARGIN REQUIREMENTS

In addition to meeting certain financial requirements that demonstrate an ability to assume the risk of short option positions, such as a minimum net worth and a minimum account balance, sellers of uncovered index options must deposit a preset amount of equity capital in their trading account when initiating such positions. This deposit is known as an *initial margin deposit.* There is no guaranty that an initial margin deposit will cover the risk of a position requiring the deposit, and a trader may be called upon by the brokerage firm to deposit additional margin, or close the position, or both. In any event, the firm has the right to close the position without the trader's knowledge or consent.

Minimum margin requirements are established by exchanges on which products requiring margin deposits are traded, but brokerage firms may require higher deposits. It is therefore essential that traders who employ strategies requiring margin deposits be familiar with their firm's policies.

A typical margin requirement for a short, uncovered index option on a broad-based market index is 100 percent of the option premium plus 15 percent of the aggregate underlying index value minus the aggregate out-of-the-money amount, if any, to a minimum of the option premium plus 10 percent of the aggregate underlying index value for calls, and the option premium plus 10 percent of the aggregate put exercise price for puts. Table 9–2 shows the margin requirement calculation for a short, uncovered *call* option on the S&P 500 index; a broad-based index option traded on the Chicago Board Options Exchange. Assuming an index level of 950 and a 975 Call sold for 8, the margin requirement of $12,550 is calculated as follows: the "option premium" is $800 (8 × $100), the aggregate underlying index value is $95,000 (950 × $100), 15 percent of the aggregate underlying index value is $14,250

Table 9–2 Margin Requirement for a Short, Uncovered Call Option on a Broad-Based Index

Assumptions: 975 Call sold for 8 with the index at 950

The margin requirement for a short, uncovered *call* option on a broad-based index is: option premium +15% of the aggregate underlying index value minus the out-of-the-money amount, if any, to a minimum of option premium plus 10% of the aggregate underlying index value.

Option premium = 8 =	$ 800
+ Aggregate underlying index value = 950 × $100 = $95,000	
× 15% 0.15	
	+14,250
– Out-of-the-money amount = (index level – strike) × $100	
= (975 – 950) × $100 =	– 2,500
= Margin requirement* =	$12,550

*In addition to the margin requirement, a minimum account equity is required.

(15% × $95,000) and the out-of-the-money amount is $2,500 [(975 − 950) × $100]. Adding the option premium to 15 percent of the aggregate underlying index value and subtracting the out-of-the-money amount produces the margin requirement of $12,550. The minimum margin is calculated by adding the option premium to 10 percent of the aggregate underlying index value (or 10 percent of the aggregate put exercise amount in the case of a short put). If the amount derived using the minimum calculation exceeds the amount calculated using the primary formula (15 percent of the aggregate underlying index value less any out-of-the-money amount), the requirement is that generated by the minimum calculation. In this example, the requirement derived by the primary calculation exceeds the amount rendered under the minimum calculation; therefore, the requirement is that generated by the primary calculation. The methodology for calculating a margin requirement is generally the same for all short options; however, the primary and minimum percentage amounts will vary depending on the underlying index. These figures do not include the minimum equity requirement of the firm.

MARGIN CALL

If the underlying index rises (falls), the margin requirement for a short call (put) will increase. A brokerage firm, however, will not require a customer to increase the account equity immediately. But if the account equity drops to a predetermined level known as the *minimum margin level,* the brokerage firm will require a customer to deposit additional funds into the account so that the account equity will be increased to a level known as the *maintenance margin level.* Such a request is known as a *margin call.* If a customer fails to increase the account equity within a defined time period as requested, the brokerage firm will close some or all of the position.

PROFIT MEASUREMENT INTRODUCED

Profit and loss results are frequently stated in annualized percentage terms, because annualized percentages take into account differences in investment capital and in time. To calculate the annualized percentage results of a strategy, its profit or loss is divided by the initial investment, and the resulting quotient is multiplied by an annualization factor, which is the quotient of the days per year divided by the number of days the trade was open. The results of such calculations are sometimes an impressive annualized return, and traders should note that it is unlikely that such performance can be repeated for an entire year. In fact, the purpose of such calculations is not to estimate what annualized percentage profits will be, but to compare two or more alternative strategies.

Consider the profitable trading results of two traders who purchased options. The first trader, John, purchased an option for 6, or $600, and sold it 90 days later for 12, or $1,200. The second trader, Ramona, purchased an option for 15 and sold it 75 days later for 25. Since John and Ramona invested different amounts and held their options for different periods of time, the typical method of comparing these trades is to look at the annualized percentage profits.

For John, his profit of $600 is divided by his investment of $600, and the quotient, 1.00, is multiplied by 365 divided by 90 (the number of days John's position was held). The result is a 400 percent annualized profit. For Ramona, her profit of $1,000 is divided by her investment of $1,500, and the quotient, 0.67, is multiplied by 365 divided by 75 (the number of days Ramona's position was held). Ramona's result is a 324 percent annualized profit. Note that these impressive annualized returns are for only one trade. It is most unlikely that such results can be repeated over the course of a year of making several trades. The only purpose of these calculations is to compare John's and Ramona's results, and the comparison indicates that John's profit was higher on an annualized percentage basis. It should also be noted that this comparison does not include other criteria that may lead to a different conclusion, such as absolute dollar profit or the ratio of profitable to losing trades.

Table 9–3 Calculation of Annualized Percentage Profit Potential*

Assumptions:
Profit (option premium received)	$ 800
Investment (margin requirement)	$12,550
Days per year	365
Days until expiration	60

$$\text{Annualized percentage profit potential} = \frac{\text{profit}}{\text{investment}} \times \frac{\text{days per year}}{\text{days to expiration}}$$

$$= \frac{\$800}{\$12,550} \times \frac{365}{60}$$

$$= 0.387, \text{ or } 38.7\%$$

*Assumes sold option expires without being assigned.

Note: Annualized percentage calculations assume that results can repeated during the course of a year, which is unlikely. Calculations of this nature are for comparison purposes only.

MEASURING THE PROFIT POTENTIAL OF SHORT OPTIONS

The same formula can be used to evaluate the profit potential of a strategy involving short options. Assuming the option expires without being assigned, the "profit" is the option premium received. The "investment" is the margin requirement. Assuming the position will be held to expiration, the annualization factor is the number of days in a year divided by the number of days to expiration.

The calculation of the annualized percentage profit potential is shown in Table 9–3. The example assumes a 60-day 975 Call sold for 8, and a margin requirement of $12,550, as calculated in Table 9–2.

INTERPRET RETURN CALCULATIONS CAREFULLY

Potential percentage returns such as those in Table 9–3 should not be seen as enticements to employ short option strategies, because selling uncovered index options involves substantial risk, and is suitable only for experienced, well-capitalized traders. Furthermore, a decision between two short option trades should not be based on annualized percentage calculations. It is only possible to compare alternatives if all other factors are equal, and this is almost never true. Rarely, if ever, are forecasts for different indexes exactly the same.

The advantage of annualized percentage return calculations is that they are specific. The disadvantage is that they do not include subjective elements, such as a market forecast and tolerance for risk. These subjective considerations are the most important elements of trading decisions. With experience, traders can use annualized percentage return calculations as part of a subjective decision-making process.

Now that the basics of short option positions and profit measurement have been reviewed, we will follow a trader through the process of establishing a short option position and tracking it as market conditions change. Since it is impossible to know in advance what will happen after a position is established, three possible outcomes will be examined.

A SHORT OPTION TRADING EXAMPLE

Michelle is a public relations specialist with a major bank in Colorado. She is an experienced option trader who frequently takes aggressive positions. In this example we will accept Michelle's market forecast as given. She is, of course, taking the risk that her forecast is wrong and that a loss will result. But Michelle is not hesitant about taking a loss if her forecast does not materialize. She will first analyze three options that she might sell to profit from her forecast and then choose one. Three possible outcomes will be presented: an optimistic scenario, a pessimistic scenario, and an expected scenario. We will watch Michelle's analysis and action in each situation.

Michelle follows the Russell 2000 Index, ticker symbol RUT. European-style options on this index are traded at the CBOE. In this example, the RUT Index is at 315, and Michelle is forecasting that it will trade between 312 and 325 for the next 24 days until option expiration. Michelle also believes the implied volatility of RUT options will decline. Consequently, she is planning the sale of puts to profit from her forecast.

Table 9–4 shows the information Michelle has gathered on implied volatility. Columns 1 and 2 contain recent closing levels of the OEX Index and the Volatility Index (VIX), CBOE's proprietary index of OEX implied volatility, which was discussed in Chapter 6. Columns 3 through 6 contain information about the RUT Index and an at-the-money call option. Column 3 lists closing RUT Index levels. Column 4 identifies the at-the-money (ATM) strike price that is nearest to the closing index level in column 3. Column 5 contains the days to expiration of the call in column 4, and column 6 shows the closing price of that call. Note that on Day 16 the number of days to expiration increases from 36 to 63. This occurs because Michelle has chosen an option with a further out expiration to use in her table. Although other

Table 9–4 Michelle's Implied Volatility Tracker

Day	Col. 1: OEX	Col. 2: VIX	Col. 3: RUT	Col. 4: ATM Strike	Col. 5: Days to Exp.	Col. 6: Call Price	Col. 7: Implied Volatility
1	647.53	15.20	346.61	345	50	8⅜	13.14
2	653.79	15.08	347.72	345	49	9⅛	13.49
3	651.08	15.71	346.94	345	48	8¾	13.85
4	648.22	15.76	344.80	345	47	7⅝	14.19
5	633.38	18.10	339.78	340	46	7⅝	14.64
6	628.69	18.39	336.68	335	45	9¼	16.30
7	630.03	17.30	336.44	335	44	8¾	15.73
8	633.42	16.46	332.71	335	43	6⅝	15.61
9	622.93	18.81	324.58	325	42	7¾	16.76
10	623.49	18.26	323.69	325	41	7⅛	16.62
11	606.07	22.65	314.72	315	40	7⅞	17.96
12	605.70	22.05	310.12	310	39	8	18.30
13	612.36	20.97	318.19	320	38	7	17.96
14	620.28	18.33	322.92	325	37	6⅝	17.34
15	616.72	18.48	321.54	320	36	8¼	17.19
16	611.18	21.53	317.65	320	63	9¾	19.06
17	602.70	24.43	311.72	310	62	11½	19.05
18	602.96	22.83	307.77	310	61	9⅛	18.74
19	608.07	20.10	311.58	310	60	11	18.59
20	613.00	18.62	315.00	315	59	9⅞	18.40

Dividend yield, 1.7%; interest rate, 5%.

traders may select the days to expiration differently, Michelle has chosen to keep track of 30-60 day options so that the information is consistent.

From the information in columns 3 through 6 and the interest rate and dividend yield listed at the bottom of the table, the implied volatility in column 7 is calculated using OP-EVAL3™ as described in Chapters 4 and 6. Although some traders may disagree, Michelle believes that concrete information about the VIX and the implied volatility level of the index options she trades is helpful in making trading decisions.

The daily information-gathering process takes Michelle about five minutes. She gets the closing index levels and closing option prices either by looking in a national business newspaper, by calling her broker, or by checking the CBOE's Web site at http://www.cboe.com. Information on VIX is available in Monday's *Barron's* or on CBOE's home page.

In Michelle's opinion, Table 9–4 and her knowledge of market conditions indicate that the implied volatility of RUT options has stopped rising and is likely to decline. She believes that since her forecast is for neutral market action, she can profit from both a decline in implied volatility and time erosion. The risk is that Michelle's forecast is wrong and she will have a losing trade. Furthermore, an unexpected adverse move in the index could mean that Michelle's loss will be substantially bigger than she expects. Prepared to take these risks, Michelle begins her analysis of three options.

Options under Consideration

It is 24 days prior to August expiration, and Michelle is considering the sale of either the RUT 310 Put for 3⅜, the RUT 315 Put for 5½, or the RUT 320 Put for 8¼. Table 9–5 shows the delta, gamma, vega, theta, margin requirement, and annualized percentage profit potential for each put. It is evident that these three put positions are not directly comparable! Each has a different delta and a different annualized percentage profit potential. The short 320 Put has the highest maximum profit potential, but that potential is not realized unless the index is above 320 at expiration, five index points above the current index level. Also, that highest potential profit is accompanied by the highest short-term market exposure. A short 320 Put has a positive delta of +0.607, compared to +0.472 and +0.338 for short 315 and 310 Puts, respectively. A short 310 Put, while having the lowest delta, and therefore the

Table 9–5 Position Greeks: Short 1 310 Put, Short 1 315 Put, Short 1 320 Put*

	Short 1 310 Put	Short 1 315 Put	Short 1 320 Put
Price	3⅜	5½	8¼
Delta	+0.338	+0.472	+0.607
Gamma	−0.025	−0.027	−0.027
Vega	−0.296	−0.321	−0.311
Theta	+0.764	+0.817	+0.744
Margin requirement	$4,563	$5,225	$5,550
Annual. % profit potential†	112%	146%	226%

*Index level, 315; dividend yield, 1.7%; volatility, 18%; interest rates, 5%; days to expiration, 24.

†Annualized percentage profit potential assumes the index is above the strike price at expiration and the option expires without assignment.

lowest short-term market exposure, also has the lowest profit potential both in absolute dollar terms and in annualized percentage terms. How does Michelle choose between alternatives that are not directly comparable? She must make a subjective decision based on her forecast and her tolerance for risk.

Since her forecast is for "neutral price action in a range between 312 to 325," Michelle decides to sell five 310 Puts at 3⅜ each. This is a subjective decision that only Michelle can make, and we will accept her decision as given and proceed with watching the three scenarios develop. It is important to note that Michelle did not automatically choose the strategy with the highest annualized profit potential. She chose the strategy best suited to her market forecast.

Preparing the Trade

Having chosen to sell five 310 Puts at 3⅜ each, Michelle prepares Table 9–6, which shows her initial risk exposures, that is, the Greeks, and margin requirement. The delta of +1.690 indicates that if factors other than the index level remain constant, Michelle's short put position will profit by $169 if the market rises by one index point and lose $169 if the market falls by one point. The negative gamma means that the position delta will change in the opposite direction of the change in the index level. Specifically, if the index level rises by one point, the position delta will decline by 0.125 from +1.690 to +1.565. The vega of −1.480 means the position will theoretically lose $148 if volatility rises by 1 percent and profit by this amount if volatility decreases by 1 percent. The theta of +3.820 means that $382 will be earned from the decrease in option value if 7 days pass and other factors remain constant. The Greeks indicate whether or not a position meets a trader's risk parameters. It takes some practice to understand what they are saying, but, given time, anyone can learn to interpret these numbers.

Table 9–6 Position Greeks: Short 5 310 Puts

	Short 5 310 Puts
Total premium received	$1,687.50
Position delta	+ 1.690
Position gamma	− 0.125
Position vega	− 1.480
Position theta	+ 3.820
Total margin requirement	$ 22,713

Index level, 315; dividend yield, 1.7%; volatility, 18%; interest rates, 5%; days to expiration, 24.

Table 9–7 Theoretical Values of 310 Put at Various Index Levels and Days to Expiration

Row	Index Level	Col. 1: 24 Days	Col. 2: 20 Days	Col. 3: 16 Days	Col. 4: 12 Days	Col. 5: 8 Days	Col. 6: 4 Days	Col. 7: Exp.
1	327	7/8	5/8	3/8	1/4	1/16	0	0
2	324	1 1/4	7/8	5/8	3/8	1/8	0	0
3	321	1 3/4	1 3/8	1	3/4	3/8	1/16	0
4	318	2 1/2	2	1 5/8	1 1/4	3/4	1/4	0
5	315	3 3/8	2 7/8	2 1/2	1 7/8	1 3/8	5/8	0
6	312	4 1/2	4	3 1/2	3	2 3/8	1 3/8	0
7	309	5 7/8	5 3/8	4 7/8	4 3/8	3 3/4	2 3/4	1
8	306	7 1/2	7	6 5/8	6 1/8	5 1/2	4 3/4	4
9	303	9 3/8	9	8 5/8	8 1/8	7 3/4	7 1/4	7

Dividend yield, 1.7%; volatility 18%; interest rates, 5%.

Michelle's next step is to create Table 9–7, which shows estimated prices of the 310 Put at different index levels and days to expiration. Although Michelle's forecast is for the RUT Index to stay above 312, Table 9–7 contains option price estimates down to an index level of 303, because she wants to estimate what her potential losses will be if her forecast is wrong. The index, of course, could drop significantly, and Michelle's loss could be substantially larger than estimated in Table 9–7. As stated earlier, this is the risk Michelle is taking.

Using Table 9–7 and the Call/Put Pricer page of OP-EVAL3™, Michelle can estimate how her short option position will behave and how her risk exposures will change under various scenarios.

Scenario 1: Better Than Planned

In this scenario, Michelle's neutral-to-bullish forecast is too conservative. The RUT Index rallies to 324 in 4 days, and her puts decline in price to 7/8 (row 2, column 2 in Table 9–7) for an unrealized profit of 2½ per option, or $1,250 on five options, not including commissions. What should Michelle do?

Although Michelle has many alternatives, in this scenario she is choosing between holding her short put position and closing the position by repurchasing them at 7/8. There are a number of factors to consider when making this decision. First, has the forecast changed? Second, has the target been achieved? Third, if the trade is profitable, what percentage of the total maximum profit could be realized if the position is closed, and fourth, regardless of whether the trade is profitable, how do the current risk measures—the Greeks—compare to the position's original risk measures? If the trade is unprofitable, have the risks changed sufficiently to warrant closing the position and realizing a loss? We will address these questions in order.

1. *Has the forecast changed?* As mentioned above, forecasting the market is a subjective process, which is not within the scope of this book. If Michelle changes her forecast, then the possibilities are endless. We will, therefore, assume that Michelle has not changed her forecast.

2. *Has the target been achieved?* A target, of course, could be stated in terms of either an index level or an option price. In Michelle's case, she picked an index level of 325 as the top of her predicted range. Her forecast, remember, was that the index would trade in a range from 310 to 325. With the index now at 324, this forecast implies that the index is more likely to decline from its current level of 324 than to rise. Has the target being achieved? The answer is a definite yes! Although it is possible for the index to decline at a sufficiently slow rate that time erosion of the options is greater than the tendency of the puts to rise with a downward move in the index, such a prediction is far too precise to be reliable. Since the index target of 325 has very nearly been reached, many traders would close the position by repurchasing the puts at ⅞ each and move on to the next trade.

3. *What percentage of the total maximum profit has been realized?* Michelle's maximum profit potential is 3⅜ per put. With the put now at ⅞, the decline of 2½ represents approximately 74 percent of the maximum profit potential (2½/3⅜). And, since only 4 out of 24 days has passed, Michelle has earned 74 percent of her maximum potential profit in just 17 percent of the expected time (4 days/24 days). While an opinion about these percentages is subjective, many traders would think that getting this much, this soon is too good to pass up. This is a second argument in favor of closing the position.

4. *Has the market exposure changed?* The answer is a definite yes! Everything has changed. Table 9–8 compares Michelle's short put position under the new market conditions to the position when initiated. With the rise in the index and the decrease in the put price, the total premium has declined to $437.50 from $1,687.50. The delta is now +0.665, approximately 40 percent of the original delta of +1.690. The new gamma and vega indicate less risk exposure, and the new theta indicates that $238 will be made from time erosion in the next 7 days, compared to $382 in the original position.

Table 9–8 Outcome 1: Better Than Expected

	Current Position	Original Position
Option price	⅞	3⅜
Total premium	$437.50	$1,687.50
Position delta	+ 0.665	+ 1.690
Position gamma	− 0.075	− 0.125
Position vega	− 0.840	− 1.480
Position theta	+ 2.380	+ 3.820
Margin requirement	$17,738	$22,813

Current index level, 324; current days to expiration, 20; dividend yield, 1.7%; volatility, 18%; interest rates, 5%.

Although the response is ultimately subjective, the answers to these four questions seem to strongly indicate a decision in favor of covering the short put position, realizing the profit, and moving on to the next trade. In real trading situations, of course, the answers may not indicate a course of action as clearly as they do in this situation, but when they do, traders should act accordingly.

Scenario 2: Worse Than Expected

In this scenario, the RUT Index falls to 309 in 8 days, and Michelle's puts rise in price to 4⅞ (row 7, column 3 in Table 9–7) for an unrealized loss of 1½ per option, or $750 on five options, not including commissions.

Table 9–9 shows Michelle's risk exposures under the new market conditions. First, the position delta has increased from +1.690 to +2.555. Assuming other factors remain constant, this delta estimates that another six-point decline in the index, from 309 to 303, will cause Michelle's position to lose $1,533 ($600 × 2.555). This loss is twice as big as the loss caused by the six-point drop from 315 to 309. Michelle's short put position now has more risk! The slight change in vega, from −1.480 to −1.290, means less exposure to an adverse change in volatility, but this slight benefit is outweighed by the increase in delta risk.

What should Michelle do in this case?

First, Michelle must maintain a rational view of the situation. Given that she did not predict the decline in the index (her low estimate of the range

Table 9–9 Outcome 2: Worse Than Expected

	Current Position	Original Position
Option price	4⅞	3⅜
Total premium	$2,437.50	$1,687.50
Position delta	+ 2.555	+ 1.690
Position gamma	− 0.170	− 0.125
Position vega	− 1.290	− 1.480
Position theta	+ 5.270	+ 3.820
Margin requirement	$25,613	$22,813

Current index level, 309; current days to expiration, 16; dividend yield, 1.7%; volatility, 18%; interest rates, 5%.

was the 312 level), the simple fact is that Michelle's forecast is wrong. The biggest mistake Michelle could make is to become emotionally involved in this losing trade ("This really is a good trade") or look for more reasons to hang on ("I wasn't wrong, I was just early").

Second, Michelle must know her stop-loss limit, the point at which, no matter what else she may think, she recognizes that she is wrong and that it is time to close the position, realize a loss, and move on to the next trade.

Setting stop-loss limits.   There are no firmly established rules about stop-loss limits, but some traders establish such limits in relation to the potential profits of a trade. It makes little sense, for example, to risk $10,000 on a trade that has a maximum profit potential of $1,000. Consequently, given that Michelle's five short puts have a maximum profit potential of 3⅜, or $337.50, each, then a stop-loss limit at 5⅜, a loss of 2, or $200 each, seems reasonable. A stop-loss limit at 8⅜, a loss of 5, or $500 each, is, arguably, too high.

Actual or mental stop-loss orders.   Although Michelle should have a maximum loss point in mind, this does not necessarily mean that she should place a stop-loss order with her broker. First, some brokerage firms do not accept stop-loss orders. Second, stop-loss orders are inflexible, and flexibility is sometimes an advantage for traders. If a broker has a stop-loss order, then its specific instructions must be followed if certain market conditions are met. If, on the other hand, a trader is watching the market and can give the broker a market order, then the trader has flexibility as to timing.

There is, however, a difference between being flexible and lacking discipline. Closing a trade "at or near a maximum-loss point" is being flexible.

Lacking discipline, in contrast, is failing to close a position until a margin call is received.

In Michelle's case, her forecast for the RUT Index to trade in a range between 312 and 325 was made when the index was at 315. Consequently, with the index at 309, it has declined more than she predicted. Also, the maximum profit potential of Michelle's short 310 Puts was $3\frac{3}{8}$, the price at which she sold them to establish the position. With these puts now trading a $4\frac{7}{8}$, her unrealized loss of $1\frac{1}{2}$ per option is almost 45 percent as great as her potential profit. Consequently, a strong case can be made for Michelle to close the position, realize the loss, and move on to the next trade. Of course, only Michelle can make this decision, but experienced traders know that losing trades are inevitable. There is an old saying: "Your first loss is your best loss." Arguably, in this worse-than-expected scenario, Michelle should take her 1.5-point loss, close her short put position by repurchasing them in the market, and move on to the next trade.

Scenario 3: About As Expected

In the third scenario, the market is living up to the neutral point in Michelle's forecast. The RUT Index has fluctuated little from where it started, and with only 12 days to expiration, the RUT Index is at 315, and Michelle's 310 Puts are trading at $1\frac{7}{8}$ (row 5, column 4 in Table 9–7). In this case Michelle has an unrealized profit of $1\frac{1}{2}$ per option, or $750 on five options, not including commissions. Remembering that "success is no excuse for complacency," Michelle should review the initial premises on which she based her strategy selection and ask herself if anything has changed. The four factors introduced above will be reviewed in order. These questions will help Michelle to decide between keeping the position open and closing it.

1. *Has the forecast changed?* As mentioned above, forecasting the market is a subjective process, which is not within the scope of this book. In real trading situations, forecasts change frequently. Traders must constantly study the market. Even though Michelle's forecast has been accurate so far in this example, she must still look for clues that things are about to change. To complete the decision-making process, we assume that Michelle has not changed her forecast.

2. *Has the target been achieved?* The second question is moot, because there has been no change in the RUT. Michelle originally picked an index level of 325 as the top of her predicted range. Consequently, the answer to this question is a definite no. Given that her forecast has not changed, this is a point in favor of keeping the position open.

3. *What percentage of the total maximum profit has been realized?*
   Michelle's maximum profit potential is 3⅜ per put. With the put now
   at 1⅞ and 12 of 24 days having passed, this means that 40 percent of
   the maximum profit potential has been earned in 50 percent of the
   time. Realistically, if the position were to be closed today, the actual
   percentage may be lower if bid-ask spreads and transaction costs are
   taken into account. Right now, it appears that if she holds the position for the remaining 50 percent of the time, she could realize the
   balance of 60 percent of the original maximum profit potential if the
   index is above 310, the strike price of the put, at expiration. Her
   future profit potential over the next 12 days is greater than her results
   over the past 12 days, assuming the index cooperates. Another argument in favor of keeping the position open.

4. *Has the market exposure changed?* Table 9–10 shows Michelle's risk
   exposures under the new market conditions. The position delta has
   decreased slightly from +1.690 to +1.475. This should be expected;
   as explained in Chapter 5, absolute values of deltas of out-of-the-
   money options decline toward zero as expiration approaches. The
   gamma has increased slightly, which means that the delta will now
   change slightly faster than before, and the smaller absolute value of
   the vega indicates a reduced sensitivity to volatility. The higher theta
   means that more profit will be earned if factors other than time are
   unchanged for the next 7 days relative to the first 7 days after the
   position was established. This is another argument in favor of keeping the position open.

Table 9–10 Outcome 3: About As Expected

	Current Position	Original Position
Option price	1⅞	3⅜
Total premium	$ 937.50	$1,687.50
Position delta	+1.475	+1.690
Position gamma	−0.165	−0.125
Position vega	−0.990	−1.480
Position theta	+5.620	+3.820
Margin requirement	$22,063	$22,813

Current index level, 315; current days to expiration, 12; dividend
yield, 1.7%; volatility, 18%; interest rates, 5%.

The weight of evidence in this scenario is clearly in favor of keeping the position open. The key assumption, though, is that Michelle's forecast has not changed.

SUMMARY

Uncovered short option positions have limited profit potential and substantial or unlimited risk potential. When considering strategies that involve short options, traders must think differently about capital management, risk, and profit potential than when buying options. Traders who sell uncovered index options must meet minimum financial requirements and maintain a minimum account equity. Policies in this regard vary by brokerage firm, so traders must be fully informed about their firm's requirements.

Traders should select strategies based on their market forecast and their tolerance for risk rather than on annualized percentage return calculations of a strategy's profit potential.

After a short option position is established, it should be monitored closely, and the decision to keep it open or to close it and realize a profit or loss should be based on four considerations. First, has the forecast changed? Second, has the target been achieved? Targets can be stated either in terms of an index level or in terms of an option price. Third, if the trade is profitable, what percentage of the maximum profit potential will be realized if the position is closed, and is the profit sufficient to justify closing the trade? Fourth, regardless of whether the trade is profitable or not, how do the position's current risk measures compare to the original measures? If the trade is unprofitable, has the risk changed sufficiently to warrant closing the position and taking a loss?

Although risk sensitivity numbers—the Greeks—are difficult to understand at first, with practice, any trader can learn to interpret and use these numbers.

Ten

Vertical Spreads

INTRODUCTION

S am made what is, perhaps, the most common mistake in trading options. He purchased 10 Bull Call spreads, because they were "cheaper" than simply buying 10 at-the-money calls. When the market moved up as Sam predicted, the at-the-money calls rose nicely, but his call spread hardly moved! We will spend a lot of time with Sam in this chapter discussing his motivations, his market forecast, and his alternatives. In the process, many aspects of vertical spreads will be explained.

The goal of this chapter is to explain the unique aspects of vertical spreads, how to analyze them, and how to determine when they are appropriate for a particular market forecast and when they are not. First, the term "vertical spread" will be defined, and four basic examples will be presented. Second, commonly used terminology regarding vertical spreads will be defined. Third, the chapter will explain the differences in risk between vertical spreads with American-style options and those with European-style options. Fourth, price behavior of vertical spreads will be examined. And finally, the impact of changes in volatility on vertical spreads will be discussed.

The examples in this chapter do not include commissions, other transaction costs, or margin requirements. Since vertical spreads involve two option positions, transaction costs and margin requirements can be higher than for single option positions. Consequently, these factors can significantly impact the desirability of the strategies discussed in this chapter, and they must be included in the analysis of any real strategy involving real options.

VERTICAL SPREAD DEFINED

A *vertical spread* involves the purchase of one option and the sale of a second option of the same type with the same underlying and same expiration but with a different strike price. The term "vertical" describes the relationship of the strike prices, one being higher, over, or "vertical to" the other. Also, unless stated otherwise, vertical spreads are one-to-one vertical spreads in which one option is purchased and one is sold. *Ratio vertical spreads,* as the name implies, involve the purchase (or sale) of one option and the sale (or purchase) of more than one of a second option. Ratio vertical spreads will be discussed in Chapter 12.

There are four basic vertical spreads.

Bull Call Spread

The purchase of one call and the simultaneous sale of a second call with the same underlying and expiration but with a higher strike price is known as a *bull call spread.* Figure 10–1 illustrates an SPX 850–860 Bull Call spread, in which one SPX 850 Call is purchased and one SPX 860 Call is sold. SPX options are European-style options on the S&P 500 Index, which are traded at the CBOE.

The term "bull call spread" describes three aspects of the position. First, this is a *bull* call spread, because the position has a tendency to profit as the underlying instrument rises in price. In Figure 10–1, for example, the bull call spread achieves its maximum profit potential at expiration only if the index is at or above 860. Second, this is a bull *call* spread, because only call options are involved, the SPX 850 and 860 Calls in this example. Third, this

**Figure 10–1 Bull Call Spread: Long 1 850 Call at 14 and Short 1 860
          Call at 10**

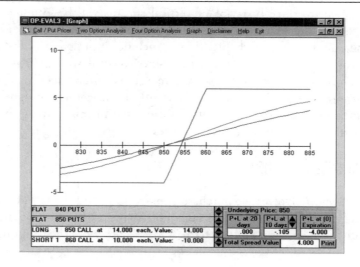

is a *spread*, because two different options are involved. The term "spread" is used loosely to describe a wide range of multiple-option positions, but, in this example, it refers to the 10-point difference, or spread, between the strike prices of the 850 and 860 Calls.

Bull call spreads are sometimes referred to as "debit call spreads," because they are established for a net cost, or net debit. The spread in Figure 10–1, for example, is established by purchasing the 850 Call for 14, or $1,400, and simultaneously selling the 860 Call at 10, or $1,000, for a net cost, or net debit, of 4, or $400. Also, it is common practice to describe a spread using the lower strike first regardless of whether calls or puts are involved; hence, the position in Figure 10–1 is called an 850–860 Bull Call spread.

At expiration, there are three possible outcomes. The index can be at or below the lower strike, above the lower strike but not above the higher strike, or above the higher strike. The straight lines in Figure 10–1 illustrate these possibilities.

1. *If the index is at or below the lower strike* of a bull call spread at expiration, then the maximum potential loss is incurred: both calls expire worthless and the full amount paid for the position, $400 plus commissions in this example, is lost.

2. *If the index is above the lower strike but not above the higher strike* at expiration, then the long call (lower strike) is exercised, and the short call (higher strike) expires worthless. The index level at expiration at which a bull call spread breaks even is equal to the lower strike price plus the net premium paid for the position. In Figure 10–1, for example, the break-even index level at expiration is 854, the lower strike of 850 plus the net cost of 4.

3. *If the index is above the higher strike* at expiration, then the long call is exercised, and the short call is assigned and the maximum profit potential is realized. If the SPX Index is 868 at expiration, for example, then exercising the 850 Call results in a cash receipt of 18, or $1,800, and assignment on the 860 Call results in a cash payment of 8, or $800, for a net receipt of 10, or $1,000. The cost of the position, $400 in this example, is subtracted from the $1,000 received, and the result is the net profit of 6, or $600.

Note that the maximum profit potential of a bull call spread is equal to the difference between the strike prices less the net cost of the position. Also, the maximum profit is realized at expiration if the underlying index is at or above the higher strike.

Bear Call Spread

The sale of one call and simultaneous purchase of a second call with the same underlying and same expiration but with a higher strike is known as a *bear call spread*. Figure 10–2 illustrates an SPX 850–860 Bear Call spread, in which one SPX 850 Call is sold for 14, and one SPX 860 Call is purchased for 10. The term *bear* means the position has a tendency to profit as the underlying instrument declines in price. In Figure 10–2, the bear call spread achieves its maximum theoretical profit at expiration only if the index is at or below 850. The maximum loss is realized at expiration if the index is at or above the higher strike, 860 in this example.

Bear call spreads are sometimes referred to as "credit call spreads," because they are established for a net receipt of premium, or net credit. The spread in Figure 10–2, for example, is established for a net credit of 4, or $400.

At expiration, there are three possible outcomes. The index can be at or below the lower strike, above the lower strike but not above the upper strike, and above the upper strike. The straight lines in Figure 10–2 illustrate these possibilities.

1. *If the index level is at or below the lower strike* of a bear call spread at expiration, then both calls expire worthless and the net premium received, $400 in this example, is kept as income.

Figure 10–2 Bear Call Spread: Short 1 850 Call at 14 and Long 1 860 Call at 10

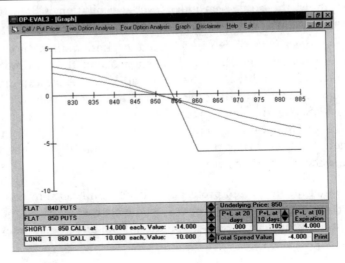

2. *If the index is above the lower strike but not above the upper strike* at expiration, then the short call (lower strike) is assigned and the long call (higher strike) expires worthless. The index level at expiration at which a bear call spread breaks even is equal to the lower strike price plus the net premium received. In Figure 10–2, the break-even index level at expiration is 854, the lower strike of 850 plus the net premium received of 4.

3. *If the index is above the higher strike* at expiration, then the short call is assigned, and the long call is exercised. If the SPX Index is 865 at expiration, for example, then assignment of the 850 Call results in a cash payment of 15, or $1,500. Exercise of the 860 Call results in a cash receipt of 5, or $500, for a net payment of 10, or $1,000. The net cash payment at expiration, $1,000 in this example, is subtracted from the $400 net received when the position was established, and the result is the net loss of 6, or $600.

Note that the maximum potential loss of a bear call spread is equal to the difference between the strike prices less the net premium received for establishing the position. Also, this maximum loss is realized at expiration if the index is at or above the higher strike.

Bear Put Spread

The purchase of one put and simultaneous sale of a second put with the same underlying and same expiration but with a lower strike price is known as a *bear put spread.* Figure 10–3 illustrates an SPX 840–850 bear put spread, in which one SPX 850 Put is purchased for 13 and one SPX 840 Put is sold for 9¼.

Bear put spreads are sometimes referred to as "debit put spreads," because they are established for a net cost, or net debit. The spread in Figure 10–3, for example, is established by purchasing the 850 Put for 13, or $1,300, and simultaneously selling the 840 Put at 9¼, or $925, for a net cost, or net debit, of 3¾, or $375, not including transaction costs. Remember, it is common practice to describe a vertical spread using the lower strike first regardless of whether calls or puts are involved; hence, the position in Figure 10–3 is called an 840–850 Bear Put spread.

At expiration, there are three possible outcomes. The index can be at or above the higher strike, below the higher strike but not below the lower strike, or below the lower strike. The straight lines in Figure 10–3 illustrate these possibilities.

**Figure 10–3 Bear Put Spread: Long 1 850 Put at 13 and Short 1 840
Put at 9¼**

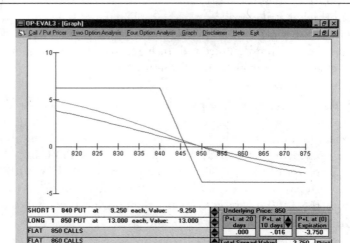

1. *If the index level is at or above the upper strike* of a bear put spread at
   expiration, then the maximum potential loss is realized: both puts
   expire worthless, and the full amount paid for the position, $375 plus
   transaction costs in this example, is lost.

2. *If the index is below the higher strike but not below the lower strike* at expiration, then the long put (higher strike) is exercised, and the short put
   (lower strike) expires worthless. The index level at expiration at which
   a bear put spread breaks even is equal to the higher strike price minus
   the net premium paid for the position. In Figure 10–3, the break-even
   index level at expiration is 846¼, the higher strike of 850 minus the net
   cost of 3¾.

3. *If the index is below the lower strike* at expiration, then the long put is
   exercised and the short put is assigned and the maximum profit potential is realized. If the SPX Index is 837 at expiration, for example, then
   exercising the 850 Put results in a cash receipt of 13, or $1,300, and
   assignment on the 840 Put results in a cash payment of 3, or $300, for
   a net receipt of 10, or $1,000. The cost of the position, $375 in this
   example, is subtracted from the $1,000 received, and the result is the
   net profit of 6¼, or $625, not including commissions.

Note that the maximum potential profit of a bear put spread is equal to
the difference between the strike prices less the net cost of the position. Also,

this maximum profit is realized at expiration if the index is at or below the lower strike. The maximum loss is realized at expiration if the index is at or above the higher strike, 850 in this example.

Bull Put Spread

The sale of one put and simultaneous purchase of a second put with the same underlying and same expiration but with a lower strike price is known as a *bull put spread*. Figure 10–4 illustrates an SPX 840–850 Bull Put spread in which one SPX 850 Put is sold for 13 and one SPX 840 Put is purchased for 9¼.

Bull put spreads are sometimes referred to as "credit put spreads," because they are established for a net receipt, or net credit. The spread in Figure 10–4, for example, is established by selling the 850 Put for 13, or $1,300, and simultaneously purchasing the 840 Put at 9¼, or $925, for a net receipt, or net credit, of 3¾, or $375, not including commissions. Once again, it is common practice to describe a vertical spread using the lower strike first regardless of whether calls or puts are involved; hence, the position in Figure 10–4 is called an 840–850 Bull Put spread.

At expiration, there are three possible outcomes. The index can be at or above the higher strike, below the higher strike but not below the lower strike, or below the lower strike. The straight lines in Figure 10–4 illustrate these possibilities.

Figure 10–4 Bull Put Spread: Short 1 850 Put at 13 and Long 1 840 Put at 9¼

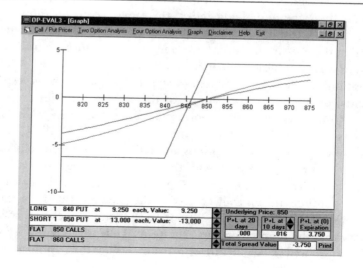

1. *If the index level is at or above the upper strike* of a bull put spread at expiration, then the maximum potential profit is realized: both puts expire worthless and the full amount received, $375 less transaction costs in this example, is kept as income.

2. *If the index is below the higher strike but not below the lower strike* at expiration, then the short put (higher strike) is assigned, and the long put (lower strike) expires worthless. The index level at expiration at which a bull put spread breaks even is equal to the higher strike price minus the net premium received. In Figure 10–4, the break-even index level at expiration is 846¼, the higher strike of 850 minus the 3¾ received.

3. *If the index is below the lower strike* at expiration, then the short put is assigned and the long put is exercised. If the SPX Index is 834 at expiration, for example, then assignment of the 850 Put results in a cash payment of 16, or $1,600, and exercising the 840 Put results in a cash receipt of 6, or $600, for a net payment of 10, or $1,000. The credit received, $375 in this example, is subtracted from the $1,000 paid, and the result is the net loss of 6¼, or $625, not including commissions.

Note that the maximum potential loss of a bull put spread is equal to the difference between the strike prices less the net credit received. Also, this maximum loss is realized at expiration if the index is at or below the lower strike.

RISKS OF VERTICAL SPREADS INVOLVING AMERICAN-STYLE OPTIONS

European-style index options cannot be exercised early. Therefore, short European-style index options can be covered by long options of the same type with the same underlying index, the same expiration month, and a lower strike in the case of calls or a higher strike in the case of puts. This means that the one-to-one vertical spreads described above are truly limited-risk strategies if European-style index options are used.

Positions involving short American-style index options, however, involve substantial or unlimited risk because of the early-exercise feature of these options. Consequently, it is important to understand the risks of these options as described in Chapter 1, where the term "covered" is discussed. Even if American-style index options are sold on a one-to-one basis against other options of the same type, with the same underlying, same expiration, and a lower strike in the case of calls or a higher strike in the case of puts, these short options are not truly covered in the same way that European-style index options or American-style options on individual stocks are covered.

Now that the terminology and the profit and risk potential of spreads have been reviewed, we will return to Sam and his less than optimal situation.

SAM'S SITUATION

Sam trades TXX options. These are European-style options on the Technology Index, which are traded at the Philadelphia Stock Exchange. Since Sam is a short-term trader who closes positions prior to expiration, the straight-line expiration profit and loss diagrams in Figures 10–1 through 10–4 do not offer sufficient information for Sam to select a strategy. And although the curved lines in these exhibits indicate how a spread might behave prior to expiration, Sam needs a specific estimate of a spread price given forecasted changes in market conditions. The Call/Put Pricer and the Two Option Analysis pages in OP-EVAL3™ are just Sam what needs.

Tables 10–1, 10–2, and 10–3 were created using the Two Option Analysis page in OP-EVAL3™. They contain theoretical values of a 180 Call, a 190 Call, and a 180–190 Bull Call spread, respectively, at different index levels and different days prior to expiration. The values in Table 10–3 appear in the Spread Value box on the Two Option Analysis page, but they can also be calculated by subtracting a 190 Call value in Table 10–2 from the corresponding 180 Call Value in Table 10–1. The value of 7 in Table 10–3, column 1, row 1, for example, is the difference between the 180 Call value of 13⅞ and the 190 Call value of 6⅞ in the corresponding boxes in Tables 10–1 and 10–2. Sam could use tables such as these to estimate the results of different strategies for different forecasts.

Table 10–1 Theoretical Values of 180 Call at Various Index Levels and Days to Expiration

Row	Index Level	Col. 1: 30 Days	Col. 2: 25 Days	Col. 3: 20 Days	Col. 4: 15 Days	Col. 5: 10 Days	Col. 6: 5 Days	Col. 7: Exp.
1	192	13⅞	13½	13⅛	12¾	12⅜	12⅛	12
2	190	12¼	11⅞	11½	11	10½	10⅛	10
3	188	10¾	10¼	9¾	9¼	8⅞	8¼	8
4	186	9¼	8⅞	8½	7⅞	7¼	6½	6
5	184	7⅞	7⅜	6⅞	6¼	5⅝	4¾	4
6	182	6⅝	6⅛	5⅝	5	4¼	3⅜	2
7	180	5½	5	4½	3⅞	3⅛	2⅛	0
8	178	4½	4	3½	2⅞	2⅛	1¼	0
9	176	3⅝	3⅛	2⅝	2	1⅜	⅝	0

Dividend yield, 0%; volatility, 25%; interest rates, 5%.

Table 10–2 Theoretical Values of 190 Call at Various Index Levels and Days to Expiration

Row	Index Level	Col. 1: 30 Days	Col. 2: 25 Days	Col. 3: 20 Days	Col. 4: 15 Days	Col. 5: 10 Days	Col. 6: 5 Days	Col. 7: Exp.
1	192	6⅞	6⅜	5¾	5⅛	4⅜	3½	0
2	190	5¾	5¼	4¾	4	3¼	2¼	0
3	188	4¾	4½	3¾	3	2⅜	1⅜	0
4	186	3⅞	3⅜	2⅞	2¼	1⅝	⅞	0
5	184	3⅛	2⅝	2⅛	1⅝	1	⅜	0
6	182	2½	2	1⅝	1⅛	⅝	³⁄₁₆	0
7	180	1⅞	1½	1⅛	¾	⅜	¹⁄₁₆	0
8	178	1⅜	1⅛	¾	½	¼	nil	0
9	176	1	¾	½	¼	⅛	nil	0

Dividend yield, 0%; volatility, 25%; interest rates, 5%.

Table 10–3 Theoretical Values of 180–190 Bull Call Spread at Various Index Levels and Days to Expiration

Row	Index Level	Col. 1: 30 Days	Col. 2: 25 Days	Col. 3: 20 Days	Col. 4: 15 Days	Col. 5: 10 Days	Col. 6: 5 Days	Col. 7: Exp.
1	192	7	7⅛	7⅜	7⅝	8	8⅝	10
2	190	6½	6⅝	6¾	7	7¼	7⅞	10
3	188	6	5¾	6	6¼	6½	6⅞	8
4	186	5⅜	5½	5⅝	5⅝	5⅝	5⅝	6
5	184	4¾	4¾	4¾	4⅝	4⅝	4⅝	4
6	182	4⅛	4⅛	4	3⅞	3⅝	3³⁄₁₆	2
7	180	3⅝	3½	3⅜	3⅛	2¾	2¹⁄₁₆	0
8	178	3⅛	2⅞	2¾	2⅜	1⅞	1¼	0
9	176	2⅝	2⅜	2⅛	1¾	1¼	⅝	0

Dividend yield, 0%; volatility, 25%; interest rates, 5%.

Higher Profit or Higher Risk?

At the start of this chapter, we learned that Sam purchased 10 180–190 Bull Call spreads rather than 10 180 Calls. When Sam was facing this decision, it was 30 days prior to expiration, the TXX Index was 178, and Sam was predicting a six-point rise in the index in 5 days. Tables 10–1 and 10–3 show why Sam got a smaller profit from purchasing 10 bull call spreads than from purchasing 10 180 Calls.

Table 10–1 shows that with the TXX Index at 178 30 days prior to expiration (column 1, row 8), the 180 Call is 4½. Five days later, with the index at 184 (column 2, row 5), the call is 7⅜. Purchasing 10 of these calls at 4½ and selling them at 7⅜ results in a profit of 2⅞, or $287.50, per option or $2,875 on 10 options not including commissions.

Table 10–3 shows that with the index at 178 at 30 days to expiration and at 184 at 25 days, the 180–190 Call spread is 3⅛ and 4¾, respectively. Purchasing 10 of these calls at 3⅛ and selling them at 4¾ results in a profit of 1⅝, or $162.50, per spread, or $1,625 on 10 spreads not including commissions.

Had Sam done this simple analysis before making his decision, he would have known what to expect. This analysis does not imply, however, that Sam made the "wrong" decision, because the purchase of 10 180 Calls involves a greater maximum theoretical risk and greater short-term risk than purchasing 10 180–190 Bull Call spreads. The maximum risk of purchasing 10 180 Calls is the total cost paid, which is $4,500 plus commissions in this example. The maximum theoretical value of purchasing bull call spreads involving calls subject to European-style exercise is also the total cost paid plus commissions. In this example, the cost of 10 180–190 Bull Call spreads is $3,112.50 plus commissions.

Regarding short-term risk, Tables 10–1 and 10–3 indicate that if Sam's forecast is incorrect and the index declines two points in 5 days, then 10 long 180 Calls suffer a greater loss than 10 bull call spreads. According to Table 10–1, if the index declines from 178 at 30 days to 176 at 25 days, then the 180 Call is estimated to decline from 4½ to 3⅛ for a loss of $1,375 on the purchase of 10. And according to Table 10–3, under the same circumstances, the 180–190 Bull Call spread is estimated to decline from 3⅛ to 2⅜ for a loss of $750 on the purchase of 10 spreads. These strategies, therefore, involve different short-term profit and risk potentials, so they are not directly comparable. Consequently, a choice between them should not be based solely on cost. Rather, Sam should subjectively weigh his confidence in his market forecast and his tolerance for risk.

Using the Greeks

Another way to evaluate Sam's choices is to use the Greeks to analyze the profit and risk potentials of his alternatives. Table 10–4 shows the delta, gamma, vega, and theta of the 180 Call, the 190 Call, and the 180–190 Bull Call spread. Having a bullish forecast, Sam's first concern should be delta—

Table 10–4 Delta, Gamma, Vega, and Theta

	180 Call	190 Call	180–190 Bull Call Spread
Price	4½	1⅜	3⅛
Delta	+0.475	+0.207	+0.268
Gamma	+0.031	+0.023	+0.008
Vega	+0.203	+0.148	+0.055
Theta	−0.707	−0.459	−0.248

and the 180 Call and the 180–190 Bull Call spread have significantly different deltas! The delta of 1 long 180 Call is +0.475, so the delta of 10 long 180 Calls is +4.750, equivalent to 4.75 long futures contracts on the underlying index if futures were available on this index. The delta of 1 180–190 Bull Call spread, however, is +0.268. This is calculated by subtracting the delta of the 190 Call (+0.207) from the delta of the 180 Call (+0.475). Consequently, the delta of 10 spreads is +2.68, slightly more than half the delta of 10 180 Calls. Had Sam done this analysis, this would have been his first indication that the bull call spreads would underperform relative to the 180 Calls.

Table 10–4 also shows that the gammas of the call and the bull call spread are very different. One 180 Call has a gamma of +0.031, so 10 180 Calls have a gamma of +0.310. This means that as the underlying index rises one point, the delta of the 10 long 180 Calls rises by 0.310. Consequently, as the index rises six points, from 178 to 184, the delta of the 10 Call position rises from +4.750 to approximately +6.610. This is calculated by adding the beginning delta to the index point change times the gamma. In this example, the beginning position delta is +4.750, the index point change is 6, from 178 to 184, and the position gamma is +0.310. Consequently, the ending delta is 4.750 + (6 × 0.0310) = +6.610. The 10 long 180 Calls started out equivalent to long 4.75 futures and ended up equal to long 6.610 futures.

In contrast, the gammas of +0.008 for 1 180–190 Bull Call spread and +0.080 for 10 spreads indicate a much smaller rise in the delta of this position. Specifically, with a six-point rise in the index from 178 to 184, the delta of 10 180–190 Bull Call spreads starts at +2.680 and rises to approximately +3.160 [2.680 + (6 × 0.080)].

To summarize, there are two reasons that Sam's predicted rise in the TXX Index caused the 10 long 180 Call position to earn a larger profit than the 10 180–190 Bull Call spreads. First, the 10 long calls started with a higher delta and, second, that delta increased more rapidly as the index rose. But, again, this analysis explains why one strategy performed better than the other strategy. It does not mean that purchasing 10 180 Calls is a "better" choice. As discussed above, the 10 180 Calls involved more risk than the 10 Bull Call spreads. Nevertheless, had Sam done this analysis rather than just consider the "cost" of the positions, he would have realized that the strategies have different profit/loss potentials. He still might have made the same choice, but, having done this analysis, he would have been prepared for the outcome.

CAPITAL MANAGEMENT AND STRATEGY ALTERNATIVES

Suppose that Sam had approached this trading decision differently. If, for example, he had decided that he was willing to invest and risk $4,000 on this trade, then he could have chosen between alternatives with approximately the same maximum theoretical risk.

Although Sam has many alternatives involving calls and puts with different strike prices and expiration dates not shown in Tables 10–1 to 10–3, for the sake of simplicity, these tables will be used to examine only three strategies: buying 180 Calls, buying 190 Calls, and buying 180–190 Bull Call spreads. The purpose of this example is to demonstrate how the price behavior of vertical spreads differs from the price behavior of at-the-money and out-of-the-money options. And although this example uses call options to illustrate several points, the concepts apply equally to puts.

Identifying the Alternatives

Using the prices in Tables 10–1 to 10–3, and assuming that Sam has approximately $4,000 to invest and risk, not including commissions, he can evaluate three strategies: the purchase of 9 180 Calls, the purchase of 29 190 Calls, and the purchase of 13 180–190 Call spreads. The maximum number of units of each strategy is determined by first dividing the capital available by the cost of the strategy and then rounding to the nearest whole number.

The number of 180 Calls that can be purchased, for example, is calculated by dividing the capital of $4,000 by the 180 Call price of 4½, or $450. Rounding the result of 8.88 to 9 indicates that 9 180 Calls can be purchased for $4,050 (9 × $450), not including commissions. By the same process, it is calculated that 29 190 Calls can be purchased at 1⅜, or $137.50, each for a total of $3,987.50 (29 × $137.50). Finally, 13 180–190 Bull Call spreads can be purchased for $4,062.50 (13 × $312.50), not including commissions. All three strategies cost approximately $4,000, not including commissions.

Estimating Results

Sam can now use Tables 10–1 to 10–3 to estimate the results of these strategies under different market forecasts. Sam's initial forecast will be analyzed first, and then the same price rise over a longer time period will be analyzed.

Sam's initial forecast was that the market would rise from 178 at 30 days prior to expiration to 184 at 25 days. Column 2, row 5 of Table 10–1 estimates that, after the predicted move, the 180 Call price will be 7⅜. The corresponding boxes in Tables 10–2 and 10–3 indicate that the 190 Call and 180–190 Bull Call spread will be 2⅝ and 4¾, respectively.

Assuming these estimates are accurate, the conclusion is that purchasing 29 190 Calls yields the highest profit. Purchasing these calls at 1⅜ and selling them at 2⅝ yields a profit of 1¼, or $125, per option, for a total profit of $3,625, before commissions on the purchase and sale of the options. This compares favorably to the purchase and sale of 9 180 Calls at 4½ and 7⅜, respectively, for a profit of 2⅞ each, or $2,587.50 total. Purchasing 13 180–190 Bull Call spreads at 3⅛ each and selling them at 4¾ results in the lowest total profit of the three strategies of $2,112.50 before commissions.

Different Forecast, Different Strategy

Suppose that Sam accurately forecasts the five-point rise in the index but that his timing is off. If the rise takes 15 days instead of 5, the index will be at 184 at 15 days to expiration. In this case column 4, row 5 of Tables 10–1, 10–2, and 10–3, estimates that the 180 Call, the 190 Call, and the 180–190 Bull Call spread will be 6¼, 1⅝, and 4⅝, respectively.

This forecast suggests a different strategy for achieving the highest profit. Purchasing 29 190 Calls at 1⅜ and selling them at 1⅝ yields a profit of ¼, or $25, on each, for a total profit of $725, not including commissions. The purchase and sale of 9 180 Calls at 4½ and 6¼, respectively, results is a profit of 1¾ on each, or $1,575 total. Purchasing 13 180–190 Bull Call spreads at 3⅛ each and selling them at 4⅝ results in a profit of $1,950.

Under the new forecast, the bull call spread rose from last place to first place! The conclusion is that, assuming a constant amount of capital, short, sharp price rises favor out-of-the-money calls over at-the-money calls or bull call spreads. Smaller price rises over a longer time period favor bull call spreads. At-the-money calls are favored when the forecast predicts a price movement somewhere in between.

Until now the examples have assumed a constant volatility. The next example will show the impact of changes in volatility on vertical spreads.

CHANGING THE VOLATILITY

What should traders consider when they have a strong opinion about market direction but are worried about an adverse change in volatility? Such a situation may arise when an economic report is eagerly awaited.

Refer to Sam's original forecast for a six-point rise in the index in 5 days. This time, however, assume Sam is forecasting a decrease in implied volatility from 25 percent to 20 percent. Sam might consider such a change possible if several companies in the index were to release earnings at the same time, forecasting that after the news is out, the implied volatility will drop. With this new element factored into the forecast, Sam will choose a different strategy, even though the price change and time period elements are the same.

Figure 10–5 is a Two Option Analysis page from OP-EVAL3™ in which the options are priced with Sam's new assumptions. The index is now 184, up from 178. The days to expiration have declined from 30 to 25, and the volatility has declined from 25 percent to 20 percent. The interest rates, dividends, and strike prices remain the same. The price of the 180 Call will be 6.539, or approximately 6½. The 190 Call price is estimated at 1.792, or approximately 1¾, and the 180–190 Bull Call spread price is estimated at 4.747, or approximately 4¾.

A comparison of the values in Figure 10–5 and Tables 10–1 through 10–3 shows that the decrease in volatility greatly affects the prices of the 180 and 190 Calls but not the price of the bull call spread.

Figure 10–5 Sam's Forecast, with a Decrease in Implied Volatility

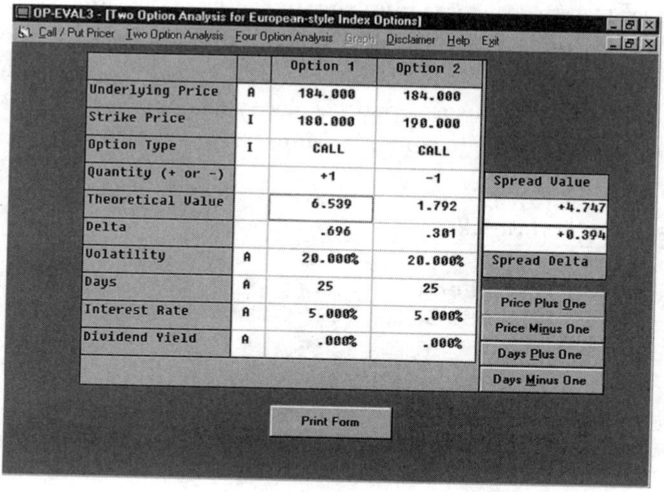

If Sam's original forecast of an index rise from 178 to 184 in six days also includes a decrease in implied volatility from 25% to 20%, the prices in Figure 10–5 indicate that Sam should purchase 13 180–190 Bull Call spreads rather than 29 190 Calls or 9 180 Calls. Purchasing 29 190 Calls at 1⅜ and selling them at 1¾ yields a profit of ⅜, or $37.50, on each, for a profit of $1,087.50 before commissions. The purchase and sale of 9 180 Calls at 4½ and 6½, respectively, results in a profit of 2 on each, for a total of $1,800. Purchasing 13 180–190 Bull Call spreads at 3⅛ each and selling them at 4¾ results in a total profit of $2,112.50, the highest of the three strategies for this forecast.

The conclusion is that one-to-one vertical spreads can be much less sensitive to changes in volatility than single-option positions. *When traders think that volatility risk is high, one-to-one vertical spreads may be the strategy of choice!*

A LOOK AT THE GREEKS

Table 10–5 presents the Greeks of the three strategies discussed above. The vegas of the three strategies provide a clue that the 180–190 Bull Call spread is least sensitive to changes in volatility. The vega of the bull call spread is the smallest, less than half that of the 180 Call position and less than one-sixth that of the 190 Call position. But once again, this does not make the bull call spread the "better" choice. The smallest vega is only one aspect of the bull call spread. This strategy also has the smallest delta of the three strategies. This means that in a sharply rising market in which implied volatility remains constant, this strategy will underperform the other two.

The conclusion to be drawn from Table 10–5 is that despite being almost equal in terms of maximum theoretical risk, the three strategies still offer trade-offs, some relatively positive attributes, and some relatively negative ones when compared to each other. Although the Greeks are difficult to interpret initially, with some practice, every trader will find that they are of great benefit in making trading decisions.

Table 10–5 Position Greeks

	Long 9 180 Calls	Long 29 190 Calls	Long 13 180–190 Bull Call Spreads
Price (total)	40½	39⅞	40⅝
Delta	+4.2755	+6.003	+3.484
Gamma	+0.297	+0.667	+0.104
Vega	+1.827	+4.292	+0.715
Theta	−6.363	−13.311	−4.524

CREDIT SPREADS VERSUS SELLING UNCOVERED OPTIONS

Many traders ask which is better, selling vertical spreads or uncovered options? Unfortunately, there is no simple answer to this question because the strategies involve different short-term risks and different maximum theoretical risks. Uncovered short index options involve substantial or unlimited risk, and this strategy is only suitable for experienced traders who are financially and psychologically capable of assuming those risks. Credit spreads with American-style index options have substantial or unlimited theoretical risk, because, as discussed earlier in this chapter and in Chapter 1, short American-style index options cannot be covered in the same way that short European-style index options can be covered.

Figure 10–6 illustrates a short DTX 275 Call, Figure 10–7 shows a DTX 275–285 Bear Call spread, and Table 10–6 compares the Greeks of the two strategies. The DTX Index is based on the Dow Jones Transportation Average, and European-style options are traded at the CBOE.

There are many differences between these two strategies. First, the uncovered short 275 Call is sold for 7¼ in this example, and the 275–285 Bear Call spread is sold for 4. Second, the risk of the uncovered 275 Call is unlimited, while the risk of the 10-point Bear Call spread involving European-style index options is limited to 6, or $600, in this example. Third, Table 10–6 shows how the short-term market exposures, the Greeks, are different.

Figure 10–6 Short 1 275 Call at 7¼

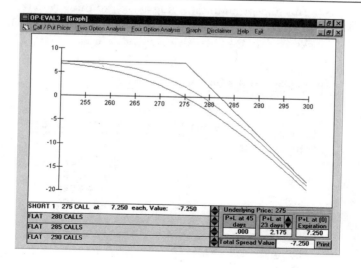

Figure 10–7 275–285 Bear Call Spread at 4

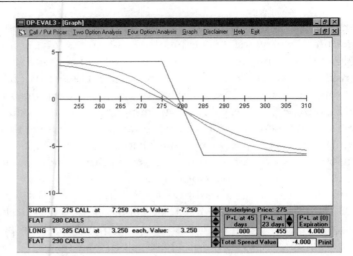

Table 10–6 reveals that the short 275 Call is more sensitive to all factors than the call spread. Its delta, gamma, and vega are all smaller (higher absolute value), which means that it has more risk than the bear call spread. But its higher theta means it profits more if factors other than time remain constant.

Which is "better"? Neither. These two strategies offer a choice between two sets of trade-offs. Choosing between them is a personal decision that can be made only by traders themselves based on their market forecast and tolerance for risk. This may be an unsatisfying answer to those who want a clear choice. Unfortunately, there are rarely "clear" choices in trading whether it be options, stocks, or futures. One advantage of options is that they provide

Table 10–6 Short Call versus Bear Call Spread

	Short 275 Call	275–285 Bear Call Spread
Theoretical value	7¼	4
Delta	−0.536	−0.224
Gamma	−0.023	−0.002
Vega	−0.383	−0.040
Theta	+0.621	+0.100

Index, 275; dividend yield, 2%; volatility, 17.5%; interest rates, 5%; days to expiration, 45.

traders with a wide range of alternatives. But only a trader can decide which alternative is "best" for a particular forecast. And, of course, there is always the risk that the forecast will be wrong and a loss incurred.

SUMMARY

There are four basic one-to-one vertical spreads. Assuming the same underlying and expiration date, a bull call spread consists of a long call with a lower strike and a short call with a higher strike. A bear call spread consists of a short call with a lower strike and a long call with a higher strike. A bear put spread consists of a long put with a higher strike and a short put with a lower strike. A bull put spread consists of a short put with a higher strike and a long put with a lower strike. Regardless of whether calls or puts are involved, it is common practice to refer to vertical spreads using the lower strike first.

The prices of vertical spreads behave differently than at-the-money or out-of-the-money single options because their Greeks are different. Consequently, the same three-part forecasting technique including a price forecast, a time forecast, and a volatility forecast must be used with vertical spreads as with individual options. Different forecasts will lead to the selection of different strategies.

Vertical spreads tend to be less sensitive to changes in implied volatility than single-option positions. This means that vertical spreads may be a preferred choice when a forecast calls for a decrease in implied volatility. In most cases the market price of an in-the-money vertical spread will not go to its maximum value until very close to expiration.

Selling vertical spreads and selling uncovered options are not directly comparable because they involve different risks, that is, different Greeks, and different profit potential. Although the Greeks are difficult to interpret initially, with practice any trader will find that they offer valuable information quickly and easily, thereby speeding up trading decisions.

There are no "better" strategies. Traders must make individual judgments about the level of their confidence in forecasts and their tolerance for risk when choosing between alternative strategies.

Eleven

Straddles and Strangles

INTRODUCTION

O ption traders tend to fall into one of three categories. The first group has heard of straddles and strangles but has no idea what they are. The second group has seen expiration profit and loss diagrams of the strategies but has never traded them. And the third group has used them but lost money! The goal of this chapter is to create a fourth group: option traders who have realistic expectations about straddles and strangles and which forecasts they are and are not suited for. Every option strategy has its own set of advantages and disadvantages, and straddles and strangles are no exception.

This chapter will discuss long and short straddles and strangles. Each strategy will be defined first, and expiration profit and loss diagrams will be presented. Next, a table of theoretical values will be used to explain price behavior prior to expiration. Some forecasts will be tested using the Greeks, delta, gamma, vega, and theta. Finally, straddles and strangles will be compared.

The examples in this chapter do not include commissions, other transaction costs, or margin requirements. Since straddles and strangles involve two option positions, transaction costs and margin requirements can be higher than for single-option positions. Consequently, these factors can significantly impact the desirability of the strategies discussed in this chapter, and they must be included in the analysis of any real strategy involving real options.

LONG STRADDLES

A *long straddle* involves the simultaneous purchase of one call and one put with the same strike, same expiration, and same underlying. Figure 11–1 illustrates a long XCI 430 straddle. XCI is the Computer Technology Index on which European-style options are traded at the American Stock Exchange.

195

This long straddle is established by purchasing one 430 Call for 13½, or $1,350, and simultaneously purchasing one 430 Put for 11½, or $1,150, for a total cost of 25, or $2,500. It is common practice to describe a straddle using the strike price, because the strike price is the same for both the call and put. Hence the name for the position in Figure 11–1. "Long" indicates that both options are purchased.

"Straddle" is an appropriate name, because it means taking both sides at the same time, a strategy that has the potential of profiting from either an up or down movement.

Profit or Loss at Expiration

At expiration, there are three possible outcomes. The index can be above the strike, below the strike, or at the strike. The straight lines in Figure 11–1 illustrate these possibilities. If the index level is above the strike at expiration, then the call is exercised and the put expires worthless. If the index is 470 at expiration, for example, then exercising the 430 Call results in a cash receipt of 40, or $4,000, and the 430 Put expires worthless. The cost of the position, $2,500 in this example, is subtracted from the $4,000, and the result is a net profit of 15, or $1,500. If the index level is above the strike but below the upper break-even point at expiration, then the result is a loss. In Figure 11–1, the upper break-even index level at expiration is 455. This is calculated by adding the total price paid of 25 to the strike of 430.

Figure 11–1 Long 430 Straddle

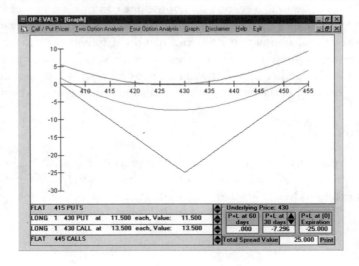

If the index level is below the strike at expiration, then the put is exercised, and the call expires worthless. If the index is 380 at expiration, for example, then exercising the 430 Put results in a cash receipt of 50, or $5,000, and the 430 Call expires worthless. The cost of the position, $2,500 in this example, is subtracted from the $5,000 received, and the result is a profit of 25, or $2,500. If the index level is below the strike but above the lower break-even point at expiration, then the result is a loss. In Figure 11–1, the lower break-even index level at expiration is 405: the strike of 430 minus the total cost of 25.

If the index is exactly at the strike at expiration, then both the call and put expire worthless, and the full amount paid, $2,500 in this example, is lost.

Expiration profit and loss analysis is beneficial because it reveals the index levels where the best possible and worst possible outcomes occur at expiration. Such analysis, however, does not help short-term traders understand how the strategy behaves prior to expiration. The following discussion addresses pricing issues that short-term traders should consider.

Buying Straddles

Alex is confident and unsure at the same time!

He is confidently predicting that the XCI Index will move sharply in response to the earnings reports of several high-tech companies this week, but he is unsure about the direction. He is thinking, "News good, XCI up; news bad, XCI down; but which will it be?" Consequently, he is considering the purchase of a 60-day XCI 430 straddle. "As long as the market moves," Alex says, "I'll make a profit."

Table 11–1 tends to confirm Alex's logic, but a loss can still result if the market does not move sufficiently in either direction. Table 11–1 was created using the Two Option Analysis page in OP-EVAL3™. The value in each box is the sum of a 430 Call value and a 430 Put value assuming the indicated inputs. Alex's starting position is column 1, row 5: a 430 straddle value of 25.

Table 11–1 estimates how the 430 straddle value changes over a range of index levels at different days prior to expiration, assuming dividends, volatility, and interest rates remain constant. If, for example, the index rises 15 points in 10 days to a level of 445 at 50 days prior to expiration (column 2, row 4), then the straddle is estimated to be 26⅞ for a profit of 1⅞, not including commissions. If, however, it takes 30 days for the index to rise 15 points, then the straddle is estimated to be 22⅜ (column 4, row 4), for a loss of 2⅜ before commissions.

Table 11–1 makes an important point about straddles. Assuming the index is at the strike when a straddle is purchased, down moves generally

Table 11–1 Theoretical Values of 430 Straddle (1 430 Call and 1 430 Put)

Row	Index Level	Col. 1: 60 Days	Col. 2: 50 Days	Col. 3: 40 Days	Col. 4: 30 Days	Col. 5: 20 Days	Col. 6: 10 Days	Col. 7: Exp.
1	490	62¾	62⅛	61½	61	60⅝	60⅜	60
2	475	49¼	48⅛	47¼	46⅜	45¾	45⅜	45
3	460	37½	35⅞	34⅜	32⅞	31½	30⅜	30
4	445	28⅞	26⅞	24¾	22⅜	19¾	16⅞	15
5	430	25	22¾	20⅜	17⅝	14½	10¼	0
6	415	26½	24¾	22⅞	20¾	18½	16⅛	15
7	400	33⅝	32½	31½	30⅝	29⅞	29⅝	30
8	385	44⅝	44⅜	44⅛	44⅛	44¼	44⅝	45
9	370	58¼	58⅜	58⅝	58⅞	59¼	59⅝	60

Dividend yield, 2%; volatility 18%; interest rates, 5%.

have to be larger than up moves in order for the same profit to be realized. In the example above, a 15-point rise in the index in 10 days resulted in a profit of 1⅞. However, Table 11–1 indicates that with a 15-point fall in the index in 10 days, a small loss results. Column 2, row 6, is 50 days to expiration with the index at 415, and the estimated 430 straddle value is 24¾, down ¼ from the initial value of 25 in this example. The reasons for this asymmetrical price action will be discussed later when the Greeks are reviewed.

How much of a change in the index and what period of time justify the purchase of a straddle? Unfortunately, there is no objective answer to this question. Alex must consider his forecast and make a personal assessment of the potential profits and risks. Value estimates as shown in Table 11–1 are helpful in making this decision, but an analysis of the Greeks also provides valuable information.

THE GREEKS

Table 11–2 summarizes the delta, gamma, theta, and vega of a long 430 Call, a long 430 Put, and a long 430 straddle. This information was taken from the Call/Put Pricer page in OP-EVAL3™. The numbers for the long 430 straddle are the sums of the numbers for the long 430 Call and long 430 Put. The Greeks of a multiple-part option position are equal to the sum of the Greeks of the individual options in the position. The straddle delta of

Table 11–2 Position Greeks

	Long 430 Call	Long 430 Put	Long 430 Straddle
Price	13½	11½	25
Delta	+0.541	−0.451	+0.090
Gamma	+0.031	+0.023	+0.054
Vega	+0.203	+0.148	+0.351
Theta	−0.707	−0.459	−1.166

+0.090, for example, is the sum of the 430 Call delta of +0.541 and the 430 Put delta of −0.451.

What does Table 11–2 reveal about the straddle? First, notice the relatively large vega, the position's sensitivity to changes in volatility. Second, notice the relatively low theta (high absolute value), the position's sensitivity to the passage of time. And, third, notice the delta, which is slightly positive.

The vega of +0.351 indicates that the straddle value will increase or decrease by this amount if volatility rises or falls by 1 percent, respectively, and other factors remain constant. A large vega should be expected, because the straddle position consists of two long options.

The theta of −1.166 estimates that the straddle value will decrease by this amount if 7 days pass and other factors remain constant. A low theta (high absolute value) should also be expected because of the two long options.

The near-zero delta is the sum of the positive call delta and the negative put delta. It means that for "small" changes in the index, there will be little or no change in the straddle value. Only after a sufficient move will the gamma effect, the change in delta, come into play, and only then will the straddle value change.

The delta of the straddle does not equal zero exactly when the index is at the strike, as many newcomers to options expect, because of technical factors in the Black-Scholes option pricing formula. An explanation of these factors is beyond the scope of the book, but it is correct to expect that a straddle's delta will be slightly positive when an underlying index is exactly at the strike price. This positive delta explains why a straddle has an upward bias and why equal up and down movements in the underlying index do not change the straddle value equally.

What are the implications for risk of the large vega, the low theta, and the near-zero delta? Simply stated, for straddle buyers, these factors mean that a "big move" must occur in a "short" time with "little or no decline in implied volatility." Otherwise a loss will be incurred.

TESTING SCENARIOS

OP-EVAL3™ can be used to test various scenarios. Suppose, for example, that in scenario one Alex forecasts that the XCI Index will be 15 points higher or lower in 7 days and volatility will decline 4 percent. As mentioned above, Alex's forecast for the change in the index is based on his belief that the earnings reports will be good or bad and that the market will react strongly. His forecast for a decrease in implied volatility could be based on his knowledge that implied volatility has risen in recent days, perhaps in anticipation of the reports, and on his belief that implied volatility will "return to normal" after the reports.

Table11–3 shows how OP-EVAL3™ might be used to test this forecast. Column 1 contains the initial inputs and outputs. Columns 2 and 3 contain new inputs and outputs reflecting a 15-point increase and decrease in the index level. What is the conclusion? If Alex believes this is likely to happen, Table 11–3 indicates that he should not buy the 60-day 430 straddle! Both the up market scenario and the down market scenario result in a loss.

But if Alex believes that there will be a 30-point rise or fall in the index in 10 days, with a 4 percent decrease in implied volatility, he may draw a different conclusion. Table 11–4 estimates that if the index rises 30 points in 10 days, then the 430 straddle rises to 33⅜ for a profit of 8⅜, or $837.50 before commissions. If the index declines 30 points in 10 days, the straddle rises to 29⅞ for a profit of 4⅞, or $487.50 before commissions.

Which scenario should Alex believe? That is a subjective decision that only he can make based on his conviction in his forecast and his tolerance

Table 11–3 Scenario 1: 15-Point Change in the XCI in 7 Days, Implied Volatility Down 4%

	Col. 1: Initial Status		Col. 2: Market Up		Col. 3: Market Down
Inputs					
Index level	430	→	445	→	415
Strike price	430				
Dividend yield	2%				
Volatility	18%	→	14%	→	14%
Interest rates	5%				
Days to expiration	60	→	53	→	53
Outputs					
430 Call price	13½	→	20	→	3⅞
430 Call price	11½	→	3¼	→	17
430 straddle	25	→	23¼	→	20⅞

Table 11–4 Scenario 2: 30-Point Change in the XCI in 10 days, Implied Volatility Down 4%

	Col. 1: Initial Status		Col. 2: Market Up		Col. 3: Market Down
Inputs					
Index level	430	→	460	→	400
Strike price	180				
Dividend yield	2%				
Volatility	18%	→	14%	→	14%
Interest rates	5%				
Days to expiration	60	→	50	→	50
Outputs:					
430 Call price	13½	→	32½	→	⅞
430 Put price	11½	→	⅞	→	29
430 straddle	25	→	33⅜	→	29⅞

for risk. The important lesson for all traders is that the analysis involved a three-part forecast, for the change in the index, for the timing of the expected change, and for the implied volatility. When trading straddles, parts two and three of this analysis are especially important, because straddles involve two options.

SHORT STRADDLES

A *short straddle* involves the simultaneous sale of one call and one put with the same strike, same expiration, and same underlying. Since a short index straddle contains short, uncovered index options, this strategy involves unlimited risk and is only suitable for traders who can meet specific requirements such as a minimum net worth and a substantial minimum account equity and who receive the appropriate approval of their brokerage firm. Figure 11–2 illustrates a short 430 straddle, which is established by selling one 430 Call for 13½ and one 430 Put for 11½ for a total amount received of 25.

Profit or Loss at Expiration

At expiration, there are three possible outcomes. The index can be above the strike, below the strike, or at the strike. The straight lines in Figure 11–2 illustrate these possibilities. If the index level is above the strike at expiration, then the call is assigned and the put expires worthless. If the index is 435 at expiration, for example, then assignment of the 430 Call results in a cash payment of 5, or $500, and the 430 Put expires worthless. This payment is

Figure 11–2 Short 430 Straddle

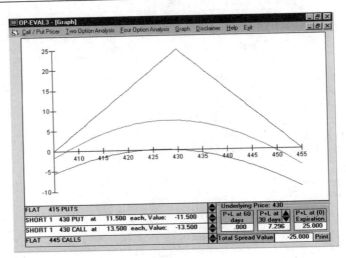

subtracted from the amount received initially, $2,500 in this example, and the result is a net profit of 20, or $2,000. If the index level is above the upper break-even point at expiration, then the result is a loss. In Figure 11–2, the upper break-even index level at expiration is 455. This is calculated by adding the total amount received of 25 to the strike of 430.

If the index level is below the strike at expiration, then the put is assigned, and the call expires worthless. If the index is 422 at expiration, for example, then assignment of the 430 Put results in a cash payment of 8, or $800, and the 430 Call expires worthless. This payment is subtracted from the $2,500 received initially, and the result is a profit of 17, or $1,700. If the index level is below the lower break-even point at expiration, then the result is a loss. In Figure 11–2, the lower break-even index level at expiration is 405, the strike of 430 minus the initial amount received of 25.

If the index is exactly at the strike at expiration, then the maximum profit potential is realized: both the call and put expire worthless, and the full amount received initially, $2,500 in this example, is kept as income.

Selling Straddles

Selling straddles is, essentially, the opposite of buying straddles. Whereas the straddle buyer hopes for a big move in either direction and an increase in implied volatility, the straddle seller hopes for no movement at all and a decrease in implied volatility.

Table 11–1 offers some clues as to the type of forecast that leads to the sale of a straddle. Assuming the 430 straddle is sold for 25 at 60 days prior to expiration when the index is 430 (column 1, row 5), then Table 11–1 indicates that the index must stay within a 30-point range between 415 and 445 (between rows 4 and 6) for 20 to 30 days before the straddle value declines noticeably.

The delta, gamma, vega, and theta of a short straddle are the opposite of those of a long straddle. Using the figures in Table 11–2, the delta of a short 430 straddle is −0.090; the gamma is −0.054; the vega is −0.351; and the theta is +1.166. While the high theta may be enticing to some traders ("Look how much I can make from time decay!"), this potential benefit is balanced by the risk of an increase in volatility and of a large move in either direction.

Traders who sell options in general and straddles in particular are well advised to have as much information as possible about implied volatility levels. They should be confident that they are selling options when implied volatility is "high" in their opinion. There are no guarantes that this knowledge will avoid a loss, but the purpose of studying implied volatility levels is to reduce this risk factor as much as possible.

LONG STRANGLES

A *long strangle* involves the simultaneous purchase of one call of a given strike and one put with the same expiration and same underlying but with a lower strike. Figure 11–3 illustrates a long 415–445 strangle, which is established by purchasing one 415 Put for 5⅝ and one 445 Call for 7¼ for a total cost 12⅞. It is common practice to describe a strangle using the lower strike price first. Hence the name for the position in Figure 11–3 is a long 415–445 strangle. "Long" indicates that both options are purchased. The origin of the term "strangle" is unknown, but it starts with the same letters as straddle and may have been coined for convenience.

At expiration, there are three possible outcomes. The index can be above the higher strike, below the lower strike, or at or between the strikes. The straight lines in Figure 11–3 illustrate these possibilities. If the index level is above the higher strike at expiration, then the call is exercised and the put expires worthless. If the index is 475 at expiration, then exercising the 445 Call results in a cash receipt of 30, or $3,000, and the 415 Put expires worthless. The cost of the position, 12⅞, or $1,287.50, is subtracted from the $3,000, and the result is a net profit of 17⅛, or $1,712.50. If the index level is above the higher strike but below the upper break-even point at expiration, then the result is a loss. In Figure 11–3, the upper break-even index level at

Figure 11–3 Long 415–445 Straddle

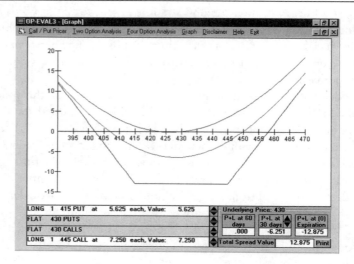

expiration is 457⅞. This is calculated by adding the total price paid of 12⅞ to the higher strike of 445.

If the index level is below the lower strike at expiration, then the put is exercised and the call expires worthless. If the index is 400 at expiration, then exercising the 415 Put results in a cash receipt of 15, or $1,500, and the 445 Call expires worthless. The cost of the position, $1,287.50 in this example, is subtracted from the $1,500 received, and the result is a profit of 2⅛, or $212.50. If the index level is below the strike but above the lower break-even point at expiration, then the result is a loss. In Figure 11–3, the lower break-even index level at expiration is 402⅛, the strike of 415 minus the total cost of 12⅞.

If the index is exactly at either strike or between the strikes at expiration, then the maximum loss is realized: both the call and put expire worthless, and the full amount paid, $1,287.50 in this example, is lost.

SHORT STRANGLES

A *short strangle* involves the simultaneous sale of one call of a given strike and one put with the same expiration and same underlying but with a lower strike. Figure 11–4 illustrates a short 415–445 strangle, which is established by selling one 415 Put for 5⅝ and one 445 Call for 7¼ for a total amount received of 12⅞.

Since a short index strangle contains short, uncovered index options, this strategy involves unlimited risk and is only suited for traders who can meet the requirements for short straddles described above.

At expiration, there are three possible outcomes. The index can be above the higher strike, below the lower strike, or at or between the strikes. The straight lines in Figure 11–4 illustrate these possibilities. If the index level is above the higher strike at expiration, then the call is assigned and the put expires worthless. If the index is 452 at expiration, then assignment of the 445 Call results in a cash payment of 7, or $700, and the 415 Put expires worthless. This payment is subtracted from the amount received initially, $1,287.50 in this example, and the result is a net profit of 5⅞, or $587.50. If the index level is above the upper break-even point at expiration, then the result is a loss. In Figure 11–4, the upper break-even index level at expiration is 457⅞. This is calculated by adding the total amount received of 12⅞ to the strike of 445.

If the index level is below the lower strike at expiration, then the put is assigned and the call expires worthless. If the index is 411 at expiration, for example, then assignment of the 415 Put results in a cash payment of 4, or $400, and the 445 Call expires worthless. This payment is subtracted from the $1,287.50 received initially, and the result is a profit of 8⅞, or $887.50. If the index level is below the lower break-even point at expiration, then the result is a loss. In Figure 11–4, the lower break-even index level at expiration is 402⅛, the lower strike of 415 minus the initial amount received of 12⅞.

Figure 11–4 Short 415–445 Straddle

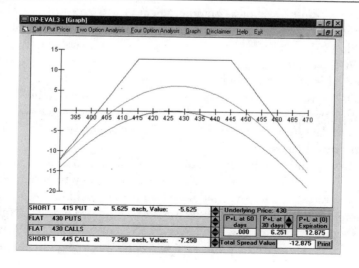

If the index is exactly at either strike or between the strikes at expiration, then both the call and put expire worthless and the full amount received initially, $1,287.50 in this example, is kept as income.

STRADDLES VERSUS STRANGLES

A comparison of the expiration profit and loss diagrams reveals that straddles and strangles offer different sets of trade-offs. This discussion will focus on long, or purchased, straddles and strangles, but similar reasoning applies to short straddles and strangles.

First, compare the expiration profit and loss diagrams in Figures 11–1 and 11–3. The straddle is purchased for 25 and the strangle is purchased for 12⅞. The straddle is more expensive, a disadvantage, but its break-even points are 455 and 405, closer together than the strangle's break-even points of 457⅞ and 402⅛. The relative closeness of the straddle's break-even points is an advantage.

Also, what are the chances that the outcome for the straddle will be a total loss of the premium paid? In order for this to occur, the index level must be 430 exactly at expiration. For the strangle to incur its maximum loss, however, the index can be at or between the two strikes. Whatever the chances are that the long straddle will incur its maximum loss, the chances that the long strangle will do so are greater.

The conclusion is that neither strategy is "better" in an absolute sense. A long straddle costs more than a comparable long strangle, but its break-even points at expiration are closer together. Also, there is less of a chance that the maximum loss of a straddle will be incurred. Now consider the profit and risk potential of the two strategies for short-term traders.

Table 11–5 contains 415–445 strangle values comparable to the straddle values in Table 11–1. The value in each box in Table 11–5 is the sum of a 415 Put value and a 445 Call value assuming the indicated inputs. Just as Table 11–1 estimates how the 430 straddle value changes, Table 11–5 estimates how the 415–445 strangle value changes over a range of index levels at different days prior to expiration, assuming dividends, volatility, and interest rates remain constant.

Assuming an initial index level of 430 and 60 days to expiration (column 1, row 5), then a 45-point rise or fall in the index in any time frame yields a higher absolute profit for the straddle. At 50 days with an index level of 475, for example, the straddle value is 48⅛, up 23⅛, compared to the strangle value of 34¼, up 21⅜. In this case the larger investment in the straddle earned a higher profit. However, the profit as a *percentage* was higher for the strangle.

Table 11–5 Theoretical Values of 415–445 Strangle (1 415 Put and 1 445 Call)

Row	Index Level	Col. 1: 60 Days	Col. 2: 50 Days	Col. 3: 40 Days	Col. 4: 30 Days	Col. 5: 20 Days	Col. 6: 10 Days	Col. 7: Exp.
1	490	48⅜	47⅝	46⅞	46¼	45¾	45⅜	45
2	475	35⅜	34¼	33⅛	32	31⅛	30⅜	30
3	460	24⅜	22⅞	21¼	19⅝	17⅞	16¼	15
4	445	16½	14⅝	12⅝	10½	8⅛	5½	0
5	430	12⅞	10⅞	8⅞	6⅝	4⅛	1½	0
6	415	14¼	12⅝	10⅞	9	7	4¾	0
7	400	20½	19⅜	18⅜	17¼	16¼	15⅜	15
8	385	30¾	30⅜	30	29⅝	29½	29⅝	30
9	370	43¾	43¾	43⅞	44	44¼	44⅝	45

Dividend yield, 2%; volatility, 18%; interest rates, 5%.

Over a longer time period, the same holds true. At 20 days with an index level of 475, for example, the straddle value is 45¾, up 20¾, compared to the strangle value of 30⅜, up 19½. As before, the straddle value increased more in absolute terms, but the strangle value increased more in percentage terms.

But the situation is different in unprofitable outcomes. If the index is at 445 at 10 days to expiration, then both strategies incur a loss. The straddle value has declined to 16⅞, an absolute loss of 8⅛ and a 33 percent loss of the initial investment. In comparison, the strangle value declined to 5½, a lower absolute loss of 7⅜, but a higher percentage loss of 57 percent.

This difference in profit measurement when absolute results are compared to percentage results is significant, because it emphasizes the need for traders to define their profit goals in advance of a trade. Any forecast will tend to favor one strategy over another depending on how the profit target is stated.

STRADDLES VERSUS STRANGLES: THE GREEKS

What do the Greeks reveal? Table 11–6 compares the delta, gamma, vega, and theta of the two strategies. The numbers for the long 430 straddle are taken from Table 11–2, and those for the long 415–445 strangle were calculated in a similar fashion.

What is so striking about the information in Table 11–6 is how close together the numbers are. The vega of the long 430 straddle, for example, is +0.351, not much greater than the vega of the long 415–445 strangle of

Table 11–6 Position Greeks: Straddle versus Strangle

	Long 430 Straddle	Long 415–445 Strangle
Price	25	12⅞
Delta	+0.090	+0.080
Gamma	+0.054	+0.038
Vega	+1.351	+0.238
Theta	−1.166	−1.133

Index, 430; dividend yield, 2%; volatility, 18%; interest rate, 5%; days to expiration, 60.

+0.238. Consequently, a rise or fall in volatility will have a similar absolute effect on both strategies. The percentage effect, however, will be greater on the strangle.

Space restrictions prohibit an examination of changes in all inputs on all strategies, so readers are encouraged to work through a variety of scenarios on their own. Comparing the behavior of straddles and strangles over a range of index prices, time periods, and volatility levels is a valuable experience.

SUMMARY

Long straddles involve the purchase of a call and put with the same underlying, expiration, and strike price. Short straddles involve the sale of both. Strangles are different from straddles in that they involve calls and puts with different strike prices. When considering these strategies, it is important to draw an expiration profit and loss diagram first so that the best and worst possible outcomes are fully understood. Short straddles and strangles involve unlimited risk and are suitable only for experienced traders who are financially and psychologically capable of assuming this level of risk and who receive approval from their brokerage firm to use these strategies.

To study straddles, this chapter used the same method of analysis that readers were taught in previous chapters. First, have a three-part forecast: a target for the underlying index, a prediction for the time period, and an outlook for implied volatility. Second, estimate the price of each option in a position and then calculate the estimated profit or loss. Third, evaluate a number of alternative strategies and select the one which best fits your personal risk-reward parameters.

Straddles and strangles involve different trade-offs. Long straddles are more expensive than comparable long strangles, but the break-even points of straddles are closer together and the risk of total loss of investment for a straddle is lower. Short-term traders should also be aware that absolute results and percentage results differ between the two strategies. Consequently, it is important to state a profit target in advance. A comparison of the delta, gamma, vega, and theta of straddles and strangles indicates that changes in individual factors tend to have a greater percentage impact on strangle values.

Twelve

Ratio Spreads

INTRODUCTION

Ratio spreads involve the purchase of one quantity of an option with a given strike and the sale of a different quantity of a second option of the same type, with the same underlying and expiration but a different strike. As the name implies, the difference in quantity is expressed as a ratio, such as 1 × 2 or 2 × 3. Although there are numerous ratio possibilities, this chapter will focus on 1 × 2 ratio spreads. The method of analysis and strategy selection for these ratio spreads can be applied to other ratio spreads as well.

Some of the strategies discussed in this chapter involve the sale of uncovered index options, the risk of which is unlimited, and these are suitable only for those traders who are psychologically and financially capable of assuming the risks of these strategies and who meet the requirements of their brokerage firm.

The examples in this chapter do not include commissions, other transaction costs, or margin requirements. Since ratio spreads involve two or more option positions, transaction costs and margin requirements can be higher than for single-option positions. These factors can significantly impact the desirability of any investment or trading strategy, and they must be included in the analysis of any real strategy involving options.

RATIO VERTICAL SPREADS

A 1 × 2 *ratio vertical spread with calls* involves the purchase of one call with a given strike and the sale of two calls with the same underlying and expiration but with a higher strike. A 1 × 2 *ratio vertical spread with puts* involves the purchase of one put with a given strike and the sale of two puts with the same underlying and expiration but with a lower strike. Ratio vertical spreads involve unlimited risk in the case of calls and substantial risk in the case of puts. Traders who use these strategies must be approved by their brokerage firms for the risk of uncovered index options prior to initiating these positions.

Note that the term "vertical" means more than a description of the relationship of the strike prices. When applied to ratio spreads, *vertical* means that the greater quantity of options is sold. Although there is nothing in the strict definition of the word "vertical" to connote this meaning, this is common terminology in the options business.

Figure 12–1 illustrates an XAU 95–100 1 × 2 ratio vertical spread with calls. XAU is the Gold and Silver Stock Index on which American-style options are traded at the American Stock Exchange. In this strategy, one XAU 95 Call is purchased for 3⅜ and two XAU 100 Calls are sold for 1½ each. This means that the spread is established for a ⅜ net debit, not including commissions. The term "net debit" means that the difference between the amount paid for options and the amount received from the sale of options is an amount *paid*. A "net credit" means that the difference between the amount paid and the amount received is an amount *received*.

Remember, the amount paid or received when a position is established is not necessarily equal to the risk or profit potential of a strategy. Net profit or net loss is the difference between the net revenue from a strategy and the net cost of that strategy. People too often think "buy first at a cost and sell later for a revenue," but this thinking does not always apply to ratio spreads,

**Figure 12–1 95–100 1 × 2 Ratio Vertical Spread with Calls
(Long 1 95 Call and Short 2 100 Calls)**

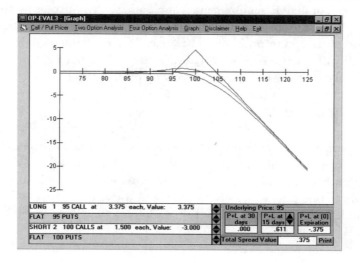

which can be established for a debit or credit and subsequently closed for either a debit or credit. It can get confusing if you do not take the time to understand each step along the way.

The following explanation of strategy mechanics focuses on ratio vertical spreads with calls, but the explanation is similar when puts are involved.

Profit or Loss at Expiration

At expiration, there are three possible outcomes for ratio vertical spreads with calls. The index can be at or below the lower strike, above the lower strike but not above the upper strike, or above the upper strike. The straight lines in Figure 12–1 illustrate these possibilities. If the index level is at or below the lower strike at expiration, then all calls expire worthless and the full amount paid for the position, ⅜ in this example, is lost. However, this is not the maximum potential risk of this strategy! The maximum risk of a ratio spread with calls is unlimited. As illustrated in Figure 12–1, losses increase as the underlying index rises above the upper break-even point.

If the index is above the lower strike but not above the upper strike, then the long call (lower strike) is exercised and the two short calls (higher strike) expire worthless. In Figure 12–1, if the XAU Index is at 97 at expiration, then exercising the 95 Call results in a cash receipt, or credit, of 2, or $200. The 100 Calls expire worthless, so the net result of the strategy is calculated by subtracting the cost of the position, ⅜, from the credit, 2, which is received from exercising the 95 Call. The result is a net profit of 1⅝, or $162.50, before commissions.

If the index is above the higher strike at expiration, then the long call (lower strike) is exercised and the two short calls (higher strike) are assigned. As Figure 12–1 illustrates, either a net profit or net loss can result if the index is above the higher strike. If the index is at 102 at expiration, for example, then exercising the 95 Call results in a credit of 7, and assignment on the two 100 Calls results in a debit of 2 each, or 4 total. These two events close the position and result in a net credit of 3, or $300. The net profit or loss is then calculated by subtracting the initial net debit of ⅜ from the ending net credit of 3. The net result, therefore, is a net profit of 2⅝, or $262.50, not including commissions.

A net loss is the result, however, if the index is at 107 at expiration. In this case, the 95 Call is exercised for a net credit of 12 and the two short 100 Calls are assigned for a debit of 7 each, or 14 total. These two events close the position and result in a net debit of 2, or $200. The net loss is calculated by adding the initial net debit of ⅜ to the ending net debit of 2. The result, a total debit of 2⅜, or $237.50 before commissions, is the loss in this example.

Break-Even Points and Maximum Profit Potential

In Figure 12–1 there are two index levels at which the strategy breaks even at expiration. The lower break-even point, 95⅜ in this example, is calculated by adding the net debit paid for the strategy, ⅜, to the lower strike, 95.

In order to calculate the upper break-even index level at expiration, it is necessary to know the maximum profit potential of the strategy. The maximum profit of a 1 × 2 ratio spread with calls is realized at expiration if the index is exactly at the higher strike, because, as the index rises above the higher strike, the increase in value of the two short calls more than offsets the increase in value of the one long call. Consequently, the maximum profit potential in index points is calculated by subtracting the lower break-even point from the higher strike. In this example, the lower break-even index level of 95⅜ is subtracted from the upper strike of 100, and the maximum potential profit, therefore, is 4⅝ index points, or $462.50, not including commissions.

Now that the maximum potential profit in index points has been determined, the upper break-even point is calculated by adding the maximum profit in index points to the upper strike. In this example, the upper break-even point is 100 plus 4⅝, or 104⅝. If the index is above this level at expiration, then a loss results.

Price Behavior

Table 12–1 contains theoretical values of a 95–100 1 × 2 ratio vertical spread with calls at various index levels and days to expiration. This table was created using the Two Option Analysis page in OP-EVAL3™. The value in each box assumes that one 95 Call is purchased and two 100 Calls are sold. Column 1, row 8, for example, assumes an index level of 95.00 and 30 days to expiration. Although the individual call values are not shown, purchasing one 95 Call at 3⅜ and selling two 100 Calls at 1½ each results in a net debit of ⅜, not including commissions, and ⅜ is the number that appears in this box. Consequently, under the assumptions stated above, the strategy could be established for a net debit of ⅜ not including commissions.

Parentheses in Table 12–1 indicate that the strategy could be established for a net credit. The number in parentheses appearing in column 1, row 5, for example, indicates that purchasing one 95 Call and selling two 100 Calls results in a net credit of 1½ before commissions.

Table 12–1 can be difficult to interpret. One way of avoiding confusion is to use the terms "open" and "close" rather than "buy" and "sell." Calculation of profit or loss for a 1 × 2 ratio vertical spread involves properly adding or subtracting the opening debit or credit to or from the closing debit or

Table 12–1 Theoretical Values of 95–100 Ratio Vertical Spread with Calls (Long 1 95 Call and Short 2 100 Calls)

Row	Index Level	Col. 1: 30 Days	Col. 2: 25 Days	Col. 3: 20 Days	Col. 4: 15 Days	Col. 5: 10 Days	Col. 6: 5 Days	Col. 7: Exp.
1	112.50	(8½)	(8¼)	(8)	(7⅞)	(7⅝)	(7½)	(7½)
2	110.00	(6⅜)	(6⅛)	(5¾)	(5½)	(5¼)	(5)	(5)
3	107.50	(4½)	(4⅛)	(3¾)	(3⅜)	(3)	(2⅝)	(2½)
4	105.00	(2⅞)	(2½)	(2)	(1½)	(⅞)	(⅜)	(0)
5	102.50	(1½)	(1⅛)	(⅝)	(⅛)	(⅝)	1½	2½
6	100.00	(⅝)	(⅛)	¼	¾	1⅜	2⅜	5
7	97.50	0	⅜	¾	⅞	1½	2	2½
8	95.00	⅜	⅝	¾	1	1⅛	1⅛	0
9	92.50	½	⅝	⅝	¾	⅝	⅜	0

Dividend yield, 1%; volatility, 30%; interest rates, 5%.

credit. Opening a position for a debit is a cash outflow, but opening a position for a credit is a cash inflow. Closing a position at a debit is a cash inflow, and closing a position for a credit is a cash outflow. Let's work through some examples.

First, assume the ratio vertical spread is opened in column 1, row 8 of Table 12–1 and closed in column 6, row 7. The position is opened for a debit of ⅜, which means that ⅜ is paid. The position is then closed at a debit of 2, which means that 2 is received. The result is ⅜ paid and 2 received for a net received, or net profit, of 1⅝. Alternatively, 2 received when closing minus ⅜ paid when opening equals a net credit of 1⅝, which is a net profit.

Second, assume the ratio vertical spread is opened in column 1, row 5 and closed in column 6, row 7. The position is opened for a credit of 1½, which means that 1½ is received. The position is then closed at a debit of 2 which means that 2 is received. The result is 1½ received and 2 received for a total received, or profit, of 3½. Alternatively, the 2 received when closing plus the 1½ received when opening equals a total credit of 3½, which is a profit.

Third, assume the ratio vertical spread is opened in column 1, row 9 and closed in column 3, row 1. The position is opened for a debit of ½, which means that ½ is paid. The position is then closed at a credit of 8, which means that 8 is paid. The result is ½ paid and 8 paid for a total paid, or loss, of 8½. Alternatively, the 8 paid when closing plus the ½ paid when opening equals a total debit of 8½, which is a loss.

Finally, assume the ratio vertical spread is opened in column 2, row 4 and closed in column 5, row 5. The position is opened for a credit of 2½, which means that 2½ is received. The position is then closed at a credit of ⅝, which means that ⅝ is paid. The result is 2½ received and ⅝ paid for a net received, or net profit, of 1⅞. Alternatively, the ⅝ paid when closing subtracted from the 2½ received when opening equals a net credit of 1⅞, which is a profit.

The conclusion from Table 12–1, which is supported by Figure 12–1, is that ratio vertical spreads with calls perform best when the underlying trades in a narrow range around the strike of the short calls. Traders must, therefore, forecast this kind of market action in order to choose this strategy.

The Greeks

Table 12–2 summarizes the delta, gamma, theta, and vega of the long 95 Call, the short 100 Calls, and the ratio vertical spread. The information in columns 1 and 2 was taken from the Call/Put Pricer page in OP-EVAL3™, and the numbers in column 3 are the sum of the numbers in column 1 plus two times the numbers in column 2. The Greeks of a multiple-part option position are equal to the sum of the Greeks of the individual options that make up the position. The vega, for example, is calculated by adding +0.108 and –0.192 (2 × –0.096), which equals –0.084.

What does Table 12–2 reveal about the ratio vertical spread? First, the negative vega indicates that the position will benefit from a decrease in implied volatility and be hurt by an increase if other factors remain constant. Second, the positive theta means that the position will profit from time erosion if other factors remain constant. Third, the negative gamma means that the position will be hurt by a sharp move up or down. The conclusion is that the ideal scenario for a ratio vertical spread is for the underlying index to trade in a narrow range around the strike of the short options with declining volatility until expiration.

Table 12–2 Position Greeks

	Col. 1: Long 1 95 Call	Col. 2: Short 2 100 Calls	Col. 3: 95–100 1 × 2 Ratio Vertical Spread
Theoretical value	3⅜	1½ (each)	⅜
Delta	+0.532	–0.302 (each)	–0.072
Gamma	+0.048	–0.044 (each)	–0.040
Vega	+0.108	–0.096 (each)	–0.084
Theta	–0.440	+0.366 (each)	+0.292

Index, 95.00; dividend yield, 1%; volatility, 30%; interest rates, 5%; days to expiration, 30.

Testing Scenarios

Let us now test some forecasts to estimate how successful the use of a ratio vertical spread with calls might be. OP-EVAL3™ can be used to test various scenarios. Suppose, for example, that Pauline, an experienced trader who is suited to assume the risk of selling uncovered index options, is forecasting neutral to slightly bullish movement of the XAU Index. In this example, assume 20 days to expiration, an index level of 92.50, a 20-day 95 Call price of 1⅝, and a 20-day 100 Call price of ½. This means that Pauline can purchase one 95 Call and sell two 100 Calls for a net debit of ⅝, not including commissions. This situation is consistent with column 3, row 9, in Table 12–1.

Pauline forecasts that the XAU Index will rise gradually to 100 in the next 20 days, but because an inflation report is scheduled for release in 10 days, Pauline wants to test some negative scenarios to estimate her risk.

Table 12–1 estimates that if in 5 days the index rises 12.50 points to 105 at 15 days to expiration (column 4, row 4), then the spread value will drop to a credit of 1½ for a loss of 2⅛. This is a risk Pauline feels comfortable with, but the numbers in Table 12–1 assume implied volatility remains constant at 30 percent. Pauline wants to estimate the result if implied volatility increases to 38 percent.

Table 12–3 shows how OP-EVAL3™ might be used to test this scenario. Column 1 contains the initial inputs. Column 2 contains Pauline's forecast. With the new inputs, the 95 Call is estimated to be trading at 10½ and the 100 Call is estimated to be trading at 6⅜. The ratio vertical spread, therefore, is estimated to be trading for a credit of 2¼. This is calculated by assuming

Table 12–3 Forecast Based on an Increase in Implied Volatility

	Col. 1: Initial Situation		Col. 2: Pauline's Forecast
Inputs			
Index level	92.50	→	105.00
Strike price	95/100		
Dividend yield	1%		
Volatility	30%	→	38%
Interest rates	5%		
Days to expiration	20	→	15
Outputs			
95 Call price	1.625	→	10.500
100 Call price	0.500	→	6.375
1 × 2 ratio vertical spread	0.625	→	(2.250)

that one 95 Call is purchased for 10½ and two 100 Calls are sold at 6⅜ each, or 12¾ total, for a net spread credit of 2¼. Paying ⅝ to open the ratio vertical spread and paying 2¼ to close it means that a loss of 2⅞ is incurred. This loss is ¾ greater than the 2⅛ loss calculated above from Table 12–1.

Pauline can use this information as part of her subjective decision-making process. If she does not consider this additional risk too great, and if she has confidence in her forecast, then she may employ the ratio vertical spread strategy. If, however, this changes her attitude toward the risk-reward ratio, then she may look for another strategy or decide to sit this one out and do nothing for the time being.

We have seen that ratio vertical spreads are suited for neutral market forecasts. The ratio volatility spread, which is discussed next, is suited for a different market environment.

RATIO VOLATILITY SPREADS

A 1 × 2 *ratio volatility spread with calls* involves the sale of one call with a given strike and the purchase of two calls with the same underlying and expiration but with a higher strike. A 1 × 2 *ratio volatility spread with puts* involves the sale of one put with a given strike and the purchase of two puts with the same underlying and expiration but with a lower strike.

When applied to ratio spreads, *volatility* means that the greater quantity of options is purchased. This meaning has become common terminology, because this strategy profits from a "large move" in the underlying index, that is, high volatility.

Figure 12–2 illustrates a DTX 250–255 1 × 2 ratio volatility spread with calls. The DTX Index is based on the Dow Jones Transportation Average, and European-style options are traded at the CBOE. In this strategy, one DTX 250 Call is sold for 9 and two DTX 255 Calls are purchased for 6¾ each. This means that the spread is established for a "4½ net debit," or amount paid, not including commissions.

The following explanation of strategy mechanics focuses on ratio volatility spreads with calls, but the explanation is similar when puts are involved.

Profit or Loss at Expiration

At expiration, there are three possible outcomes for a ratio volatility spread with calls. The index can be at or below the lower strike, above the lower strike but not above the upper strike, or above the upper strike. The straight lines in Figure 12–2 illustrate these possibilities. If the index level is at or

Figure 12–2 250–255 1 x 2 Ratio Volatility Spread with Calls
(Short 1 250 Call and Long 2 255 Calls)

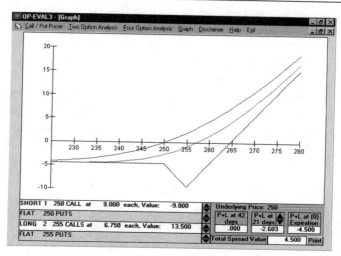

below the lower strike of a ratio volatility spread at expiration, then all calls expire worthless and the full amount paid for the position, 4½ in this example, is lost. However, this is not the maximum potential risk of this strategy! The maximum risk will be calculated shortly.

If the index is above the lower strike but not above the upper strike, then the short call (lower strike) is assigned and the two long calls (higher strike) expire worthless. In Figure 12–2, for example, if the DTX Index is at 253 at expiration, then assignment of the short 250 Call results in a cash payment, or debit, of 3, or $300. The 255 Calls expire worthless, so the profit or loss result is calculated by adding the cost of the position, 4½, to the debit of 3 for a total loss of 7½, or $750.00, not including commissions.

The maximum loss occurs if the index is exactly at the higher strike at expiration. With the index at 255 at expiration, assignment of the 250 call results in a debit of 5. Since the 255 Calls expire worthless with the index at 255 at expiration, the debit of 5 is added to the initial debit of 4½ for a total loss of 9½. Figure 12–2 confirms that 255 is the index level at expiration where the maximum loss occurs.

If the index is above the higher strike at expiration, then the short call (lower strike) is assigned and the two long calls (higher strike) are exercised. As Figure 12–2 illustrates, either a net profit or a net loss can result if the index is above the higher strike. If the index is at 256 at expiration, for example, then assignment of the 250 Call results in a debit of 6 and exercising the two 255

Calls results in a credit of 1 each, or 2 total. These two events close the position and result in a net debit of 4, or $400. The final result is calculated by properly combining credits (amounts received) and debits (amounts paid). In this case, with the index at 256, the initial net debit of 4½ is added to the closing net debit of 4 for a total loss of 8½, not including commissions.

A net profit is the result, however, if the index is at 268 at expiration. In this case, the 250 Call is assigned for a net debit of 18, and the two long 255 Calls are exercised for a credit of 13 each, or 26 total. These two events close the position and result in a net credit of 8, or $800. The net profit is then calculated by subtracting the initial net debit of 4½ from the ending net credit of 8. The result is a net profit of 3½, or $350, not including commissions.

Break-Even Points and Maximum Profit Potential

In Figure 12–2 the ratio volatility spread breaks even at 264½ at expiration. This is calculated by adding the maximum potential loss of 9½ to the higher strike of 255. Above an index level of 255 at expiration, the net position is long 1 255 Call, because the short 250 Call is offset by one of the two long 255 Calls. The value of the second long 255 Call equals the maximum potential loss of 9½ at the break-even index level of 264½ (255 + 9½). Above the break-even point, the profit potential is unlimited.

Price Behavior

Table 12–4 contains theoretical values of a 250–255 1 × 2 ratio volatility spread with calls at various index levels and days to expiration. This table was created using the Two Option Analysis page in OP-EVAL3™. The value in each box assumes that one 250 Call is sold and two 255 Calls are purchased. Column 1, row 7, for example, assumes an index level of 250 and 42 days to expiration. Although the individual call values are not shown, selling one 250 Call at 9 and purchasing two 255 Calls at 6¾ each results in a net debit of 4½, not including commissions, and 4½ is the number that appears in this box. Consequently, given the assumptions stated above, the strategy could be established for a net debit of 4½.

Parentheses in Table 12–4 indicate that the strategy could be established for a net credit. The number in parentheses appearing in column 6, row 7, for example, indicates that selling one 250 Call and purchasing two 255 Calls results in a credit of ⅜. Table 12–4 can be difficult to interpret. Calculating

Table 12–4 Theoretical Values of 250–255 Ratio Volatility Spread with Calls (Short 1 250 Call and Long 2 255 Calls)

Row	Index Level	Col. 1: 42 Days	Col. 2: 35 Days	Col. 3: 28 Days	Col. 4: 21 Days	Col. 5: 14 Days	Col. 6: 7 Days	Col. 7: Exp.
1	280	23⅜	22⅝	22	21⅜	20¾	20¼	20
2	275	19¼	18½	17⅝	16⅞	16	15⅜	15
3	270	15½	14⅝	13¾	12¾	11⅝	10½	10
4	265	12	11⅛	10⅛	9	7¾	6¼	5
5	260	9⅛	8⅛	7⅛	6	4⅝	2¾	0
6	255	6⅝	5⅝	4¾	3⅝	2¼	⅝	(5)
7	250	4½	3¾	2⅞	1⅞	⅞	(⅜)	0
8	245	3	2⅜	1⅝	⅞	⅛	(⅜)	0
9	240	1⅞	1⅜	¾	¼	(⅛)	(¼)	0

Dividend yield, 0%; volatility, 25%; interest rates, 5%.

profit or loss requires knowing the cash debit or credit when a position is opened and when it is closed and then combining them together correctly.

The conclusion from Table 12–4, which is supported by Figure 12–2, is that ratio volatility spreads with calls perform best when the underlying rises sharply beyond the break-even point. Consequently, traders must be forecasting this kind of market action in order to choose this strategy. If the market trades in a narrow range around the higher strike, then, as expiration approaches, ratio volatility spreads with calls will result in a loss.

The Greeks

Table 12–5 summarizes the delta, gamma, theta, and vega of the short 250 Call, the long 255 Call, and the ratio volatility spread. This information confirms the conclusions from Figure 12–2 and Table 12–4. First, the positive vega indicates that the position will profit from an increase in volatility. Second, the negative theta means that time erosion will cause a loss to result if factors other than time are unchanged. Third, the positive gamma means that the position will benefit from a sharp move in either direction in the index. The ideal scenario for a ratio volatility spread is for the underlying index to move sharply beyond the strike of the long options. In the case of ratio volatility spreads with calls, this is up. When puts are involved, the desired direction is down.

Table 12–5 Position Greeks

	Col. 1: Short 1 250 Call	Col. 2: Long 2 255 Calls	Col. 3:* 250–255 1 × 2 Ratio Volatility Spread
Theoretical value	9	6¾ (each)	4½
Delta	−0.544	+0.450 (each)	+0.356
Gamma	−0.019	+0.019 (each)	+0.019
Vega	−0.336	+0.336 (each)	+0.336
Theta	+0.840	−0.820 (each)	−0.800

Index level, 250; dividend yield, 0%; volatility, 25%; interest rates, 5%;
days to expiration, 42.
*The numbers in column 3 are calculated by adding the numbers in column 1 to two
times the numbers in column 2. The delta in column 1, for example, is calculated as
follows: (−0.544) + (2 × 0.450) = +0.356. Close attention should be paid to plus and
minus signs as they can be confusing.

SUMMARY

Ratio spreads involve the purchase of one quantity of an option with a given
strike and the sale of a different quantity of a second option of the same type,
with the same underlying and expiration but with a different strike. In ratio
vertical spreads, the larger number of options is sold. In ratio volatility
spreads, the larger number of options is purchased.

Ratio vertical spreads involve substantial or unlimited risk because they
involve an uncovered short option. The ideal scenario for a ratio vertical
spread is for the underlying index to trade in a narrow range around the
strike of the short options, with declining volatility until expiration.

The risk of ratio volatility spreads is limited, but it can be greater than
the debit amount paid to establish the position. The ideal scenario for a ratio
volatility spread is for the underlying index to move sharply beyond the
strike price of the long options.

The short-term price behavior of ratio spreads can be analyzed by creating theoretical value tables similar to those for single options. The numbers
in the tables are, however, sometimes difficult to interpret, because ratio
spreads can be established for either a debit or credit. Consequently, calculating profit and loss can be confusing when a position is opened for a debit
and closed at a credit or vice versa.

Various market scenarios should be tested and the information should be used as part of the subjective decision-making process. As with single-option positions, traders should use a three-part forecast when trading ratio spreads. They should have a forecast for the change in the index level, a forecast for the time it will take for the predicted move to occur, and a forecast for the implied volatility level after the move.

Thirteen

Time Spreads

INTRODUCTION

ime spreads are not well known other than to experienced traders, but they are appropriate, and indeed optimal, for a few market forecasts. This chapter will first show how a time spread position is established. Second, strategy mechanics and the special need for planning will be explained. Third, the price behavior of time spreads will be reviewed by using theoretical value tables similar to those used in previous chapters and by analyzing the sensitivities of time spreads (the Greeks). Finally, a trading example will be presented. The goal of this chapter is to help you develop realistic expectations for risk, profit potential, and timing when using time spreads. It is important to understand the price behavior of time spreads and the impact of changes in volatility on them before attempting to use them. This chapter will describe time spreads that involve only calls, but the concepts apply equally to time spreads involving puts.

As will be explained in this chapter, the maximum risk of a debit time spread is limited to the amount paid including commissions. The risk of credit time spreads, however, is unlimited if the short position is held after the long position expires or if American-exercise options are involved and the short option is assigned early. For this reason traders who use credit time spreads must receive approval from their brokerage firm to write uncovered index options.

Time spread positions must be established in a margin account, and because two options are involved, transaction costs may be higher than for single-option positions. The examples in this chapter do not include commissions, other transaction costs, or margin requirements, but these factors can significantly impact the desirability of the strategies discussed in this chapter and must be included in the analysis of any strategy involving real options.

225

TIME SPREADS DEFINED

Time spreads involve the purchase of one option and the sale of another option of the same type with the same underlying and strike price but with a different expiration. An example of a time spread is the sale of one SPX September 900 Call for 19¼ and the simultaneous purchase of one SPX October 900 Call for 29. SPX is the symbol for the Standard and Poor's 500 Index, on which European-style options are traded at the CBOE.

It is common practice to describe time spreads using the underlying symbol first, the shorter-term expiration second, the longer-term expiration third, the strike price fourth, and the option type fifth. The time spread presented above, for example, is described as the "SPX September-October 900 Call time spread."

The terms *long time spread, debit time spread* and *purchased time spread* refer to time spreads in which the option with the shorter-term expiration is sold and the option with the longer-term expiration is purchased. Since the longer-term option has a higher value, long time spread positions are established for a net cost, or net debit. The SPX September-October 900 Call time spread described above is an example of a long call time spread. This spread was "purchased for 9¾," the difference between the amount paid for October 900 Call—29—and the amount received for the September 900 Call—19¼.

Short time spread, credit time spreads and *sold time spread* describe time spreads in which the shorter-term option is purchased and the longer-term option is sold. An NDX June-July 990 Call time spread could be "sold for 7," for example, by purchasing one NDX June 990 Call for 9 and simultaneously selling one NDX July 990 Call at 16. For margin purposes, the short option in a short time spread is traded as being uncovered.

RISKS AT EXPIRATION

If European-style options are involved, a time spread ceases to exist on the expiration date of the shorter-term option. On that day, the shorter-term option is either exercised or assigned, if it is in-the-money, or expires worthless, if it is out-of-the-money. In either case, after the expiration of the shorter-term option, a time spread becomes a single-option position with all of the profit potential and risks of that position.

If a time spread consists of options subject to American-style exercise, then early exercise or assignment will cause the time spread position to be converted into a single-option position prior to expiration of the shorter-term option. Traders must plan for this possibility.

PROFIT OR LOSS AT EXPIRATION

Figure 13–1 is a diagram of the theoretical profit or loss of a long-call time spread at the expiration of the shorter-term option. The profit and loss line is not straight, because the delta of the unexpired call is between 0 and 1. In profit and loss diagrams in which options with the same expiration date are involved, horizontal straight lines indicate that an option has expired worthless, and has a zero delta. Diagonal straight lines indicate that an option is in-the-money at expiration and has been exercised or assigned and has become a position in the underlying with a delta of +1 or −1.

OP-EVAL3™ can be used to evaluate the price behavior of time spreads, but it cannot graph time spread positions, because the graphing feature of the program requires that options have the same number of days to expiration. To use the Two Option Analysis and Four Option Analysis pages to evaluate prices of time spreads, simply change the A to I in the Days row, and the number of days to expiration can be set independently for each option in a position.

Figure 13–1 Long Time Spread (with Calls)

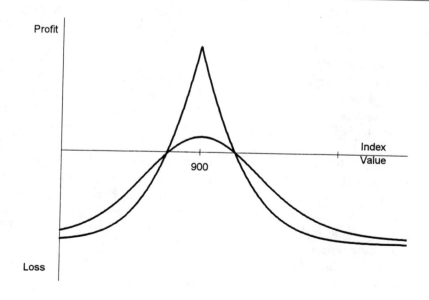

At expiration of the shorter-term option, there are two possible outcomes. The index can be at or below the strike or above the strike.

In the case of a long-call time spread, if the index level is at or below the strike, then the short shorter-term call expires worthless and the long longer-term call remains open. If the index is above the strike, then the short shorter-term call is assigned and the long longer-term long call remains open. In either case, the open long-call position is subject to the potential profits and risks of market movement without the countervailing impact of the short call that existed before that call expired or was assigned.

In the case of a short-call time spread, if the index level is at or below the strike, then the long shorter-term call expires worthless and the short longer-term call remains open. If the index is above the strike, then the long shorter-term call is exercised and the short longer-term call remains open. In either case, the short-call position remains open and is subject to the potential profits and risks of market movement without the countervailing impact of the long call.

Profit or loss cannot definitely be determined until both option positions are closed, but theoretical value tables similar to those presented in previous chapters can be used to illustrate how values of time spreads change prior to expiration.

PRICE BEHAVIOR OF LONG TIME SPREADS

Tables 13–1, 13–2, and 13–3 were created using the Two Option Analysis page in OP-EVAL3™. Table 13–1 contains values of a September 900 Call at various index levels and times to expiration. Table 13–2 contains values of an October 900 Call at the same index levels but at different times to expiration. In this example, October expiration is 28 days after September expiration; hence, every column in Table 13–2 is 28 days farther from expiration than the corresponding column in Table 13–1. For example, column 1 is 24 days prior to expiration in Table 13–1 and 52 days prior to expiration in Table 13–2.

The values in Table 13–3 came from the Spread Value box on the Two Option Analysis page, but they can also be calculated by subtracting a September 900 Call value in Table 13–1 from the corresponding October 900 Call value in Table 13–2. The value of 9¾ in column 1, row 5, of Table 13–3, for example, is the difference between the values of 19¼ and 29 in the corresponding cells of Tables 13–1 and 13–2, respectively.

Table 13–3 shows how time spread values change prior to expiration and exhibit some unique behavior. First, column 1 shows that the September-

Table 13–1 Theoretical Values of September 900 Call at Various Index Levels and Days to Expiration

Row	Index Level	Col. 1: 24 Days	Col. 2: 20 Days	Col. 3: 16 Days	Col. 4: 12 Days	Col. 5: 8 Days	Col. 6: 4 Days	Col. 7: Exp.
1	980	82⅝	82	81½	81	80⅝	80¼	80
2	960	64	63⅛	62⅛	61⅜	60¾	60¼	60
3	940	46⅝	45⅜	44	42⅝	41⅜	40½	40
4	920	31½	29⅞	21⅛	26¼	24	21¾	20
5	900	19¼	17⅝	15⅝	13½	11	7⅝	0
6	880	10½	9	7⅜	5½	3½	1⅜	0
7	860	5	3⅞	2¾	1¾	¾	⅛	0
8	840	2	1⅜	¾	⅜	⅛	nil	0
9	820	⅝	⅜	⅛	nil	nil	nil	0

Dividend yield, 1.8%; volatility, 20%; interest rates, 5%.

Table 13–2 Theoretical Values of October 900 Call at Various Index Levels and Days to Expiration

Row	Index Level	Col. 1: 52 Days	Col. 2: 48 Days	Col. 3: 44 Days	Col. 4: 40 Days	Col. 5: 36 Days	Col. 6: 32 Days	Col. 7: 28 Days
1	980	87⅞	87⅛	86⅜	85⅝	84⅞	84	83⅜
2	960	70¾	69¾	68¾	67⅞	66⅞	65⅞	65
3	940	56	53⅞	52¾	51⅝	50⅜	49¼	47⅞
4	920	41	39¾	38½	37¼	35⅞	34½	33
5	900	29	27⅞	26⅝	25¼	24	22½	21
6	880	19½	18⅜	17¼	16	14⅝	13⅜	12
7	860	12¼	11¼	10¼	9¼	8¼	7⅛	6⅛
8	840	7⅛	6⅜	5⅝	4⅞	4⅛	3⅜	2⅝
9	820	3¾	3¼	2¾	2¼	1⅞	1⅜	1

Dividend yield, 1.8%; volatility, 20%; interest rates, 5%.

October 900 Call time spread has a value of 9 with the index at 880, a value of 9¾ with the index at 900, and a value of 9½ with the index at 920. This change in value is very small compared to the changes in value of the individual calls. The September 900 Call rises from 10½ to 31½ and the October 900 Call rises from 19½ to 41 as the index rises from 880 to 920.

Table 13–3 Theoretical Values of September-October 900 Call Time Spread at Various Index Levels and Days to Expiration

Row	Index Level	Col. 1: 52–24 Days	Col. 2: 48–20 Days	Col. 3: 44–16 Days	Col. 4: 40–12 Days	Col. 5: 36–8 Days	Col. 6: 32–4 Days	Col. 7: 28–0 Days
1	980	5¼	5⅛	4⅞	4⅝	4¼	3¾	3⅜
2	960	6¾	6⅝	6⅝	6½	6⅛	5⅝	5
3	940	8⅜	8½	8¾	9	9	8¾	7⅞
4	920	9½	9⅞	10⅜	11	11⅞	12¾	13
5	900	9¾	10¼	11	11¾	13	14⅞	21
6	880	9	9⅜	9⅞	10½	11⅛	12	12
7	860	7¼	7⅜	7½	7½	7½	7	6⅛
8	840	5⅛	5	4¾	4½	4	3⅜	2⅝
9	820	3⅛	2⅞	2⅝	2¼	1⅞	1⅜	1

Dividend yield, 1.8%; volatility, 20%; interest rates, 5%.

Second, at any time prior to expiration of the September call, the value of the call time spread is highest when the underlying index is at the strike price of 900. Also, the spread value increases when the index is at the strike as expiration approaches. If the index rises above the strike or declines below the strike as expiration approaches, then the spread value decreases.

The conclusion to be drawn from Table 13–3 is that a long time spread is a "neutral" or "gradual-movement" strategy. In an ideal scenario, a trader purchases a time spread when it is near-the-money and watches the index gradually move to the strike price at the expiration of the shorter-term option.

Suppose, for example, it is 24 days to September expiration, 52 days to October expiration, the SPX Index is 860, and Ann, an experienced index option trader, is forecasting that the index will rise to 900 in 24 days. Ann could attempt to profit from her forecast by purchasing one October 900 Call for 12¼ and simultaneously selling one September 900 Call for 5, thus creating a long September-October 900 Call time spread for 7¼, not including commissions. This situation is created in column 1, row 7 of Table 13–3.

If European-style options are used, purchasing the time spread for 7¼ involves less risk than buying only the October 900 Call for 12¼. Also, if Ann's forecast is accurate, then the tables indicate that the profit potential is greater. If, for example, the index rises to 900 in 24 days at September expiration, then the September 900 Call expires worthless, and if the October 900 Call is sold at 21, as indicated in Table 13–2 (column 7, row 5), then a profit of 13¾ is realized. In contrast, if the October 900 Call were purchased for 12¼ and sold for 21, then a profit of 8¾ would be realized.

Some, but not all, other outcomes also result in a larger profit for the long call time spread than for the long October 900 Call. If the index rise does not meet Ann's expectations and rises only to 880 at expiration, then Table 13–3 indicates the time spread will rise to 12 for a profit of 4¾. Under the same circumstances, the October 900 Call suffers a loss of ¼.

What if the index rises farther or sooner than Ann predicts or both? In several cases the long October 900 Call will perform better than the long call time spread. If, for example, the index rises from 860 to 920 in 20 days, which is 4 days prior to September expiration, then column 6, row 4 in Table 13–2 indicates that the October 900 Call will rise to 34½ for a profit of 22¼. In contrast, the estimated profit for the long call time spread in Table 13–3 in the corresponding cell is only 5½!

PRICE BEHAVIOR OF SHORT TIME SPREADS

Table 13–3 can also be used to estimate the results of short call time spreads; however, the numbers must be reversed, that is, viewed as credits. The number 9¾, which appears in column 1, row 5, for example, is a net debit, because the assumption is that this is a long time spread in which the October 900 Call is purchased for 29 and the September 900 Call is sold for 19¼. A short-call time spread, however, would be created by selling the October 900 Call and buying the September 900 Call for a net credit of 9¾.

Since short time spreads are generally established for a net credit, or cash inflow, and closed for a net debit, or cash outflow, Table 13–3 can be interpreted for short-call time spreads by thinking in terms of selling first and buying second.

Suppose, for example, it is 24 days to September expiration, 52 days to October expiration, the SPX Index is 900, and Adam is forecasting that the index will fall to 840 in 24 days. Adam could attempt to profit from his forecast by purchasing one September 900 Call for 19¼ and simultaneously selling one October 900 Call for 29, thus creating a short September-October 900 Call time spread for a credit of 9¾, not including commissions. If the index declines to 840, as Adam predicts, then the tables indicate that the September 900 Call will expire worthless and the October 900 Call will be trading at 2⅝. If Adam closes the short October 900 Call by repurchasing it at 2⅝, then he will realize a net profit of 7⅛ on his short call time spread: the purchased September 900 Call will expire worthless for a loss of 19¼, and the short October 900 Call will be closed by being repurchased at 2⅝ for a profit of 26⅜.

As Table 13–3 indicates, the ideal scenario for a short time spread is for the position to be established when the index is exactly at the strike and then for the index to rise or fall sharply at the expiration of the shorter-term option.

The general conclusion to be drawn from Table 13–3 is that long time spreads are neutral market strategies and short time spreads are volatile market strategies.

THE GREEKS: TIME SPREADS WITH CALLS

Table 13–4 summarizes the delta, gamma, theta, and vega of the September 900 Call, the October 900 Call, and both the long and short time spreads involving these calls. The information in columns 1 and 2 is taken from the Call/Put Pricer page in OP-EVAL3™. The numbers for the long time spread in column 3 are calculated by subtracting the numbers in column 1 from the numbers in column 2. The delta of +0.012 in column 3, for example, is calculated by subtracting +0.527 from +0.539. The numbers in column 4 are calculated by subtracting column 2 from column 1. The vega of −0.427 in column 4, for example, is calculated by subtracting +1.345 from +0.918.

Table 13–4 explains why time spreads behave the way they do. First, the very low delta and positive theta in column 3 explain why the long time spread is considered to be a neutral market strategy. The low delta means that little price change will occur if the underlying index changes by one point and other factors remain constant, and the positive theta means that the position will benefit from the passing of time if other factors remain constant.

The risks of the long time spread are explained by the positive vega and the negative gamma. The positive vega indicates that the position will benefit from an increase in implied volatility and be hurt by a decrease. Although there is no known correlation between short-term price action and changes in implied volatility, it is possible for sideways price action in an underlying instrument to result in a change in market sentiment that leads to a decrease in implied volatility. Consequently, traders who use long time spreads must forecast that implied volatility will remain constant or increase. When might such market behavior occur? If a government report or a series of earnings reports is anxiously awaited, it is possible for underlying prices to trade in a narrow range, while an increase in anxiety over the pending report results in an increase in the implied volatility of options as ever-anxious option buyers raise their bids and reluctant option sellers raise their offers.

Although very close to zero, the negative gamma means that a large price change in the underlying will have adverse consequences for a long time

Table 13–4 Time Spreads and Position Greeks

	Col. 1: Sept. 900 Call 24 Days	Col. 2: Oct. 900 Call 52 Days	Col. 3: Long* Time Spread	Col. 4: Short** Time Spread
Price	19¼	29	9¾ debit	9¾ credit
Delta	+0.527	+0.539	+0.012	−0.012
Gamma	+0.009	+0.006	−0.003	+0.003
Vega	+0.918	+1.345	+0.427	−0.427
Theta	−3.180	−2.147	+1.033	−1.033

Index level, 900; dividend yield, 1.8%; volatility, 20%; interest rates, 5%.

*The numbers in column 3 are calculated by subtracting the numbers in column 1 from those in column 2. The delta in column 3, for example, is calculated as follows: +0.539 − (+0.527) = +0.012.

**The numbers in column 4 are calculated by subtracting the numbers in column 2 from those in column 1. The theta in column 4, for example is calculated as follows: −3.180 − (−2.147) = −1.033.

spread, and this is verified by Table 13–3. The spread values in rows 1 and 9, when the index is out-of-the-money or in-the-money, are much smaller than in row 5 when the index is at-the-money. Consequently, a long time spread that is established when the index is at-the-money will result in a loss if the index moves substantially up or down.

Column 4 in Table 13–4 shows that the Greeks of a short time spread are opposite those of the corresponding long time spread. A short time spread position has a near-zero delta that is slightly negative instead of slightly positive; a positive gamma, which indicates that it will benefit from a large price change in the underlying; a negative vega, which means it will be hurt by an increase in volatility; and a negative theta, which means it will be hurt by the passage of time, if factors other than time remain constant. The combination of these factors means that a short time spread benefits from a large price move in the underlying but is hurt by the passage of time and an increase in implied volatility.

When might a substantial change in the level of an index be accompanied by a decrease in implied volatility? One possible time is after an anxiously awaited economic report. Good or bad, the news may move the underlying substantially, but the general decrease in anxiety after the news is out could cause a decrease in implied volatility as then-anxious option sellers lower their offers and then-reluctant option buyers also lower their bids.

As with other strategies, the results of time spreads can be estimated with OP-EVAL3™. The following example will show how a trade involving a long time spread might be analyzed.

TESTING SCENARIOS

Matthew is an experienced trader who uses a margin account and is able to assume the risk of short index options in time spread positions. For this example, assume 24 days to September expiration, 52 days to October expiration, an SPX Index level of 900, a September 900 Call price of 19¼, and an October 900 Call price of 29. This means that Matthew can purchase one October 900 Call and sell one September 900 Call for a net debit of 9¾, not including commissions. This situation is consistent with column 1, row 5 of Table 13–3.

Because the last major economic report for the summer has been released, and because the next series of earnings reports is not due for several weeks, Matthew forecasts that the SPX Index will trade in a narrow range and implied volatility will remain constant over the next 24 days. Nevertheless, Matthew is aware that there is no guarantee that the market will do as he expects, so he wants to test some negative scenarios to estimate his risk.

Table 13–3 estimates that if the index stays between 880 and 920 and other factors remain constant, then the long September-October 900 Call time spread will rise from 9 3/4 to between 12 and 21. With the index at 880 at September expiration and 28 days to October expiration, for example, Table 13–3 estimates that the September 900 Call will expire worthless and the October 900 Call will be trading for 12 (column 7, row 6). With the index exactly at 900 on the same day (column 7, row 5), Table 13–3 estimates that the September 900 Call will expire worthless and the October 900 Call will be trading for 21. Matthew is excited about the potential profit if his forecast is correct. But the values in Table 13–3 assume implied volatility remains constant at 20 percent, and Matthew wants to estimate the result if implied volatility decreases to 15 percent.

Table 13–5 shows how OP-EVAL3™ might be used to test this scenario. Column 1 contains the initial inputs and outputs. Column 2 contains Matthew's forecast with the index level at 900, volatility of 15 percent, and days to expiration of 0 for the September 900 Call and 28 for the October 900 Call. Column 3 contains Matthew's forecast with the index level at 880 instead of 900, and other factors the same as in column 2.

Column 2 of Table 13–5 indicates that with the index at 900, the September 900 Call expires worthless and the October 900 Call is estimated to

Table 13–5 Matthew's Forecast

	Col. 1: Initial Situation		Col. 2: Index 900		Col. 3: Index 880
Inputs					
Index level	900	→	900	→	880
Strike price	900				
Dividend yield	1.8%				
Volatility	20%	→	15%	→	15%
Interest rates	5%				
Days to expiration	24/52	→	0/28	→	0/28
Outputs					
September 900 Call price	19.250	→	0	→	0
October 900 Call price	29.000	→	16.000	→	7.500
Long time spread	9.750	→	16.000	→	7.500

be trading at 16. If the October 900 Call is sold at this price, then Matthew will realize a profit of 6¼. This profit is 5 less than would be earned if the October 900 Call were sold for 21. Column 3 indicates that if the index is 880 instead of 900, then the September 900 Call expires worthless and the October 900 Call is estimated to be trading at 7½. If the October 900 Call is sold at this price, then Matthew will realize a loss of 2¼. This compares to a profit of 2¼ that would be earned if the October 900 Call were sold for 12.

A decrease in implied volatility from 20 percent to 15 percent definitely changes the risk-reward ratio! Unfortunately, there is no objective method of determining whether this possible change means that Matthew should forego making the trade. This is a subjective decision that only Matthew can make. He must make a personal judgment about his confidence in his forecast, and he must make a personal judgment about the probability of implied volatility declining to 15 percent or less. Then Matthew, and only Matthew, must decide whether or not to make the trade.

SUMMARY

Time spreads involve the purchase of one option and the sale of another option of the same type with the same underlying and strike price but with a different expiration. Long time spreads involve the purchase of the longer-term option and the sale of the shorter-term option, and they are established for net debits. Short time spreads involve the purchase of the shorter-term option and the sale of the longer-term option. Short time spreads are established for net credits.

Long time spreads are neutral market strategies, and short time spreads are volatile market strategies. OP-EVAL3™ can be used to evaluate the price behavior of time spreads, but it cannot graph time spread positions. The price behavior of time spreads can also be analyzed with theoretical value tables. The ideal scenario for a long time spread is to establish the position when the underlying index is near-the-money and the index then gradually moves to the strike price at the expiration of the shorter-term option. The ideal scenario for a short time spread is for the underlying index to move sharply up or down away from the strike price.

The Greeks of time spreads explain why they behave the way they do. Long time spreads have slightly positive deltas, negative gammas, negative vegas, and positive thetas. This means long time spread positions benefit from little or no price movement and the passage of time, and they are hurt by large moves in either direction. Short time spreads, being the opposite of long time spreads, have slightly negative deltas, positive gammas, positive vegas, and negative thetas. Short time spread positions benefit from large price movements and a decrease in implied volatility, and they are hurt by little or no price movement and the passage of time.

Before a time spread is used, the strategy should be tested for several market forecasts. There is no objective method of using these profit and loss estimates to make trading decisions. As described throughout this book, traders should use a three-part forecast: for the change in the index level, for the time for the predicted move to occur, and for the implied volatility level after the move.

Fourteen

INTRODUCTION

I n this chapter three traders will choose among alternative index option strategies in an attempt to profit from their market forecasts. The traders will be introduced with a brief description of their background, trading style, objectives, and attitude toward risk. Each trader's forecast will be stated and the strategies under consideration will be analyzed and compared. The analysis will discuss profit potential and estimated risk within the time frame of the forecast.

Each trader's forecast will be accepted as presented. The risk of initiating any trade is that the forecast is wrong and a loss is incurred. It is assumed that the traders have been approved by their brokerage firms for the risk level that applies to the strategies being considered. No attempt will be made to review all of the possible strategies that might profit if a particular forecast is accurate. The purpose of the discussion is to illustrate an organized thought process for selecting one strategy from a number of alternatives.

In the examples presented in this chapter, commissions and other transaction costs, margin deposits, if any, and bid-ask spreads will not be included. These factors, however, can affect the desirability of any strategy, and they should be included when analyzing real strategies involving options.

SUE: TRADING WHILE WORKING

Our first trader is Sue, a financial planner with a large bank in the Midwest. Because of her work, the market is a frequent topic of conversation, and Sue tells all of her clients that she "practices what she preaches." In planning for her retirement she has 95 percent of her money allocated between conservative stocks held for the long term, aggressive stocks, some of which include conservative option strategies such as covered writing, and some high-yield bond funds. Sue actively manages these funds, and the percentage allocation varies from year to year depending on her predictions for the stock and bond markets.

The remaining 5 percent of Sue's funds is devoted to an aggressive trading account. Her goal for this account is to "assume high risk and earn a high return." In this account she makes one or more option trades per month. Last year she made 15 trades: 7 were profitable, 5 were losers, and 3 broke even. Sue's goal for this account is to make a net profit of 30 percent on the beginning account balance each year; 50 percent of the profits, if any, are added to her retirement portfolio, and 50 percent pay for a "special vacation." Sue does not always achieve her profit target. In some years she does much better, and in other years she has a loss.

Sue gets her trading ideas by "generally paying attention to the market." She reads one nationally known financial paper at home every morning, and she glances at another one at work. She also has access to charts and market opinion on the Internet. Her Internet provider has a stock market service, which includes charts on individual stocks and most major indexes such as the S&P 500 (SPX), S&P 100 (OEX), and NASDAQ 100 (NDX).

Sue thinks of herself as an aggressive, but cautious trader. To Sue, this means no uncovered short options. Her typical trade is 10–20 contracts or spreads. Her positions are typically open from 2 to 5 trading days. Sometimes, of course, she is stopped out at a loss on the first day!

Sue looks for opportunities where she believes an index can move 2.5 percent to 3.5 percent in 2 to 5 trading days, or approximately 20 to 30 points on an 800-point index. She believes that such moves in an index mean that a 50 percent profit on an at-the-money or near-the-money option is possible. If the market moves against her, Sue generally takes a loss at 20 percent to 30 percent of an option's cost. She also has a personal rule of closing a position in 5 trading days regardless of the profit or loss if her forecast has failed to materialize.

Sue has recently turned bearish on the Dow Jones Industrial Average. Some fundamentally positive government reports recently caused morning rallies of 30 to 50 DJIA Index points but there was no follow through, and, in each case, the DJIA closed virtually unchanged. Consequently, Sue has been exploring bearish strategies with DJX options. With three high-profile companies reporting earnings this week, she feels that weaker-than-expected results could tip the scales in favor of the bears.

With the DJX Index at 80.36, equivalent to 8,036 on the DJIA, Sue believes that a decline to between 77.50 and 78.50 in 5 trading days (7 calendar days) is possible. Sue has $7,500 to invest and risk, and she is looking for alternatives to profit from this forecast. Implied volatility of DJX options has been steady at 25 percent for 3 weeks, but Sue believes it will decrease to 22 percent if her forecast is realized.

It is 16 days to February expiration and 44 days to March expiration. Sue is considering three alternatives:

1. Purchase 100 February 78 DJX Puts, which are trading at ¾, or $75 each.
2. Purchase 46 March 78 Puts for 1⅝, or $162.50 each.
3. Sell 66 February 80–82 Call spreads for ⅞, or $87.50 each.

The February 80 Calls are 1⅞, or $187.50 each, and the February 82 Calls are 1.00, or $100 each. Note that selling call spreads with DJX options is a strategy with limited risk and limited profit potential because these are European-style options. Sue could consider other strategies, but the purpose of this example is to illustrate Sue's decision-making process, not to make a complete list of her alternatives.

Table 14–1 summarizes current market conditions on the DJX, Sue's forecast, the options and their prices, and how Sue arrived at the quantity of each strategy. Note that the amount that Sue is willing to risk, $7,500, is divided by the *maximum risk* of each strategy, not the *price* of each strategy. The price of the February 78 Puts and the price of the March 78 Puts equal

Table 14–1 Sue's Options

	DJX	Sue's Forecast
Index level	80.36	78.00
Implied volatility	25%	22%
Days to expiration	Feb.: 16	9 (in 5 trading days)
	Mar.: 44	37 (in 5 trading days)

Option	Feb. 78 Put	Mar. 78 Put	Feb. 80 Call	Feb. 82 Call
Price	¾	1⅝	1⅞	1
Days to expiration	16	44	16	16
Implied volatility	25%	25%	25%	25%
Capital	$7,500	$7,500	$7,500	$7,500
Risk per option	$75	$162.50	$112.50*	
Number of options†	100	46	66	
Strategy	Buy 100	Buy 46	Sell 66	
Position delta	−26.70	−15.32	−12.27	

*Risk of short 80–82 Call spread sold for ⅞ is 1⅛, or $112.50, not including commissions.
†Number of options = capital available for trade ($7,500)/risk per strategy.

the maximum risk of those strategies, but the risk of selling February 80–82 Call spreads is the difference between the strikes minus the net premium received. In this example, the difference between the strike prices is 2, or $200, and the net premium received per spread, not including commissions, is ⅞, or $87.50. Consequently, the risk of each spread is $200 minus $87.50, or $112.50. Dividing $7,500 by $112.50 yields 66, which is the number of spreads that Sue can sell.

The last row in Table 14–1 contains the position delta of each strategy. The delta can be obtained from the Two Option Analysis page or the Four Option Analysis page in OP-EVAL3™. The position delta is calculated by multiplying the delta of the strategy by the number of times the strategy is used. Each long February 78 Put, for example, has a delta of −0.267. Therefore, a position of 100 long February 78 Puts has a delta of −26.70, equal to short 26.70 futures on the underlying index. The position delta of 46 long March 78 Puts is −15.32, and short 66 February 80–82 Call Spreads have a position delta of −12.27. Sue is interested in seeing if these deltas predict which strategy will perform best if her forecast is realized.

To estimate the results of her strategies over a range of possible DJX Index levels, Sue prepares Table 14–2, which indicates various DJX Index levels from 77.50 to 81.50, equivalent to 7,750 to 8,150 on the DJIA. Strategies 1 through 3 contain Sue's estimates of how the three alternatives will perform. In each double column, the left number is the estimated price of one option or one spread and the right number is the estimated total dollar profit or loss, not including commissions, assuming the position is closed at the estimated price.

Table 14–2 can be created using the assumed inputs listed in the table note and the Call/Put Pricer page or the Two Option Analysis page in OP-EVAL3™. Table 14–2 is an analytical tool that can assist Sue in making her decision. It contains estimated profit and loss outcomes over a range of index levels. Note that Sue has included negative outcomes as well as positive outcomes in Table 14–2.

Each of the three strategies Sue is considering has advantages and disadvantages. As has been noted several times in this book, there is no "best" alternative. Strategy 1, buying 100 February 78 Puts, has the greatest estimated profit if the DJX Index declines to 77.50 in 5 trading days, but it also has the greatest estimated loss in this time frame if the index rallies to 81.50, contrary to Sue's forecast. Strategy 2, buying 46 March 78 Puts, has lower estimated profits in the positive outcomes and lower estimated losses in the negative outcomes. Consequently, a choice between buying 100 February 78 Puts and

Table 14–2 Sue Estimates Possible Outcomes

	Strategy 1: Long 100 Feb. 78 Puts (cost ¾)		Strategy 2: Long 46 March 78 Puts (cost 1⅝)		Strategy 3: Short 66 Feb. 80–82 Call Spreads (sold for ⅞)	
Index Level	Est. Price	P/L	Est. Price	P/L	Est. Price	P/L
77.50	1½	+5,000	2¼	+2,875	¼	+4,125
78.00	1	+2,500	2	+1,725	⁵⁄₁₆	+3,712
78.50	¹³⁄₁₆	+ 625	1¹³⁄₁₆	+ 862	⁷⁄₁₆	+1,237
79.00	⅝	−1,250	1⁹⁄₁₆	− 287	½	+ 825
81.50	⅛	−6,250	¹³⁄₁₆	−3,737	1⅛	−1,650

Dividend yield, 1.7%; volatility, 22%; interest rates, 5%; days to expiration: February, 9; March, 37 (5 trading days later).

buying 46 March 78 Puts is a decision about risk and reward. Both strategies have the same maximum risk of $7,500 if the options expire worthless, but, in Sue's time frame and in the index range in Table 14–2, the strategy of buying 100 Feb 78 puts is estimated to make more or lose more than the strategy of buying 46 March 78 Puts.

The estimates of outcomes for Strategy 3, selling 66 February 80–82 Call spreads, have different characteristics. In the best outcomes, Strategy 3 is estimated to make less than Strategy 1, but in the small-movement outcomes, Strategy 3 is estimated to earn a profit while Strategy 1 is estimated to incur a loss. Strategy 3 is interesting, because it has more profit outcomes than either Strategy 1 or Strategy 2. Also, it has a higher estimated profit at DJX Index levels of 78.00 and 78.50. Finally, Strategy 3 has the lowest estimated loss if the index rises to 81.50.

Choosing between Strategies 1, 2, and 3 depends on the forecast. If Sue is extremely confident that the DJX Index will decline to 77.50 or lower, and if she is willing to assume the risk of loss if her forecast is wrong, then she may be inclined to purchase 100 February 78 Puts (Strategy 1) because this has the highest estimated profit for that forecast.

But look carefully at how Sue's forecast was worded: "Sue believes that a decline to between 77.50 and 78.50 in 5 trading days (7 calendar days), is possible." This wording does not indicate extreme confidence that the index will decline to 77.50 or lower. Consequently, Strategy 3, selling 66 DJX February 80–82 Call spreads seems best suited to Sue's forecast.

PAUL: AGGRESSIVE, BUT CONSERVATIVE

Paul is a retired economics professor who divides his time between charity work, babysitting his grandchildren, taking care of his house and yard, and managing his investments. While most of Paul's investments are extremely conservative, he does have a speculative account in which he occasionally trades index options. Paul typically watches the stock market channel 1 or 2 hours a day, and he always catches the end-of-day market summary program to get the trading ideas of his favorite commentators.

Paul loves the market, and he trades index options occasionally because he feels it is the easiest way to profit from an overall market opinion and because it adds spice to his otherwise conservative investing activities. He does not rely on profits from trading index options, if any, for current income. Rather, he adds net profits to his grandchildren's college funds or to his estate.

The Airline Index (XAL) has declined recently from 540 to 490, and Paul has latched onto one TV commentator's idea that the index will stay in a trading range between 490 and 510 for the next month. He also believes that the implied volatility of XAL options will remain constant during this time period.

Paul considers this a neutral to moderately bullish forecast, and he is considering selling a put spread in August XAL options, which have 28 days to expiration. Paul chooses the strategy of selling a put spread with European-style options, because early exercise is prohibited; he does not want to assume either the risk of selling uncovered options or the risk of early assignment. Also, Paul has decided to limit his maximum theoretical risk to $5,000, not including commissions.

With the XAL Index at 490, Paul is considering selling three put spreads: the 470–480 Put spread, the 480–490 Put spread, and the 490–500 Put spread. Table 14–3 contains prices, deltas, and thetas of the August 470, 480, 490, and 500 Puts. Table 14–4 contains important information about

Table 14–3 Paul's Options

Option	Price	Delta	Theta
August 470 Put	6½	−0.27	−1.896
August 480 Put	9⅞	−0.36	−2.124
August 490 Put	14⅜	−0.47	−2.209
August 500 Put	19⅞	−0.57	−2.134

Index level, 490; dividend yield, 1%; volatility, 28%; interest rates, 5%; days to expiration, 28.

Table 14–4 Paul's Alternatives

Row	Spread	Col. 1: 470–480	Col. 2: 480–490	Col. 3: 490–500
1	Price per spread	3⅜	4½	5½
2	Quantity to sell	7	9	11
3	Maximum risk	$4,638	$4,950	$4,950
4	Maximum profit potential	$2,362	$4,050	$6,050
5	Position delta	+0.63	+0.99	+1.10
6	Position theta	+1.596	+0.085	−0.075

the put spreads themselves. Column one, row 1, shows that the net premium received, or price, of the August 470—480 Put spread is 3⅜, not including commissions. This premium is established by selling the 480 Put for 9⅞ and simultaneously buying the 470 Put for 6½ (see prices in Table 14–3).

The quantity of spreads that can be sold appears in Table 14–4, row 2. This is calculated by dividing $5,000, Paul's risk limit, by the maximum risk for one spread. The quantity to sell appearing in column 1—7—is calculated as follows: The maximum risk per spread is the difference between the strikes minus the net premium received. Consequently, if a 470–480 Put spread is sold for 3⅜, then its maximum risk is 6⅝ (10 − 3⅜). In dollars, 6⅝ is $662.50. Dividing Paul's risk limit of $5,000 by the maximum loss per spread of $662.50 produces the number 7.54. Rounding down, the number of 470–480 Put spreads that Paul can sell and stay within his risk limit of $5,000 is 7.

Row 3 shows the maximum risk of this strategy, which is calculated by multiplying the maximum risk per spread times the number of spreads: $662.50 × 7 = $4,637.50, rounded to $4,638.

Maximum profit potential (row 4) is calculated by multiplying the dollar amount of the net premium per spread times the number of spreads sold: 3⅜ translates to $337.50; $337.50 × 7 = $2,362.50, rounded down to $2,362.

Position deltas and position thetas (rows 5 and 6) are calculated from information in Table 14–3 and the Quantity to Sell amount in row 2. The 470–480 Put spread, for example, consists of a long 470 Put, which has a delta of −0.27, and a short 480 Put, which has a delta of +0.36. The spread delta is +0.09, and the position delta of seven short spreads is 7 × +0.09, or +0.63.

Note that Paul's biggest concern is risk; he does not want his maximum theoretical risk to exceed $5,000, not including commissions. Consequently, the quantity of each put spread he can sell is limited by its risk. Therefore, even though the three strategies he is considering in Table 14–4 do not have the same profit potential, delta, or theta, the strategies are equal from the standpoint of risk. Therefore, it is appropriate for Paul to be choosing between these alternatives.

Table 14–4 provides valuable information that can be evaluated before profit and loss estimates are developed. The position deltas indicate a strategy's sensitivity to change in index level, and, in this regard, the strategies are different. With the index at 490, the 470–480 Put spread can be described as out-of-the-money, the 480–490 Put spread is at-the-money, and the 490–500 Put spread is in-the-money. The position deltas are consistent with these descriptions: the 470–480 Put spread has the smallest delta and the 490–500 Put spread has the largest. This means that the 490–500 Put spread will respond the most to a change in the index level, both positively to an index rise and negatively to an index decline, while the 470–480 Put spread will respond the least.

The thetas in Table 14–4 indicate that the strategies are also different in their sensitivity to the passage of time. The 470–480 Put spread will profit from the passage of time, while the thetas of the 480–490 and 490–500 Put spreads indicate nearly zero change in those spread values if 1 week passes and other factors remain unchanged.

The conclusion to be drawn from the position deltas and thetas is that these spreads make money in different ways. The 470–480 Put spread will make some money from a rise in the index and some money from time decay. The profitability of the other two put spreads, however, depends almost totally on a rise in the index. This is important for Paul to know, because it means he must really think about his forecast: Is it more neutral, calling for little change in the index level, or is it more bullish, calling for a 10- to 20-point rise in the index? There is no correct answer to this question, but it is one that Paul must answer for himself before he selects one strategy over the others.

Paul's next step is to create a profit and loss comparison. Table 14–5 shows three estimates of how the short put spreads will perform over a range of index levels and time periods. Each double column contains an estimated price of the spread and profit or loss of the strategy, not including commissions.

For example, Strategy 1 shows a price of 5 and a profit or loss dollar amount of −1,138 after 7 days if the index is 475 (row 1, column 1). This is calculated using OP-EVAL3™. The time shown in each column head is the number of days that must be subtracted from the assumed 28 days to expiration shown in Table 14–3. The estimated dollar loss, $1,138, is calculated by multiplying the estimated loss per spread by the number of spreads. The estimated loss per spread is calculated by subtracting the price paid to close the position, assumed to be 5, from the net price received when the position was established, or 3⅜. The result is 1⅝, or $162.50; 7 times $162.50 equals $1,137.50.

Paul can now use Table 14–5 to compare the estimated profit and loss outcomes of the three strategies. It is interesting how different the estimated

Table 14–5 Paul Estimates the Performance of Three Short Put Spreads

		Col. 1: In 7 Days		Col. 2: In 14 Days		Col. 3: In 21 Days		Col. 4: In 28 Days	
Row	Index Level	Price	P/L	Price	P/L	Price	P/L	Price	P/L
Strategy 1: Sell 7 470–480 Put Spreads at 3⅜ Each									
1	475	5	−1,138	5	−1,137	5	−1,137	5	−1,138
2	485	3¾	− 263	3½	− 84	3	+ 262	0	+2,362
3	495	2⅝	+ 525	2¼	+ 787	1½	+1,312	0	+2,362
4	505	1⅞	+1,050	1⅜	+1,400	⅝	+1,925	0	+2,362
Strategy 2: Sell 9 480–490 Put Spreads at 4½ Each									
5	475	6¼	−1,575	6½	−1,800	7	−2,250	10	−4,950
6	485	5	− 450	5	− 450	5	− 450	5	− 450
7	495	3¾	+ 675	3½	+ 900	3	+1,350	0	+4,050
8	505	2¾	+1,575	2⅜	+1,912	1½	+2,700	0	+4,050
Strategy 3: Sell 11 490–500 Put Spreads at 5½ Each									
9	475	7¼	−1,925	7¾	−2,475	8½	−3,300	10	−4,950
10	485	6⅛	− 687	6½	−1,100	7	−1,650	10	−4,950
11	495	5	+ 550	5	+ 550	5	+ 550	1	+4,950
12	505	3⅞	+1,787	3⅝	+2,062	3	+2,750	0	+6,050

Dividend yield, 1%; volatility, 28%; interest rates, 5%.

results are if the index moves only five points up or down between now and expiration.

None of the three strategies are estimated to profit if the index declines five points in the first 14 days. However, the strategy of selling seven out-of-the-money 470–480 Put spreads nearly breaks even at an index level of 485 in 14 days. The short 480–490 and 490–500 Put spread positions, in comparison, have estimated losses of $450 and $1,100, respectively (rows 6 and 10).

If the market rises, the strategy with the highest delta has the highest estimated profit, as one would expect. In 7 days with the index at 505, for example, selling 11 490–500 Put spreads results in an estimated profit of $1,787, which is higher than the estimated profits of $1,575 and $1,050 for the short 480–490 and 470–480 Put spread positions, respectively (rows 4, 8, and 12).

Paul's task is to choose between the trade-offs of the three strategies. If he expects the index to rise 5 to 15 points in the next 28 days, and if he is willing to assume the risk of being wrong, then selling 11 490–500 Put spreads has the highest profit potential. However, if his forecast is more neutral, meaning that the index could be up or down five points from its current level of 490, then selling 7 of the out-of-the-money 470–480 Put spreads has the highest probability of making a profit, although the maximum risk is still approximately $5,000.

Different interpretations of Paul's forecast are possible. If one believes that a conservative person would lean toward a strategy that has a smaller profit potential with a higher probability, rather than a strategy that has a larger profit potential with a smaller probability, then Paul's selection of selling 7 470–480 Put spreads is easy to understand.

BRIAN: OUTRIGHT AGGRESSIVE

Brian, our third trader, is a software consultant in Denver. His office is in his home, and his desk is surrounded by computer screens, one of which is tuned to the stock market channel during market hours. Brian is an aggressive trader. He spends 10 to 30 minutes each morning reading a business paper and studying charts, which he gets from an on-line service. He makes at least one or two trades each week through a broker he has known for five years. Half the time he acts on his broker's recommendations, and half the time he comes up with his own trading ideas.

Brian's goal is to keep doing what he's doing. His software business is going well, and he views his index option trading as a major hobby. Every December Brian calculates his results for the year. His trading has been profitable in four of the last five years, one of which was "very profitable." Assuming he has a profit at the end of the year, Brian makes three withdrawals. The first withdrawal is for taxes; these funds are deposited in an interest-bearing account until tax time. The second withdrawal, usually equal to 33 percent of after-tax profits, is invested in a separate brokerage account that contains Brian's portfolio of quality growth stocks. This portfolio is part of Brian's long-term asset-accumulation plan for retirement. Brian has found that trading index options has increased his skill as a long-term investor, because, in the course of listening to many short-term market prognostications, he also hears some good, long-term investment advice.

The third withdrawal, also usually 33 percent, is "play money." This is Brian's reward to himself for his hard work at trading. In his most profitable year, he bought a new car. In other years, he has purchased new clothes or redecorated a room in his condominium. Brian leaves the remainder of after-tax profits, if any, in his trading account; his goal is to build his trading account equity so that he can trade more often and with bigger positions. In the year that he had a net loss, Brian did not replenish his trading account with funds from other savings. He just made fewer trades with fewer contracts per trade until his account equity grew from trading profits.

Today is 10 days to April expiration and 38 days to May expiration; the OEX Index is 900 and implied volatility is 17 percent. Brian is forecasting that a government report in 2 days will start the OEX on a 20- to 40-point move in the next 5 to 10 days. Unfortunately, Brian is not sure whether the move will be up or down, and he is worried that implied volatility will decline.

In an effort to profit from his forecast, Brian is considering three high-volatility strategies:

1. Purchase the May 900 straddle, a strategy that consists of purchasing the May 900 Call and the May 900 Put
2. Purchase the May 875–925 strangle, which consists of purchasing the May 875 Put and the May 925 Call
3. Sell the April–May 900 Call time spread, which involves purchasing the April 900 Call and selling the May 900 Call

Brian wants to commit approximately $15,000 to this trade, not including margin requirements and commissions. However, he plans to close the position and realize a loss at approximately $5,000. Brian realizes, of course, that dramatic changes in market conditions, such as a sharp decrease in implied volatility, mean that there is no guaranty about the limit of his potential loss, even if a stop-loss order is used. Prepared to accept these risks, Brian proceeds with his analysis.

Table 14–6 contains information about the options and strategies that Brian is considering. Although there are many more strike prices and expirations available, for the sake of this example Brian is limiting his analysis to those described above.

Table 14–6 shows the cost of purchasing 4 May 900 straddles, purchasing 8 May 875–925 strangles, and selling 12 April–May 900 Call time spreads.

The risk of the straddle and strangle positions is straightforward. Since these positions involve purchased options, the *maximum* risk is limited to the premiums paid plus commissions. However, there is no guaranty that Brian can *limit* his loss to his desired level of only $5,000 by selling the options in the market prior to expiration.

The risk of the time spread is more difficult to assess. Although there is risk of early assignment because American-style index options are involved, the risk of a time spread is not the same as the risk of an uncovered short index option, which is unlimited in the case of a short call and substantial in

Table 14–6 Brian's Strategy Alternatives

Option	Price	Delta	Implied Volatility	Days to Expiration
April 900 Call	10½	+0.52	17%	10
May 875 Put	8½	−0.27	17%	38
May 900 Put	18⅛	−0.46	17%	38
May 900 Call	21⅛	+0.53	17%	38
May 925 Call	10⅞	+0.34	17%	38

Strategy 1: Buy 4 May 900 Straddles

Buy 4 May 900 Calls at 21⅛ each:	4 × 21.125 =	84.50 debit
Buy 4 May 900 Puts at 18⅛ each:	4 × 18.125 =	+ 72.50 debit
		157.00 debit
Total debit (157 × multiplier of 100):		$15,700 debit

Strategy 2: Buy 8 May 875–925 Strangles

Buy 8 May 925 Calls at 10⅞ each:	8 × 10.875 =	87.00 debit
Buy 8 May 875 Puts at 8½ each:	8 × 8.50 =	+ 68.00 debit
		155.00 debit
Total debit (155 × multiplier of 100):		$15,500 debit

Strategy 3: Sell 12 April–May 900 Call Time Spreads

Sell 25 May 900 Calls at 21⅛ each:	12 × 21.125 =	253.50 credit
Buy 25 April 900 Calls at 10½ each:	12 × 10.50 =	−126.50 debit
		127.50 credit
Total credit ($127.50 × multiplier of 100):		$12,750 credit

the case of a short put. In the case of a time spread, the risk of the short option prior to being assigned early is at least partially offset by the long option. And in the case of a short time spread, a significant change in the index in either direction is, theoretically, beneficial for the position. Therefore, to assess the risk of the short April–May 900 Call time spread, Brian must estimate the price of the spread under adverse conditions.

As explained in Chapter 13, there are two market conditions that adversely affect short time spread positions: no market movement and an increase in implied volatility. Short time spreads have negative thetas and therefore tend to lose money if time passes and other factors are unchanged. They also have negative vegas, which means they lose money if implied volatility increases and other factors remain constant. Knowing this, Brian will use OP-EVAL3™ to estimate the loss of an April–May 900 Call time spread if the index level does not change and implied volatility increases.

Figure 14–1 is a Two Option Analysis page from OP-EVAL3™ that Brian might create to estimate the price change in an April–May 900 Call time spread. The Underlying Price row shows 900 because the assumption is that the index level remains unchanged from today. Today is 10 days from April expiration and 38 days from May expiration; therefore, 5 days from now will be 5 days from April expiration and 33 days from May expiration; these are the numbers in the Days row. The selection of an exact percentage for the volatility level is a subjective decision. The number 20.000 in the Volatility row indicates an implied volatility of 20 percent, a 3 percent rise from the current level of 17 percent. This is Brian's estimate, based on his trading experience, of how much volatility could rise before he would enter an order to close his position and realize a loss.

According to estimates in the Two Option Analysis page in Figure 14–1, the May 900 Call will rise to 22.845, or approximately 22⅞, and the April 900 Call will decrease to 8.599, or approximately 8⅝. Consequently, the April–May 900 Call time spread is estimated to increase from its current price of 10⅝ to 14¼, for a loss of 3⅝, or $362.50, not including commissions. For ease of calculation and to be conservative, Brian will round this number up to 4, or $400.

To calculate the number of short time spreads that do not exceed Brian's loss limit, the estimated loss per spread of $400 is divided into the target loss limit of $5,000. The result is 12.5, which Brian rounds down to 12. This means that Brian can sell 12 April–May 900 Call time spreads. There is, of

Figure 14–1 Brian Assesses the Risk of the Short April–May 900 Call Time Spread

Value rises to 14 1/4 for a loss of 4 (approx.)

		Option 1	Option 2	
Underlying Price	A	900.000	900.000	
Strike Price	A	900.000	900.000	
Option Type	I	CALL	CALL	
Quantity (+ or -)		+1	-1	Spread Value
Theoretical Value		8.599	22.845	-14.246
Delta		.512	.531	-0.019
Volatility	A	20.000%	20.000%	Spread Delta
Days	I	5	33	
Interest Rate	A	5.000%	5.000%	Price Plus One
Dividend Yield	A	1.800%	1.800%	Price Minus One

OP-EVAL3 - [Two Option Analysis for European-style Index Options]

Call / Put Pricer   Two Option Analysis   Four Option Analysis   Graph   Disclaimer   Help   Exit

Days Plus One
Days Minus One

Print Form

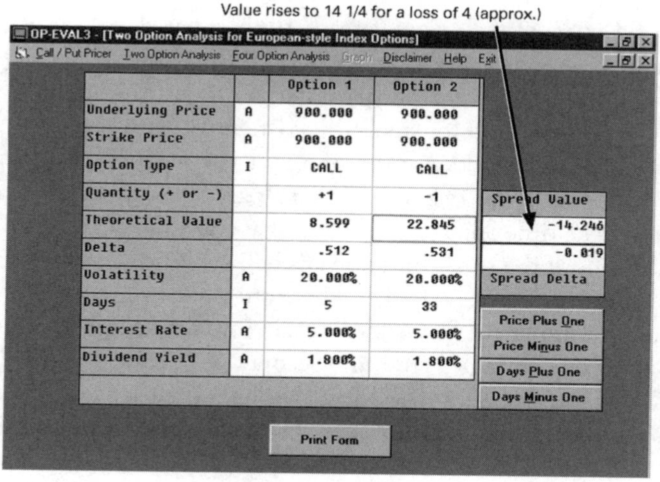

course, no guaranty that his loss will be limited to $5,000, but Brian is aware of this risk and financially and psychologically capable of withstanding a far greater loss, so he does not eliminate this strategy from consideration.

Now that Brian has identified three potential strategies—purchasing 4 May 900 straddles at 39¼ each, purchasing 8 May 875-925 strangles at 19⅜ each, and selling 12 April–May 900 Call time spreads for 10⅝ each—the next step is to use OP-EVAL3™ to estimate how each strategy will perform over a range of market outcomes.

Table 14–7 estimates how Brian's three alternatives will behave in 5 and 10 days and at five different market levels: 860, 880, 900, 920, and 940. The analysis also assumes that volatility declines to 14 percent. In each time frame and at each index level, Table 14–7 shows the estimated value of the position and dollar profit or loss. Looking at the long 4 May 900 straddles, for example, at an index level of 860 in 5 days, the straddle price is estimated to be 43⅜. The net profit or loss is calculated by subtracting the cost of the straddle, 39¼, from the estimated selling price, 43⅜, and then multiplying the difference, 4⅛, or $412.50, times 4, the number of straddles purchased. In this case, the result is a profit of $1,650, which is calculated as follows:

$$\text{Net profit/loss} = (43\tfrac{3}{8} - 39\tfrac{1}{4}) \times 4$$
$$= 16\tfrac{1}{2}$$
$$= \$1,650$$

Brian's three alternatives have different ranges of estimated profit and loss. In 5 days, for example, the most profitable result of the long 4 900 straddles is $3,400 and the worst loss is $3,600. The most profitable outcome for the long 8 875–925 strangles is $5,700 and the worst loss is $6,200. For the 12 short April–May 900 Call time spreads the estimated best and worst outcomes are *both profitable*, $9,150 and $450, respectively.

There is no one "correct" way to interpret Table 14–7, but it does provide valuable information for traders like Brian who are evaluating multiple strategies and trying to choose the one that is best suited to their market forecast and tolerance for risk. Given that Brian is an experienced, aggressive trader, selling 12 time spreads appears to have several advantages. The best estimated profit of the short time spreads is significantly higher than that of the long straddles or long strangles. There are two reasons for this. First, the short time spreads benefit from a decrease in implied volatility while the long straddles and long strangles are hurt. Second, the passage of time hurts the long straddles and strangles more than the short time spreads, because those positions consist of two long options, while the short time spread has one long option and one short option.

**Table 14–7 Estimated Outcomes of Brian's Three Strategies
(Implied Volatility 14%)**

**Strategy 1: Purchase long 4 May 900 Straddles at 39¼
(purchased at 38 days to expiration, implied volatility 17%)**

Index	In 5 Days (at 33 days to exp.)		In 10 Days (at 28 days to exp.)	
Level	Value	P/L	Value	P/L
860	43⅜	+1,650	42¼	+1,200
880	33	−2,500	31	−3,300
900	30¼	−3,600	27⅞	−4,550
920	35⅝	−1,450	33⅜	−2,350
940	46¼	+3,400	46¼	+2,800

**Strategy 2: Purchase Long 8 May 875–925 Strangles at 19⅜
(purchased at 38 days to expiration, implied volatility 17%)**

Index	In 5 Days (at 33 days to exp.)		In 10 Days (at 28 days to exp.)	
Level	Value	P/L	Value	P/L
860	22¼	+2,300	21¼	+1,500
880	13¾	−4,500	12⅛	−5,800
900	11⅝	−6,200	9¾	−7,700
920	16⅛	−2,600	14¼	−4,100
940	26½	+5,700	25	+4,500

**Strategy 3: Sell Short 12 April–May 900 Call Time Spreads at 10⅝
(sold at 10 days to April exp. and 38 days to May exp., implied volatility 17%)**

Index	In 5 Days (5 to April, 33 to May)		In 10 Days (at April exp., 28 to May)	
Level	Value	P/L	Value	P/L
860	3	+9,150	2¼	+10,050
880	7⅛	+4,200	6⅝	+ 4,800
900	10¼	+ 450	15	− 5,250
920	8⅛	+3,000	7⅞	+ 3,300
940	4¾	+7,050	4¼	+ 7,650

The primary disadvantage of the time spread is that Brian cannot be sure that his risk is limited to his target of $5,000. Remember, there is no assurance that a stop-loss order will be filled at the stop-loss price. A similar disadvantage, however, exists for the long straddles and strangles, which, in Brian's case, involve a maximum theoretical risk of $15,700 and $15,500, respectively.

Once again, there is no right or wrong answer to this strategy selection exercise. An experienced trader like Brian is likely to choose selling 12 April–May 900 Call time spreads instead of purchasing straddles or strangles, because the calculations in Table 14–7 estimate that this position has higher profits in more outcomes than the other strategies.

SUMMARY

Traders with different goals, occupations, tolerances for risk, and amounts of time available to follow the market can all trade index options. In order to choose between alternatives, a trader must first state the market forecast clearly. Second, a risk limit must be set. Risk limits can be established in terms of maximum dollar risk, implied volatility level, time, or any combination of these factors. Stop-loss orders, however, do not guarantee that a position will be closed out at a specified price or that a loss limit will not be exceeded. Also, in the case of uncovered short index options, actual risk is likely to exceed any stated maximum target. Third, a computer program such as OP-EVAL3™ can be used to estimate results of a strategy. A range of both positive and negative outcomes should be tested so that a subjective evaluation of risk and reward can be made. Finally, if a strategy is chosen, it should be the strategy that is best suited for the trader's market forecast and tolerance for risk.

Section 4

Managing Positions

Fifteen

Alternatives for Managing a Profitable Position

INTRODUCTION

Two traders are talking.

Trader one says, "I've got these calls and I'm wondering what to do."

"Look," says trader two, "You can hold 'em or fold 'em or double up. That's all you can do. Take your pick."

Is trader two right? No!

As discussed throughout this book, one advantage of options is that they give traders many different ways to trade a market forecast. The same is true for open positions. Whether an open position is profitable or unprofitable when the market forecast changes, there are alternative courses of action to simply closing the position. Of course, only time will tell what the best course of action is, because success depends on the accuracy of the market forecast.

To remain consistent with the rest of this book, the examples presented in this chapter will not include transaction costs, margin requirements, or tax considerations. These considerations can affect the desirability of entering into options transactions and should be fully examined before engaging in any strategy involving options. Also, the market forecast in each example will be accepted as presented, and the basis of the forecast will not be debated. It is assumed that prior to taking any action, the trader has made an assessment of the risk involved and is willing to assume that risk. The risk of purchasing options is limited to the total amount paid, but the risk of selling uncovered options is unlimited in the case of calls and substantial in the case of puts.

MANAGING DEFINED

Managing a position means making a trade that changes the risk profile of a position without completely closing the position. Every strategy has a profit potential, a risk potential, and a break-even point. Any trading action will change all three.

BASIC MANAGING TECHNIQUES

Consider our first trader, Sally, who employed the basic "managing" technique of reducing her position. She bought two calls last week at 5 each, and on the subsequent rally, she sold one at 7. Sally's initial break-even point on the two-call position was 5. Having sold one at 7, however, the overall break-even point on her remaining call is 3 (not including transaction costs). This simple action reduced Sally's risk, but it also reduced her profit potential, as the profit potential of one call is less than that of two.

Of course, it also works the other way. Bill, our second trader, is unhappily wondering what to do with a losing position. A few days ago he purchased two puts at 8 each, and they are now trading at 6. If he sells one, he cannot break even on the entire trade until his remaining put rises to 10. This managing technique also reduces both the risk and the profit potential of Bill's position.

"Doubling up" is another managing strategy. Typically, it means adding to an unprofitable position by an amount equal to the original trade. The benefit of doubling up is a lower break-even point, but this also increases total risk. For example, if Bill purchased more puts at 6 each, then the break-even on his four-option position would be 7, one point lower than his original break-even point of 8, but his total risk would be increased.

"Adding to a profitable position" is a strategy that increases profit potential and maximum theoretical risk and the new break-even point is below the current price. If Sally, the trader above who purchased two calls at 5 each, for example, had purchased two more calls at 7 each instead of selling one, then the break-even price on her four-option position would be 6, one point below the current price of 7. But the maximum theoretical risk of Sally's four-option position would increase to 24 ($2 \times 5 + 2 \times 7$).

WHY MANAGE A POSITION?

In each of the basic examples presented above, the "managing" action changed the profit potential, the risk, and the break-even point. Why should a trader take such an action? There is only one reason: the market forecast has changed. A trader should reduce risk only if there is less confidence in the original forecast. And risk should be increased only if there is more confidence. Since traders, almost by definition, are constantly monitoring their positions and forecasts, being aware of as many managing techniques as possible increases opportunities to take advantage of a revised forecast.

Options give traders options! And managing techniques that increase alternatives are a feature unique to options.

ALTERNATIVES FOR MANAGING A PROFITABLE LONG CALL

The following four strategies involve additional risks beyond those of purchasing options and are suitable only for experienced traders who meet the highest risk requirements of many brokerage firms. Also, in the examples involving multiple-option positions, it is generally necessary to trade in a sufficient size, that is, a large enough quantity of options, to qualify for quantity discounts on transaction costs.

To illustrate the following managing alternatives, consider the situation of Don, who trades OEX options. These are American-style cash-settled options on the S&P 100 Index. Twelve days ago, the OEX Index was 850, it was 40 days to April expiration, and Don bought an OEX April 860 Call for 19¼. It is now 28 days to April expiration, the OEX has risen to 867, and Don's call is trading at 24. Don can, of course, sell his call for 24 and realize a profit of 4¾ before commissions, but he is reviewing the OEX April call prices (Table 15–1) and looking for alternatives.

Alternative 1: Create a Bull Call Spread

Figure 15–1 illustrates a managing technique in which a long call is converted into a bull call spread by selling a call with the same underlying and expiration but with a higher strike price. Don's 860 Call originally cost 19¼, broke even at expiration at an OEX Index level of 879¼, and had unlimited

Table 15–1 OEX Call Prices

Strike	Bid	Ask
April 860 Call	24	24½
April 870 Call	18¾	19¼
April 880 Call	14⅜	14¾
April 890 Call	10⅝	10⅞

Index level, 867; dividend yield, 1.6%; volatility, 20%; days to expiration, 28.

Figure 15–1 Creating a Call Spread

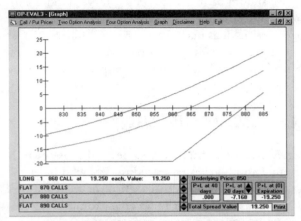

Step 1:

At 40 days to expiration with index at 850, purchase 1 860 call for 19¼

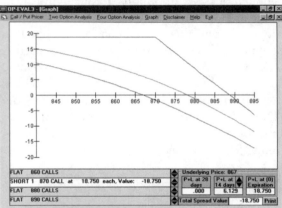

Step 2:

12 days later with index at 867, sell 1 870 call at 18¾

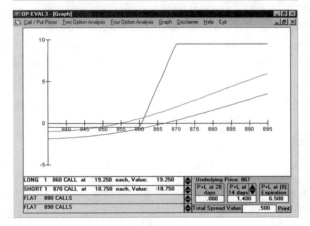

Result:

Long 860–870 call spread for ½

profit potential. The action of selling an OEX April 870 Call will change Don's profit potential, risk potential, and break-even point at expiration. If the April 870 Call is sold for 18¾, the bid price in Table 15–1, Don's net investment will be reduced from 19¼ to ½. Assuming no early assignment of the short call, his break-even point at expiration is lowered from 879¼ to 860½, and his profit potential is 9½.

In order to establish an OEX call spread, Don must be qualified by his brokerage firm to assume the risk of selling American-style index options, which must be established in a margin account and which are subject to the risk of early assignment. The theoretical risk of call spreads with American-style cash-settled options is greater than the net investment because notice of an early assignment is not received until the next morning, by which time the market may have moved significantly. If, however, Don is suitable for these risks and willing to assume them, he may determine that, given his forecast, the benefits of creating a call spread outweigh the risks.

Alternative 2: Creating a Butterfly Spread

A long-call butterfly spread consists of four options: a long call of a lower strike, two short calls of a middle strike, and a long call of a higher strike. The calls have the same expiration and the middle strike is halfway between the lower and higher strikes. A four-option position involves significant transaction costs; this makes it prohibitive for option traders who do not trade in sufficient quantity of contracts to qualify for commission discounts. It is therefore imperative to examine in advance the costs of this strategy. A butterfly spread involving American-style index options also entails the risk of early assignment on a short call, as described above.

By simultaneously selling two 870 Calls at 18¾ each and buying one 880 Call at 14¾, Don receives a net credit of 22¾, which is more than the initial 19¼ cost of his 860 Call, not including transaction costs. Don must also maintain the required margin deposit as long as the position is open. The expiration profit and loss diagram of Don's butterfly spread presented in Figure 15–2 assumes that neither of the short 870 Calls is assigned early. The maximum theoretical profit occurs if the OEX settles exactly at the middle strike at expiration and the spread remains in place without an early assignment. Since it is not very likely that the OEX will settle exactly at the middle strike at expiration, a trader who uses this strategy must be forecasting that the index will trade in a range near the middle strike of a butterfly spread.

Figure 15–2 Creating a Call Butterfly Spread

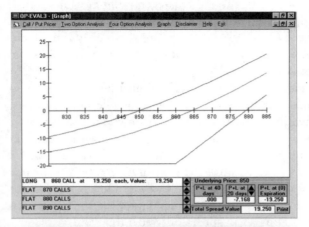

Step 1:
At 40 days to expiration with index at 850, purchase 1 860 call for 19¼

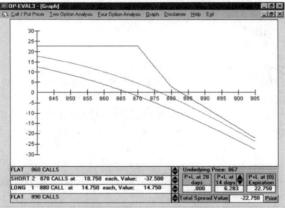

Step: 2
12 days later with index at 867, sell 2 870 calls at 18¾ ea., purchase 1 880 call for 14¾

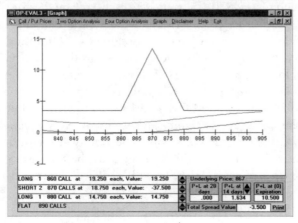

Result:
860–870–880 call butterfly for a 3½ credit

Alternative 3: Creating a Condor Spread

Condor spreads are sometimes referred to as "elongated butterflies." A long-call condor spread consists of four options with four different strikes: a long call of a lower strike, one short call of a higher strike, one short call of an even higher strike, and a long call of an even higher strike. The calls have the same expiration and the strikes are an equal distance apart. Like butterfly spreads, condor spreads involve significant transaction costs, making them prohibitive for option traders who do not qualify for commission discounts. The cost of this position must be examined before establishing it. A condor spread involving American-style index options also entails the risk of early assignment on a short call, as described above.

By selling one 870 Call at 18¾, selling one 880 Call at 14⅜, and buying one 890 Call at 10⅞, Don receives a net credit of 22¼, which is more than the initial 19¼ cost of his 860 Call, not including transaction costs. An expiration profit and loss diagram of Don's condor spread is presented in Figure 15–3 and assumes neither of the short calls is assigned early. The maximum theoretical profit occurs if the OEX settles between 870 and 880 at expiration and the spread remains in place without an early assignment.

Alternative 4: Creating a Christmas Tree Spread

A Christmas tree spread with calls consists of six options with three different strikes: a long call of a lower strike, three short calls of a higher strike, and two long calls of an even higher strike. The calls have the same expiration, and the distance between the lowest and second strike is twice the distance from the second strike to the highest strike. Christmas tree spreads involve significant transaction costs, making them prohibitive for option traders who do not qualify for commission discounts. The cost of this position must be examined before establishing it. A Christmas tree spread involving American-style index options also entails the risk of early assignment on a short call, as described above.

By selling three 880 Calls at 14⅜ each and buying two 890 Calls at 10⅞ each, Don receives a net credit of 21⅜, which is more than the initial 19¼ cost of his 860 Call, not including transaction costs. An expiration profit and loss diagram of Don's Christmas tree spread is presented in Figure 15–4 and assumes that none of the short calls is assigned early. The maximum theoretical profit occurs if the OEX settles exactly at 880 at expiration and the spread remains in place without an early assignment.

Figure 15–3 Creating a Call Condor Spread

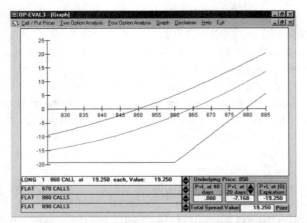

Step 1:
    At 40 days to expi-
    ration with index at
    850, purchase 1
    860 call for 19¼

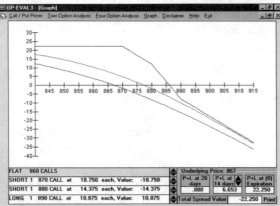

Step: 2
    12 days later with
    index at 867, sell 1
    870 call at 18¾ ea.,
    sell 1 880 call at
    14⅜, purchase 1
    890 call for 10⅞

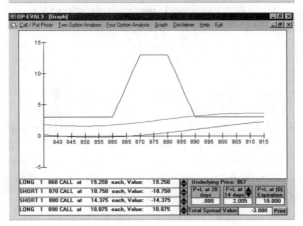

Result:
    860–870–880–890
    call condor for a 3
    credit

Figure 15–4 Creating a Call Christmas Tree Spread

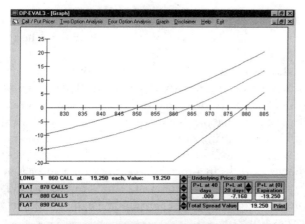

Step 1:

At 40 days to expiration with index at 850, purchase 1 860 call for 19¼

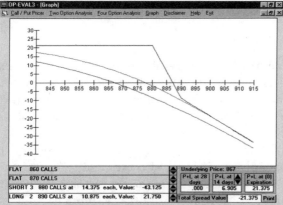

Step: 2

12 days later with index at 867, sell 3 880 calls at 14⅜ each, purchase 2 890 calls for 10⅞ ea.

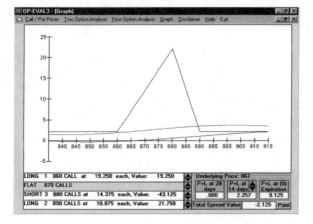

Result:

860–880–890 call Christmas tree for a 3⅜ credit

HOW TO CHOOSE?

Now that Don has four alternatives in addition to selling his call at 24 and realizing a profit in this example, what should he do? Which alternative is best?

The bad news is there is no "best" alternative! Table 15–2 compares Don's alternatives and concludes that each alternative offers different trade-offs, that is, different combinations of positives and negatives. Selling the 860 Call now at 24 and closing the position for a profit of 4¾ has the highest assured profit. The other alternatives offer the potential of a higher profit at the risk of either making less or incurring a net loss. Creating the bull call spread, for example, has the lowest profit potential of 9½ and the risk of incurring a loss of ½. Creating a butterfly spread, however, locks in a minimum profit of 3½ and has a potential maximum profit of 13½. These potentials, of course, do not include commissions. It is also important to understand conceptually why the differences exist, and this is discussed next.

ANALYZING THE TRADE-OFFS

Creating the bull call spread has the worst possible outcome and the lowest maximum profit potential. However, the bull call spread has the greatest chance of achieving its maximum profit potential, because that profit is achieved at any index level at or above 870 at expiration, assuming the short option is not assigned early.

In contrast, the butterfly spread has a higher maximum profit potential, but that profit is achieved at only one index level at expiration. For the condor spread, both the worst possible outcome and maximum profit potential fall between those of the bull call spread and the butterfly spread because the

Table 15–2 Don's Alternatives

Strategy	Amount Received	Worst Possible Outcome*	Best Possible Outcome*	Index Level Where Best Outcome Is Realized
Sell call	24	+4¾	+4¾	n.a.
Call spread	18¾	−½	+9½	≥870
Butterfly	22¾	+3½	+13½	870
Condor	22¼	+3	+13	870–880
Christmas tree	21⅜	+2⅛	+22⅛	880

*Assumes no early assignment of any short option.

condor's profit potential is achieved over a range between 870 and 880 rather than at a single point. There is a greater chance that the OEX will settle within a range than at one point.

The Christmas tree spread has the highest profit potential, but its worst possible outcome is second lowest. The Christmas tree spread's maximum profit potential is achieved at only one index point at expiration. The costs of opening and closing a six-option position are another negative aspect.

Options have given Don more alternatives, but his job has not been made any easier. He must still make a forecast and choose the strategy that he thinks is best suited to that forecast. And he accepts the risk that his forecast may not be realized.

OTHER CONSIDERATIONS

Traders who use the multiple-option strategies discussed in this chapter must treat them differently from outright purchases and sales of individual options. Butterfly, condor, and Christmas tree spreads are not "trading vehicles." These positions take time to work. Consequently, when a long option is converted into one of these positions, the trader must consciously decide to hold to expiration rather than trade.

One possible approach to these strategies is to remember that there is no requirement to do 100 percent of anything. When you are thinking of taking a profit on a long option position, consider selling half of the position and creating one of the spreads discussed above with the other half. In this way, you will realize a profit and have additional profit potential at the same time.

SUMMARY

Managing a position means taking an action that changes the profit potential, risk potential, and break-even point of a position without completely closing the position. Creating a bull call spread, a butterfly spread, a condor spread, or a Christmas tree spread is a viable alternative for experienced traders, but it involves increased transaction costs and they are not trading vehicles. Traders who use these strategies with American-style index options must be qualified by their brokerage firms to assume the risk of early assignment. There is no "best" alternative. Every strategy has its own set of trade-offs.

Sixteen

Alternatives for Managing an Unprofitable Position

INTRODUCTION

This chapter is for losers.

Not all trades will be profitable. That is the only guarantee that traders have! While closing a position and realizing a loss is the obvious alternative, traders should know about other alternatives and the circumstances in which they might be used. This chapter describes five strategies that change the risk profile of an unprofitable long option and, given a specific forecast, improve the chances for profit. The strategies discussed include three variations on rolling, the option repair strategy and creating a time spread. Each strategy will be introduced with a review of its mechanics first and an explanation of its advantages and disadvantages second. The chapter will conclude with a detailed example comparing the short-term price behavior of all five strategies.

The alternatives presented in this chapter can improve results only if the revised market forecast is accurate. The risk of some of the alternatives discussed in this chapter is greater than the risk of the original position. Also, as with previous chapters, commissions, other transaction costs, and margin requirements will not be included in the examples. These factors are important, however, because they can affect the desirability of any investment strategy, and they should be considered when analyzing real situations. The examples in this chapter deal only with calls, but the concepts apply equally to puts.

PRELUDE TO AN UNPROFITABLE SITUATION

Linda is a department manager of a garden supply wholesaler. She and two coworkers have an informal trading group. They discuss market trends and study charts of various market indexes. Two weeks ago, Linda purchased some DTX November 290 Calls for 7½. The DTX Index is based on the Dow Jones Transportation Average, and European-style options are traded at the CBOE. When Linda purchased her calls, the DTX Index was 285, it was 58 days to November expiration, interest rates were 5 percent, and the dividend yield was 2 percent. Using the OP-EVAL3™ program she ascertained that the price of 7½ for the November 290 Call indicated an implied volatility of approximately 20 percent.

Linda predicted that the DTX Index would rise 12 points in 2 weeks and that implied volatility would remain at 20 percent. Consequently, using OP-EVAL3™, she estimated that her November 290 Call would rise to 12¾. Unfortunately, the market did not behave as Linda expected.

The index hovered near 285 for a few days, but then declined to 270 over 5 trading days. Yesterday, however, the index rose five points to 275, its current level. It is now 44 days to November expiration, and even though implied volatility has risen to 22 percent, Linda's 290 Call is trading at 3⅜, down 4⅛ from her purchase price. While frustrated that her initial forecast was incorrect, Linda believes that today's action is the beginning of a further rise. She now predicts that the DTX Index will rise to 285 in 2 weeks, and she wants to maintain a bullish position in the hopes of at least recovering her losses and, hopefully, making a small profit.

ANALYSIS OF THE CURRENT POSITION

Linda's first step is to estimate how her November 290 Call will perform if her market forecast is realized. Linda enters the current market conditions in the Call/Put Pricer page of OP-EVAL3™, and determines the implied volatility level of her call (Table 16–1). Then she enters her forecast: an index level of 285 and 30 days to expiration, which is 14 days from today. With these inputs, OP-EVAL3™ estimates that Linda's November 290 Call will rise to 5¼.

While the price of 5¼ is higher than the current price of 3⅜, it is not equal to Linda's original purchase price of 7½. Given Linda's forecast that the

Table 16–1 Linda's Estimates of the Performance of Her 290 Call

	Current		Linda's Forecast
Inputs			
Index level	275	→	285
Strike price	290		
Dividend yield	2%		
Volatility	22%		
Interest rates	5%		
Days to expiration	44	→	30
Outputs			
290 Call price	3⅜	→	5¼

Table 16–2 Current Option Prices

Strike Price	November Calls (44 days to Expiration)	December Calls (72 days to Expiration)
280	6½	9⅛
285	4¾	7¼
290	3⅜	5⅝
295	2¼	4¼

Index level, 275.

index will rise to 285 in 2 weeks and implied volatility will remain constant, she is looking for a trade that will improve her prospects. Table 16–2 contains current prices of eight DTX Calls, which will be used to discuss some of Linda's alternatives.

ROLLING

The term *rolling* means simultaneously closing an existing option position and opening another option position with similar, but not identical, profit and risk characteristics. *Rolling a long call* means selling an existing long call in the market to close the position and opening a position by purchasing another call with a different strike and/or expiration. These actions change the break-even point and, ideally, improve the potential for profit. Successful results, of course, depend on the accuracy of the market forecast.

Rolling Down

In the context of a long call, *rolling down* means selling an existing call to close the position and, at the same time, opening a position by purchasing another call with the same expiration but a lower strike.

Linda could roll down to the November 280 Call by selling her November 290 Call for 3⅜ and simultaneously purchasing the November 280 Call for 6½. The cost, or net debit, of this action is 3⅛ plus commissions. This is the difference between the purchase price of the November 280 Call and the amount received for selling the November 290 Call.

After this rolling transaction is completed, Linda's position is simply long the November 280 Call. Her new break-even index level at expiration is calculated in two steps. First, the total cost of Linda's current position is calculated by adding her initial investment in the November 290 Call to the additional net investment in the rolling transaction. Second, this total cost is added to the strike price of her new call.

Linda's original investment in the November 290 Call was 7½ plus commissions, and the net cost of the roll, calculated above, is 3⅛ plus commissions. Consequently, her total cost is 10⅝ plus commissions. Adding 10⅝ to the new strike price, 280, yields the new expiration break-even price of 290⅝. This compares favorably to Linda's original expiration break-even index level of 297½, the original cost of her November 290 Call added to the strike price of 290.

The break-even point at expiration may not be relevant, however, because Linda's forecast is for a rise in the index in 2 weeks, not at expiration, which is in 6 weeks. Short-term price behavior will be analyzed after the mechanics of other alternatives are explained, but rolling down has one advantage and one disadvantage relative to maintaining the existing position. The advantage is that a call with a lower strike price has a higher delta than a call with a higher strike price and same expiration. The disadvantage is that an additional investment is required; consequently, the risk is higher. Table 16–3 summarizes Linda's position before and after the rolling-down transaction is completed.

Rolling Out

In the context of a long call, *rolling out* means selling an existing call to close the position and, at the same time, opening a position by purchasing another call with the same strike but a later expiration.

Linda could roll out to the December 290 Call by selling her November 290 Call for 3⅜ and simultaneously purchasing the December 290 Call for

Exhibit 16–3 Managing Linda's Call by Rolling Down

Initial Position: long 1 November 290 Call	7½
Original break-even index level at November expiration:	297½
Two-part action	
Sell 1 November 290 Call	3⅜
Buy 1 November 280 Call	6½
Net cost:	3⅛
Resulting position: long 1 November 280 Call	10⅝
New break-even index level at November expiration:	290⅝
Advantages: lower break-even at expiration, higher delta	
Disadvantages: Higher risk; additional investment required	

5⅝. The cost, or net debit, of this action is 2¼ plus commissions, the difference between the purchase price of the December 290 Call and the selling price of the November 290 Call.

After this rolling action is completed, Linda's position is simply long the December 290 Call. Her new break-even index level at expiration is calculated by adding the net cost of the roll to her original break-even.

As explained above, the original break-even at expiration of Linda's November 290 Call was an index level of 297½. Adding the net cost of 2¼ for rolling out to the December 290 Call results in a new break-even index level of 299¾. While 299¾ is above Linda's original break-even of 297½, the December 290 Call has an additional 28 days until its expiration. This means more time for Linda's forecast to materialize. Of course, this additional time may not be relevant, given Linda's forecast for a rise in the index in 2 weeks. Nevertheless, rolling out has two advantages and one disadvantage relative to maintaining the existing position. The first advantage is more time, and the second is a higher delta. The disadvantage is the increased cost—and, therefore, the increased risk. Table 16–4 summarizes Linda's position before and after the rolling-out transaction is completed.

Rolling Down and Out

In the context of a long call, *rolling down and out* means selling an existing call to close the position and, at the same time, opening a position by purchasing another call with a lower strike price and a later expiration.

Linda could roll down and out to the December 280 Call by selling her November 290 Call for 3⅜ and simultaneously purchasing the December 280 Call for 9⅛. The cost, or net debit, of this action is 5¾ plus commissions,

Table 16–4 Managing Linda's Call by Rolling Out

Initial position: long 1 November 290 Call	7½
Original break-even index level at November expiration:	297½
Two-part action	
Sell 1 November 290 Call	3⅜
Buy 1 December 290 Call	5⅝
Net cost:	2¼
Resulting Position: long 1 December 290 Call	9¾
New break-even index level at December expiration:	299¾
Advantages: Additional time, higher delta	
Disadvantages: Higher risk; additional investment required	

the difference between the purchase price of the December 280 Call and the selling price of the November 290 Call.

After this rolling transaction is completed, Linda's position is simply long the December 280 Call. Her new break-even index level at expiration is calculated by adding her total investment to the new strike price.

Linda's original investment in the November 290 Call was 7½ plus commissions, and the net cost of rolling down and out in this example is 5¾ plus commissions. Consequently, her total investment in the December 280 Call is 13¼ plus commissions. Adding 13¼ to the strike price of 280 yields the new break-even index level at expiration of 293¼.

Rolling down and out has three advantages and one disadvantage relative to maintaining the original position. The advantages are a lower break-even index level at expiration, additional time, and a higher delta. The disadvantage is the higher cost—and, therefore, the higher risk. Note also that the cost of this rolling alternative is higher than the previous two alternatives. Table 16–5 summarizes Linda's position before and after rolling down and out is completed.

THE OPTION REPAIR STRATEGY

While the rolling strategies discussed above offer advantages, such as a lower break-even point, more time, and a higher delta, the disadvantage of increased investment is a big hurdle for many traders who live by the well-known rule, "never add to a losing position." Is it possible to get the best of both worlds—no additional cost and a lower break-even price? That is the goal of the option repair strategy!

Table 16–5 Managing Linda's Call by Rolling Down and Out

Initial position: long 1 November 290 Call	7½
Original break-even index level at November expiration:	297½
Two-part action	
Sell 1 November 290 Call	3⅜
Buy 1 December 280 Call	9⅛
Net cost:	5¾
Resulting position: long 1 December 280 Call	13¼
New break-even index level at December expiration:	293¼
Advantages: lower break-even, higher delta, more time	
Disadvantages: higher risk; additional investment required	

The concept of the option repair strategy is that an unprofitable long call is rolled down into a bull call spread. This is accomplished by three simultaneous actions. First, the existing long call is sold in the market to close the position. Second, a new call with the same strike price and same expiration is sold to open a short position. Third, a new call with the same expiration but with a lower strike is purchased to open a position. The result is a bull call spread consisting of (1) a long call with the same expiration but a lower strike than the original call and (2) a short call with the same expiration and same strike as the original call.

Linda could implement the option repair strategy by making the following three trades simultaneously:

1. She sells her November 290 Call at $3\frac{3}{8}$ to close the position.
2. She sells a new November 290 Call at $3\frac{3}{8}$ to open a new short position.
3. She purchases a new November 280 Call for $6\frac{1}{2}$ to open a new long position.

Assuming these prices, the three trades are made for a net credit of $\frac{1}{4}$, not including commissions. $6\frac{1}{2}$ is paid for the new long 280 Call, $3\frac{3}{8}$ is received for selling the existing long 290 Call, and $3\frac{3}{8}$ is received for selling the new short 290 Call. Hence, $6\frac{1}{2}$ minus $3\frac{3}{8}$ minus $3\frac{3}{8}$ equals $-\frac{1}{4}$, or $\frac{1}{4}$ net credit.

Linda's new break-even index level at expiration and maximum profit potential are calculated in three steps. First, Linda's net investment in the bull call spread is calculated by subtracting the credit received for the three-part "repair" described above from her initial investment. Second, this net investment is added to the lower strike of the bull call spread. The result is Linda's new break-even index level at expiration. Third, the maximum profit potential is calculated by subtracting the net cost of the bull call spread from the difference between the strike prices of the two calls that create the spread.

Subtracting the $\frac{1}{4}$ credit received from Linda's original investment of $7\frac{1}{2}$ in the November 290 Call equals her net investment of $7\frac{1}{4}$. Adding this to the lower strike of 280 equals the new break-even index level at expiration of $287\frac{1}{4}$. Note that the new break-even point for the repair strategy is substantially below the new break-even points of the rolling strategies described above.

The maximum profit potential of Linda's bull call spread, in this case, is the difference between the strikes of 280 and 290 and Linda's net investment of $7\frac{1}{4}$ ($10 - 7\frac{1}{4} = 2\frac{3}{4}$). Table 16–6 shows the profit and loss at November expiration of the components of the option repair strategy and of the combined strategy.

Table 16–6 Linda's Option Repair Strategy at Expiration

Stock Price at November Expiration	Sell (to Close) 1 November 290 Call @ 3⅜	Sell (to Open) 1 November 290 Call @ 3⅜	Buy (to Open) 1 November 280 Call @ 6½	Combined Position: November 280–290 Call Spread
291	−4⅛	+2⅜	+4½	+2¾
290	−4⅛	+3⅜	+3½	+2¾
289	−4⅛	+3⅜	+2½	+1¾
288	−4⅛	+3⅜	+1½	+ ¾
287	−4⅛	+3⅜	+ ½	− ¼
286	−4⅛	+3⅜	− ½	−1¼
285	−4⅛	+3⅜	−1½	−2¼
284	−4⅛	+3⅜	−2½	−3¼
283	−4⅛	+3⅜	−3½	−4¼
282	−4⅛	+3⅜	−4½	−5¼
281	−4⅛	+3⅜	−5½	−6¼
280	−4⅛	+3⅜	−6½	−7¼
279	−4⅛	+3⅜	−6½	−7¼

The option repair strategy has two advantages and one disadvantage relative to maintaining the original position. The cost is close to zero, not including commissions, and the break-even index level at expiration is lower than the original position or than that of the other rolling strategies. But profit potential is limited; in contrast, the rolling alternatives had unlimited profit potential. The conclusion is that the option repair strategy is not "better" than other alternatives; it simply offers a different set of trade-offs. Table 16–7 summarizes Linda's position before and after the repair strategy is completed. Short-term price behavior will be analyzed after the mechanics of creating a time spread are explained.

CREATING A TIME SPREAD

A variation of both the rolling and repairing strategies has the goal of adding time at a lower cost than simply rolling out. In this strategy, the unprofitable long call is rolled out into a long-call time spread. This is accomplished by three simultaneous actions:

1. Selling the existing long call to close the position
2. Selling a new call with the same strike price and expiration to open a new short position

Table 16–7 Managing Linda's Call with the Option Repair Strategy

Initial position: long 1 November 290 Call	7½
Original break-even index level at November expiration:	297½
Three-part action	
Sell 1 November 290 Call (to close)	3⅜
Sell 1 November 290 Call (to open)	3⅜
Buy 1 November 280 Call (to open)	6½
Net credit:	¼
Resulting position	
Long 1 November 280 Call *and*	
Short 1 November 290 Call	
Net cost	7¼
New break-even index level at November expiration:	287¼
Advantages: lower break-even, little or no additional cost	
Disadvantages: limited profit potential	

   3. Purchasing a new call with the same strike price but with a later expiration to open a new long position

The result is a long-call time spread consisting of (1) a long call with the same strike but a later expiration than the original call and (2) a short call with the same strike and expiration as the original call.

Linda can roll into a time spread by making the following three trades simultaneously:

   1. She sells her November 290 Call at 3⅜ to close the position.

   2. She sells a new November 290 Call at 3⅜ to open a new short position.

   3. She purchases a new December 290 Call for 5⅝ to open a new long position.

Assuming these prices, the three trades are made for a net credit of 1⅛, not including commissions: 5⅝ is paid for the new long December 290 Call, 3⅜ is received for selling the existing long November 290 Call, and 3⅜ is received for selling the new short November 290 Call. Hence, 5⅝ minus 3⅜ minus 3⅜ equals −1⅛, or 1⅛ net credit.

   Like the other managing alternatives discussed above, the creation of a time spread has advantages and disadvantages. One advantage is that a credit is received. This means that risk is reduced if European-style options are involved. A potential advantage is an increase in time if the short option expires or is closed out at a near-zero price. If American-style options are involved, or if the short option is closed out at a price greater than the credit received for the roll, then risk is not reduced. The disadvantage is the nature of time spreads—specifically, the market forecast must be very accurate with regard to both time and price of the underlying. If the market rises too far or too fast or both, then the time spread may result in a loss, whereas an outright long call or bull call spread would show a profit. Table 16–8 summarizes Linda's position before and after rolling out to a long call time spread is completed.

SHORT-TERM PRICE PERFORMANCE

Now that the mechanics and advantages and disadvantages of each managing alternative have been discussed, the next step is to estimate how each strategy will perform if Linda's forecast is realized. The Call/Put Pricer page in OP-EVAL3™ is used to estimate the performance of one-option positions and to calculate deltas, gammas, vegas, and thetas. The Two Option Analysis page is used to estimate the performance of two-option positions. After each alternative is analyzed using Linda's forecast, the results of different forecasts will be examined.

Table 16–8 Managing Linda's Call by Creating a Time Spread

Initial position: long 1 November 290 Call	7½
Original break-even index level at November expiration:	297½
Three-part action	
Sell 1 November 290 Call (to close)	3⅜
Sell 1 November 290 Call (to open)	3⅜
Buy 1 December 290 Call (to open)	5⅝
Net credit:	1⅛
Resulting position:	
Short 1 November 290 Call *and*	
Long 1 December 290 Call	
Net cost	6⅜
New break-even index level at expiration: not applicable to time spreads	
Advantages: lowers cost, potentially adds time if near-term option expires	
Disadvantages: risk of early assignment if American-style options are involved; also, rise in index above strike reduces value of long-call time spread significantly	

A First Forecast

Table 16–9 is an expanded version of Table 16–1. Column 1 shows the initial inputs and the current prices of the individual options and spread positions discussed above, the November and December 280 and 290 Calls, the November 280–290 Bull Call spread, and the long November–December 290 Call time spread. Column 2 shows the estimated prices under the assumptions of Linda's forecast, an index level of 285 in 3 weeks, which is 30 days to November expiration and 58 days to December expiration. Column 3 shows the net or total investment in each managing alternative, and column 4 shows the profit or loss if Linda's forecast is realized. The results in column 4 are the difference between the ending price in column 2 and the net or total investment in column 3.

Assuming Linda's current forecast materializes, Table 16–9 shows that either rolling down to the November 280 Call or rolling down and out to the December 280 Call have the best results, breaking even or nearly breaking even, not including commissions. All other alternatives result in a loss. Consequently, if Linda is confident of her forecast and willing to invest and risk an additional 3⅛, not including commissions, then she would roll down to the November 280 Call. Note that the difference in results of ⅜ between

Table 16–9 Forecast 1: Estimates of Performance

	Col. 1: Current Data		Col. 2: Linda's Forecast	Col. 3: Total/Net Cost	Col. 4: Estimated Profit/Loss
Inputs					
Index level	275	→	285		
Strike price	280/290				
Dividend yield	2%				
Volatility	22%				
Interest rates	5%				
Days to expiration	44/72	→	30/58		
Outputs					
November 280 Call price	6½	→	10¼	10⅝	–⅜
November 290 Call price	3⅜	→	5¼	7½	–2¼
December 280 Call price	9⅛	→	13¼	13¼	0
December 290 Call price	5⅝	→	8¼	9¾	–1½
November 280–290 Call spread	3⅛	→	5	7¼	–2¼
November–December 290 time spread	2¼	→	3	6⅜	–3⅜

the November 280 Call and December 280 Call alternatives is deemed minor in comparison to the difference in cost of 2⅝. That is why rolling down to the November 280 Call is chosen.

Many newcomers to options ask if this result could have been anticipated without going to the trouble of creating Table 16–9. Unfortunately, the answer is no. An examination of Table 16–10, which contains the deltas, gammas, vegas, and thetas of the new positions after the managing transactions are completed, reveals that no strategy has the "best" Greeks for Linda's forecast. The December 280 Call has the highest delta, but the November 280 Call has the highest gamma, and its delta is only slightly lower than the delta of the December 280 Call. Also, even though the spreading alternatives have much lower deltas, they have near-zero thetas, so a trader would wonder how that combination would perform. As the market moves and time passes, the Greeks change, so the information in Table 16–10 is of limited value to the trader who is forecasting a several-point change in the index over several days to several weeks.

A Second Forecast

Since Linda's original forecast, which motivated her to purchase the November 290 Call, was inaccurate, she needs to test more than one scenario to estimate how the different strategies will perform if the market behaves contrary to her latest forecast. Suppose, for example, she is correct about the index rising from 275 to 285, but the move takes 4 weeks instead of 2 weeks as she predicts. Table 16–11 estimates the results in this scenario. Note that in column 2 the days to expiration are 16 and 44 instead of 30 and 58, as in

Table 16–10 Position Greeks of Positions Resulting from Linda's Managing Alternatives

	Long Nov. 280 Call	Long Nov. 290 Call	Long Dec. 280 Call	Long Dec. 290 Call	November 280-290 Call Spd.	Nov.-Dec. 290 Time Spread
Price	6½	3⅜	9⅛	5⅝	3⅛	2¼
Delta	+0.439	+0.272	+0.470	+0.333	+0.167	+0.061
Gamma	+0.019	+0.016	+0.015	+0.014	+0.003	−0.002
Vega	+0.376	+0.319	+0.484	+0.445	+0.057	+0.126
Theta	−0.741	−0.605	−0.549	−0.531	−0.036	+0.074

Index level, 275; dividend yield, 2%; volatility, 22%; interest rates, 5%; days to expiration, 44/72.

Table 16–11 Forecast 2: Estimate of Performance

	Col. 1: Current Data		Col. 2: Linda's Forecast	Col. 3: Total/Net Cost	Col. 4: Estimated Profit/Loss
Inputs					
Index level	275	→	285		
Strike price	280/290				
Dividend yield	2%				
Volatility	22%				
Interest rates	5%				
Days to expiration	44/72	→	16/44		
Outputs					
November 280 Call price	6½	→	8¼	10⅝	−2⅜
November 290 Call price	3⅜	→	3¼	7½	−4¼
December 280 Call price	9⅛	→	11⅞	13¼	−1⅜
December 290 Call price	5⅝	→	6⅞	9¾	−2⅞
November 280-290					
Call spread	3⅛	→	3⅝	7¼	−3⅝
November–December 290					
time spread	3⅜	→	3⅝	6⅜	−2¾

Table 16–9. This indicates that 2 additional weeks have passed so that it is now 16 days to November expiration and 44 days to December expiration. This difference in time changes which strategy performs best.

Table 16–11 shows that time is crucial to Linda's forecast. With the exception of the time spread, all of the other alternatives perform worse than in the 2-week time frame illustrated in Table 16–9. Instead of breaking even or nearly breaking even, rolling down to the November 280 Call results in a loss of 2⅜, not including commissions, and rolling down and out to the December 280 Call results in a loss of 1⅜. The message of Tables 16–9 and 16–11 is that Linda must think hard about the time element of her forecast. If an index level of 285 is her target, then the rise to that level had better occur in 2 weeks if she chooses to roll down to the November 280 Call. Otherwise, she should roll down and out to the December 280 Call.

A Third Forecast

Since an analysis of a second forecast revealed that the time element is so crucial, Linda should also explore the impact of a different index level in addition to a different time. What, Linda might ask, will the results be if the index rises

Table 16–12 Forecast 3: Estimate of Performance

	Col. 1: Current Data		Col. 2: Linda's Forecast	Col. 3: Total/Net Cost	Col. 4: Estimated Profit/Loss
Inputs					
Index level	275	→	290		
Strike price	280/290				
Dividend yield	2%				
Volatility	22%				
Interest rates	5%				
Days to expiration	44/72	→	16/44		
Outputs					
November 280 Call price	6½	→	12	10⅝	+1⅜
November 290 Call price	3⅜	→	5½	7½	−2
December 280 Call price	9⅛	→	15¼	13¼	+2
December 290 Call price	5⅝	→	9⅜	9¾	−⅜
November 280–290 Call spread	3⅛	→	6½	7¼	−¾
November–December 290 time spread	3⅜	→	3⅞	6⅜	−2½

to 290 in 4 weeks instead of 285? Table 16–12 answers this question. Assuming an index level of 290 at 16 days to November expiration and 44 days to December expiration, the managing alternative with the best absolute results is rolling down and out to the December 280 Call. According to Table 16–12, this strategy is estimated to yield a profit of 2, not including commissions.

A more difficult question to answer, however, is which strategy has the best risk-reward ratio? In order to achieve the profit of 2 from rolling down and out to the December 280 Call, an additional investment of 5¾ is required. The repair strategy, in contrast, nearly gets Linda back to break even with a loss of only ¾ but it requires no additional investment.

Which alternative has the best risk-reward ratio? This is a question that only Linda can answer based on her confidence in her forecast and her willingness to assume additional risk or her desire to decrease risk. The process of analyzing several scenarios, however, helps Linda in two ways. First, it gives her realistic expectations about results. Second, it clearly lays out her choices. After this analysis, Linda will have much more information which, hopefully, will improve her chances for a successful outcome depending on the accuracy of her forecast.

WHAT ABOUT IMPLIED VOLATILITY?

Each of the scenarios Linda examined assumed that implied volatility remained constant. In the real world, of course, implied volatility can change. The process of analyzing the impact of a change in implied volatility is the same as analyzing the impact of changes in index level and time to expiration. An exhibit such as Table 16–9 is created with the new assumptions, and the results are compared to the results of other scenarios. Yes, the process is time-consuming, and, yes, the possibilities are, theoretically, unlimited. However, with practice, only a few scenarios need to be analyzed. Traders with experience will make a three-part forecast that includes a forecast for change in index level, change in time to expiration, and change in the level of implied volatility. After testing one scenario, the deltas, gammas, vegas, and thetas of the alternatives will make a rough estimate of slight changes in the forecast possible. Also, with practice, the amount of time required to estimate the results of alternative strategies will decrease.

SUMMARY

When the market does not behave as forecast and a position has an unrealized loss, traders should be aware of alternatives other than closing the position and realizing the loss. Five alternatives are rolling down, rolling out, rolling down and out, the repair strategy (rolling down into a bull call spread), and rolling out into a long time spread. Each alternative has advantages and disadvantages, and successful results depend on the accuracy of the market forecast.

It is possible to estimate the short-term results of alternatives using OP-EVAL3™. Different forecasts for index level, time to expiration, and level of implied volatility will affect which alternative has the best absolute results if the forecast is realized. The decision to pick one alternative, however, should be based on an assessment of the risk-reward ratio and not on the best absolute results. Unfortunately, assessing risk-reward ratios is a subjective process that can only be made by an individual trader based on confidence in the forecast and a willingness to increase risk or a desire to decrease risk. With practice, the time required to analyze several managing alternatives will decrease.

Section 5

The Psychology of Trading

Seventeen

Thinking like a Trader

INTRODUCTION

I n the opening line of *The Road Less Traveled,* M. Scott Peck observes, "Life is difficult." The same can be said about trading.

Mastering the mechanics of options, the range of strategies, the nuances of price behavior, and the alternatives for managing positions is difficult enough. But adjusting one's thinking is, perhaps, the greatest challenge. Trading involves a unique combination of hard work, patience, and discipline—the willingness to be guided by objectivity instead of emotion.

No discussion of trading psychology can purport to answer all questions, or even to raise all issues. Yet it is reasonable to suggest guidelines for traders so they can examine their trading style and the way they *think* about trading. Successful traders make this an ongoing habit, because their goal is to improve results. More importantly, they enjoy the process.

This chapter will define trading, list the attributes of good traders, and identify the skills they must learn. Key aspects of trading psychology will be covered, including the concept of "percentage thinking," the need to treat trading like a business, and the importance of developing a dispassionate attitude about money. This chapter also presents a tool, the trading journal, which both beginning and experienced traders can use to foster a healthy psychology while evaluating their trades on a regular basis. Finally, an example of how a beginning trader might get started is presented.

How to forecast the market and select trading strategies are topics beyond the scope of this book. It is assumed that these subjects have already been studied, and that readers either hope to improve their trading or want helpful hints to get started.

WHAT MAKES A TRADER

Trading Defined

Trading is an endeavor involving a series of short-term purchase and sale transactions that are intended to profit from price changes. Essentially, *trade* means trade, buy and sell, or sell and buy. Trade does *not* mean buy and hold! While this concept may seems obvious, it is too often overlooked. No trading technique can be expected to make a profit on every trade. Traders, therefore, must believe that their method of trade selection will generate net profits after a *series* of trades, and they must trade in a manner consistent with this belief.

As the reader may recall from the introduction, trading is different than investing. First, the typical time period of a "trade" is significantly shorter than that of an "investment." Second, trading capital is managed differently than investment capital: traders typically use leverage and investors typically do not. Third, traders employ bullish, bearish, and neutral strategies, while investors use only bullish and neutral ones. Fourth, traders do not measure results against the overall market as investors tend to do. Fifth, the motivation for establishing positions is typically different: traders tend to rely more on technical analysis, while investors emphasize fundamental analysis.

Traders employ two types of trading: speculation and hedging. Speculative traders have no long-term interest in the underlying instrument on which options are traded. In the case of index options, for example, speculative traders do not own a portfolio of stocks that match the index. Conversely, hedging traders, or hedgers, do have an interest in the underlying instrument. The goal of hedging is either to lower the cost and risk of the underlying instrument or to increase the selling price. With index options, hedgers actually own or want to own a portfolio of stocks that will behave similarly to the index on which options are being traded.

Attributes of Good Traders

From the experience of the author, good traders have three key attributes: an entrepreneurial desire to succeed, a love for the markets they trade, and a dispassionate attitude about money.

Trading is not a team sport! There is not enough time for trading decisions to be made by committee, so traders must act alone. While much has been written on "the entrepreneur," with regard to trading, the key elements are independence, a willingness to risk one's own assets in the hopes of making a profit, and a desire to trade. This love for the market can only come from within, because no outside force such as a boss can mandate that the job of trading be done. There is only an individual's internal drive to look for trading opportunities. It must be fun to develop a trading system, to watch prices fluctuate, and to initiate and close positions. If the trader loves the process itself, then profitable trades will offer encouragement and losing trades will be learning experiences. The desire to "figure out the market" will provide sufficient motivation to get better at what many people find to be a frustrating challenge.

Dispassionate Attitude about Money

Since the purpose of trading is making money, some might wonder why traders must develop a dispassionate attitude about it. In a 1995 appearance on *Wall Street Week,* Steven Jobs, cofounder of Apple Computers, was asked what advice he would give entrepreneurs. He replied, "Follow your passion. That is the only hope of making a lot of money." Think about other people whose names have become synonymous with great financial success. Henry Ford was an engineer interested in making cars. Michael Jordan loves basketball. Bill Gates is obsessed with computers. Only their passion could fuel the creativity and drive necessary to overcome the obstacles inherent in the entrepreneur's path. Money was a byproduct of that passion—not the focus of it. And as long as they love what they're doing, entrepreneurs can still have fun and a sense of personal satisfaction even if they don't become millionaires. In either case, the entrepreneurs win!

This means that those who are contemplating trading must ask themselves, "Do I like trading enough? Do I like following the market enough? Am I willing to suffer the humiliations I undoubtedly will experience? Am I willing to stick it out? Is trading that much fun?" These are personal questions that can only be answered by each individual. So, look within. Think about how much you really enjoy trading. Go through the process of developing a market forecast, evaluating some alternatives, selecting a strategy, opening a position, living with its fluctuations, and closing it. Pay attention to yourself, your behavior, and your feelings. Are you excited? Are you concentrating? Is it fun? Or is it a chore?

We do what we love, and we do what we love because of the process, not because of the money. Of course, if we do not make money, we will not last long. Hence the importance of skill.

Learning the Skills to Trade

Being a "born trader" is a misconception—trading skills *can* be learned. There are three key skills that traders can acquire.

1. *The ability to act on an instinct.* Trading decisions cannot be brooded over for days, or even hours. Regardless of how specific a trading system is, conditions are never perfect. A trader must therefore develop an instinct for when to "pull the trigger"—to initiate a trade despite imperfect conditions.

2. *The ability to look forward without being unduly influenced by the past.* Looking forward is essential because continued success is not possible if a trader is psychologically paralyzed by the results of the last trade. Some trades will result in losses. Others will be closed at a fraction of their potential profit. These are frustrating experiences, but they are inevitable. A trader must look forward to the next trading opportunity objectively, regardless of the outcome of the last trade.

3. *The ability to follow a strict trading discipline.* Discipline depends on its context. *Trading discipline* means the willingness to be guided by objectivity rather than emotion. In order for a trading technique to succeed, trades must be initiated in accordance with the tenets of an individual's trading system. Positions must be closed without regard to profit or loss either when a signal to close a profitable trade is received or when it is clear that a market forecast is wrong. Otherwise, emotion will rule the day, yanking the hapless trader back and forth with every hiccup of market action.

Assuming an individual has the entrepreneurial desire to trade, these three skills—acting on instinct, looking forward, and trading with discipline—can be learned by engaging in the process. Make some trades! In the beginning, trade small, one or two options at a time. Concentrate on initiating and closing trades; do not be overly concerned with profit. Every new venture requires an investment. In the business of trading, this means making a series of losing trades.

An alternative way of testing one's abilities is *paper trading.* In paper trading, fictitious trades are recorded at estimated actual prices. Its primary purpose is to allow a trader to practice-test a trading technique without actually risking capital. Paper trading also helps new traders practice initiating trades. An estimate of commissions should be included in order to make paper trading as realistic as possible.

Although paper trading sounds good in theory, it is a valuable exercise only if the prices recorded are "totally honest," that is, recorded at the time a decision is made and not at some later time when known market action can influence what is recorded. There are numerous stories of how traders succeeded on paper but lost money in real trading! How disciplined a trader is in recording paper trades will be the first indication of how disciplined that trader will be in real trading.

Regardless of whether real trades or paper trades are made, a simple four-step technique will help beginners learn the skills of trading. First, set parameters for each trade, including a realistic profit target, a stop-loss point, and a maximum time limit to close out the position. Second, initiate a trade when, in your judgment, market conditions are consistent with your trading technique. Third, be it a winner or a loser, close the position when one of the parameters is met. Fourth, begin the process again by looking for the next trading opportunity.

By initiating a trade when you think conditions are right, you are practicing the skill of acting on instinct. By closing a position when one of the parameters is met, you are practicing the skill of trading with discipline. And by focusing on the next trading opportunity, you are practicing the skill of looking forward without being unduly influenced by the past.

If your trading technique is a good one, and if you are implementing it properly, you have a good chance of realizing net profits after a series of trades. But there are no guaranties in the business of trading. Profits will not occur on every trade; nor will they occur fast enough to satisfy impatient beginners. Yet, with continued work, results are likely to improve.

HEALTHY TRADING PSYCHOLOGY

Difficult to Learn

To be sure, trading is difficult to learn and even more difficult to implement. That's because it involves a style and pace of thinking that is different from almost any other activity. As a result, traders must consciously work at developing a healthy trading psychology that will involve unlearning old, unproductive mental habits and replacing them with new ones. For example, the maxim, "If it ain't broke, don't fix it," does not apply to trading. Short-term trends do not last forever, and a profitable trade that is not monitored and closed at a profit can rapidly become a losing trade. Thus, a profitable trade should keep a trader just as occupied as a losing trade, because the time will come in either case to close that trade and be done with it. A more apt maxim for trading is, "If a position ain't broke, watch it—and be prepared to close it."

Here is another key distinction between trading and other activities. In the course of most human events, it is generally impossible for anyone to look back and see the results of an alternative course of action. When a business manager hires someone, for example, there is no way to know whether other candidates would have been better or worse. Even if the person hired does a good job, another person might have done a spectacular job. But this can never be known.

A trader, however, can know with 100 percent certainty what "should" have been done. Checking current prices is all that is required to see how a different strategy would have performed. The bane of trading is that there will always be a strategy with more profitable results, and rarely, if ever, will a trader buy at the lowest possible price or sell at the highest. Perfect hindsight is a reality of trading. Adapting to this reality is both difficult and essential. Otherwise, a trader will waste valuable mental energy brooding over "would have, should have, could have."

Percentage Thinking

Traders must accept the idea that they will have a percentage of profitable trades and a percentage of losing trades. While this concept seems obvious, "percentage thinking" and its implications are often overlooked by novice traders.

Accepting this notion psychologically means that losses can be taken in stride and losing positions can be closed objectively when the forecast changes or when a stop-loss point is reached. Even though every trade is entered with the same confidence, experienced traders base trading decisions on current market conditions and their forecasts—not on the results of the last trade.

Traders who have not fully adapted to the psychology of percentage thinking exhibit different behavior. They tend to initiate new positions too soon after profitable trades and wait too long after losing trades. They also tend to keep a losing position open in the hopes that "it will come back" and become profitable. It is as if they are saying, "I wasn't wrong. I was just early." Certainly the market does return at times. But at other times losses continue to grow, and the results can be devastating.

Over time, the results that count are the net results of all trades. Traders must therefore learn to accept small losses and look forward to the next trading opportunity. For beginners this means two things. First, set a stop-loss point when a trade is initiated. Second, objectively close the position and realize a loss if that point is reached. If it is too difficult to accept a loss and move on, then trading may not be for you.

Building Confidence

It is much easier to talk bravely about "win some, lose some" than it is to actually handle one's emotions after making a series of trades in which some are winners and some are losers. It is reasonable, therefore, for beginners to ask how they can build the confidence necessary to continue trading after experiencing losses. Confidence in trading frequently depends on three things: knowledge about past market behavior, trading "small," and a reasoned approach to selecting trades.

Knowledge about the history of market movements builds a trader's confidence, because in financial markets history tends to repeat itself. If one has some perspective on past patterns of price action—and if one has an idea of how bad things can get when a forecasting technique gives an incorrect signal—then it is easier to ride out tough times. It is possible to get such a perspective by studying the market, learning its past, and remembering price behavior that is observed. Over time much will be learned about "typical events" and "rare events." For example, markets generally do not move straight up or straight down. Rather they make an initial move in one direction, then "retrace" part of that move before forging ahead again in the original direction. Sometimes, of course, what is predicted to be a retracement turns out to be a permanent change in direction!

Tensions can run high during such market activity. Most traders with large positions will naturally experience a higher degree of anxiety than those who are trading small. A trader who closes a position and realizes a small loss from such market behavior will learn that the experience is not as disastrous as one might imagine. Moreover, that trader will remain relatively relaxed, a mental condition that supports objective thinking. Beginning traders especially should take this point to heart, because realizing too big a loss is very discouraging.

A systematic approach to trading is the third key element that builds confidence. Such an approach means that there are specific reasons, rather than just "hunches," for making trades. A system reinforces a trader's belief that decisions will be more right (that is, profitable) than wrong (that is, losing). Consequently, developing a logical technique for forecasting the market is essential.

Develop a Market-Forecasting Technique

A successful outcome that is the result of an impulsive act is usually described as luck. The typical person who throws a beanbag at a bottle at the county fair and walks away with the stuffed animal is lucky indeed. However, a successful outcome that is the result of hard work, clear thinking, and decisiveness is described as a job well done. When Annie Oakley shot 30 consecutive bull's-eyes in 1887 to beat the British national marksman 30 to 29, that was not luck!

Traders who study the market, read books on market forecasting, track option implied volatility, keep their own charts, and stay current with market sentiment know the difference between a lucky trade and a reasoned trade. While reasoned trades can still result in losses, a series of reasoned trades should have a better chance of showing a net profit than a series of lucky trades. This is why traders must develop market-forecasting techniques that they believe will make more correct forecasts than incorrect ones.

Market-forecasting techniques can be based on any number of theories about market price action. Some traders base decisions on trending price action; others go against a trend based on a belief in range-trading price action. Some forecasting techniques include the volume of trading as a factor in making predictions. Price action in other indexes is another potential factor. Technical analysis tends to be popular among short-term traders, because the timing and occurrence of technical indicators creates opportunities more frequently than fundamental indicators. Some short-term traders also believe that technical indicators are significant, because they believe that the market anticipates fundamental news.

Every business has subjective and objective elements, and trading is no exception. Subjective elements are sometimes referred to as the art of a business. Objective elements are dubbed the science. Designing a car, for example, is art, and manufacturing it is science. The trader's art lies in developing a personal forecasting technique for the underlying instrument on which options are traded. This takes time and will frequently evolve with experience. The trader's science is understanding option price behavior and setting realistic expectations for the profit potential of a strategy. Both are essential elements of a systematic approach, albeit with a subjective element, that a trader can describe and follow.

Implied Volatility Can Help

Options do have a unique aspect—implied volatility—that traders should include in their systemic approach to market forecasting. As discussed in earlier chapters, implied volatility is the volatility percentage in a formula that explains the current market price of an option. While there is no study that the author is aware of which suggests changes in implied volatility can be used to predict rising or falling prices, changes in implied volatility of index options may be interpreted as a shift in general market psychology. A rise in implied volatility, for instance, may indicate a rise in anxiety about an upcoming event, such as a government report. Whether or not this rise is significant is another subjective determination that must be made by each trader. There is no rule that indicates whether changes in implied volatility precede or accompany changes in index levels. Each trader must observe what has happened in the past, and each must assign a probability to the possibility of similar market action happening again.

As traders consider probabilities, they should keep in mind the concepts of option pricing. The old saying "Buy on the rumor and sell on the news" is often used in traditional stock market theory to explain what appears to be contradictory price action, such as a price decline immediately after the release of good news or a price rise after bad news. In option markets, however, contradictory price action can occur in a different form. An index can rise, but call prices remain unchanged or decline. Alternatively, an index can decline, but put prices remain flat or decline. Such price behavior in option markets is explained by changes in implied volatility. Option traders must, therefore, be aware of current implied volatility levels and make a forecast of the future level.

For example, assume that the implied volatility of OEX options rose prior to the last three inflation reports and declined after the report. A trader who is considering initiating a trade prior to the fourth report must evaluate the impact of a similar change in implied volatility on the strategy under consideration. The trader must also make a prediction about whether or not history will repeat itself a fourth time. There is, of course, no guaranty that it will.

Balance and Focus

The topics discussed above take a great deal of study and reflection. For those who love the process, it is more fun than work. Yet focusing on one's trading activity should not become an obsession. Trading should be only one part of a well-balanced life that includes other important interests. Think of a business manager who has a two-year deadline for a major project such as the redesign of a product, the construction of a building, or the negotiation of a companywide labor agreement. Think of a college student with a major research paper due at the end of the semester or a homemaker in charge of the annual community charity event. These people have other important commitments in their lives. Focus on the big projects is required, but this focus must be kept in perspective. These people must do a little bit every day. They cannot wait until the last minute and hope to do everything at once.

The same is true of trading. Focusing on trading means knowing current market conditions; it does not mean trading all the time. Devoting two to four hours per week, divided into 15 to 30 minutes per day, might be enough. The broker does not have to be called every hour. Trades do not have to be made every day, every week, or even every month. There are times to be sitting on the sidelines with no open positions. Moreover, a break from the intense concentration required by active trading will do the trader's mind some good. It will then be possible to return to the market refreshed and ready for the next round.

TOOLS FOR TRADING

As discussed above, developing a healthy trading psychology means fostering key attitudes in one's own mind. The mental process can be greatly enhanced by two hands-on tools: the trading journal and the trading business plan.

The Trading Journal

The specific purpose of keeping a trading journal is to monitor trading activity so that weak points can be identified and, hopefully, improved. A trading journal should include all elements that are part of the process of planning a trade, initiating a position, and closing a position. Such data can clarify the reasons for success or failure of particular trades. A trader can then work on the specific areas that need improvement.

A trading journal should have six sections, as shown in Table 17–1: four that describe the market forecast and the trade (Trade Data, Forecast, Target Profit, and Stop-Loss Point), one that describes the actual results, and one that summarizes the results relative to the forecast. After a series of trades, the information in the trading journal will reveal strengths and weaknesses of a trading technique.

1. *The Trade Data section* contains information about opened trades. The Open Trade Date is simply the date on which a trade is initiated. The Index and Level identify the underlying index and its level when a trade is initiated. "OEX 880" or "NDX 1322" are examples of what might be entered on this line. Strategy/Price contains descriptions of strategies such as "Buy 10 SPX Sep 940 Calls at 24½" or "Sell 25 TXX Nov 450–460 Put spreads at 6⅛." Option Implied Volatility contains percentage numbers such as "22%" or "33.5%." To review the concept of implied volatility and how it is calculated, refer to Chapter 6.

Table 17–1 Trading Journal

Trade Data	Open Trade Date			
	Index and Level			
	Strategy/Price			
	Option Implied Volatility			
Forecast	Index Forecast			
	Date/Days Forecast			
	Implied Volatility Forecast			
Profit Target	Option Price Forecast			
	Total Target Profit			
Stop-Loss Point	Option Stop-Loss Price			
	Total Stop-Loss Amount			
Actual Results	Close Trade Date (Days)			
	Index Level			
	Option Price			
	Option Implied Volatility			
	$ Profit/Loss			
Summary	Profit ≥ Target			
	Profit < Target			
	Loss ≤ Stop-Loss Amount			
	Loss > Stop-Loss Amount			
	Index Forecast Accurate			
	Index Forecast Inaccurate			
	Time Forecast Accurate			
	Time Forecast Inaccurate			
	Imp. Vol. Forecast Accurate			
	Imp. Vol. Forecast Inaccurate			

2. *The Forecast section* contains the elements of the three-part forecast: index level, time, and implied volatility. This information makes it possible to compare actual results to forecasts. The Index Forecast and the Implied Volatility Forecast are simply the trader's prediction for these elements. The Date/Days Forecast may contain either a date when the index is predicted to achieve a certain level or the number of days between the date a trade is initiated and the date on which the index is predicted to achieve a certain level.

3. *The Target Profit section* contains the Option Price Forecast and the Total Target Profit. The option price forecast can be calculated by using OP-EVAL3™. First, the information required to calculate the option implied volatility in the Trade Data section is entered into the program. Second, the index level, days to expiration, and volatility are changed to the numbers in the Forecast section. With the forecast information entered, OP-EVAL3™ then estimates the price or prices of the option or options in the strategy, assuming the forecast is realized. The Forecast Option Price and the information in the Strategy/Price row are then used to calculate the Total Target Profit. If, for example, the Strategy/Price row contains "Buy 5 SPX Sep 930 Calls at 15¼" and the Option Price Forecast is "20," then the Total Target Profit is 20 minus 15¼ times 5, which equals 4¾ times 5, or "24."

4. *The Stop-Loss Point section* contains the Option Stop-Loss Price and the Total Stop-Loss Amount. There is no single right way to determine an option stop-loss price. Each trader must make a subjective decision about an amount that, in their opinion, is reasonable to risk. Of course, traders must be aware that even if stop-loss orders are used, there is no guaranty that such orders can be executed at a stated stop-loss price. Hectic market conditions during trading hours or discontinuous price action from one market close to the next market opening may result in a stop-loss order being executed at a substantially worse price than desired or not at all. A trader must be prepared to accept the risks of such occurrences. The Total Stop-Loss Amount is calculated in a manner similar to the way the Total Target Profit is calculated. If, for example, the Strategy/Price row contains "Buy 5 SPX Sep 930 Calls at 15¼" and the Option Stop-Loss Price is "12," then the Total Stop-Loss Amount is 15¼ minus 12 times 5, which equals 3¼ times 5, or "16¼."

5. *The Actual Results section* contains information about when and at what price the position is closed. Actual results will be compared to the forecast and the target profit or the stop-loss amount so that an assessment of the trade can be made. The Close Trade Date (Days) is either the date on which the position is closed or the number of days that it was open. The Index Level is the index level at the time the position is closed. The Option Price is the price at which the position is closed. The Option Implied Volatility is the implied volatility of the option at the price at which it is closed, and it is calculated with OP-EVAL3™, as described in Chapter 6. The $ Profit/Loss is the actual dollar profit or loss of the trade.

6. *The Summary section* consists of paired rows that indicate positive or negative comparisons between actual results and planned results. In Table 17–1, positive comparisons are indicated by check marks in the nonshaded rows and negative comparisons are indicated by check marks in the shaded rows. If, for example, a profit of $900 was planned and a profit of $1,100 was realized, then a check mark would be placed in the nonshaded Profit ≥ Target row. If, however, a profit of $400 was realized when a $900 profit was planned, then a check mark would be placed in the shaded Profit < Target row. Similarly, if a trade closed at a loss, then a check mark would be placed in either the nonshaded Loss ≤ Stop-Loss Amount row or in the shaded Loss > Stop-Loss Amount row. The other paired rows in the Summary relate to the accuracy of the forecasts for index level, time, and implied volatility.

After several trades, a trading journal such as the one in Table 17–1 will enable a trader to look back and identify areas of strength and weakness. Was the index forecast accurate more often than not? The number of check marks in the appropriate rows will answer this question. If losses are always greater than the stop-loss amount, then it is likely that a trader is not following the discipline of closing unprofitable trades at the preset level. If either the index or time forecasts are generally accurate or inaccurate, then this will give a trader valuable information about the market-forecasting technique being used.

Comparisons Can Be Subjective

There is some subjectivity to placing check marks in the paired rows of the trading journal. If implied volatility was forecast to rise from 15 percent to 20 percent, for example, and it actually rose to 21 percent, then a trader can check the Imp. Vol. Forecast Accurate row with a feeling of satisfaction. Similarly, if implied volatility decreased to 13 percent, then the forecast was unarguably inaccurate. However, what if implied volatility rose to 17 percent or 18 percent? At some point a trader must decide if the forecast was "more accurate" or "more inaccurate." Over time there should be enough trades so that a few "questionable" check marks will not distort the results of the trading journal.

Since some entries in the trading journal are subjective, traders must be honest with themselves. This is, perhaps, a trader's first test of trading discipline! As a result, keeping the trading journal may be frustrating in the beginning. But do not give up on the trading journal. Its goal is to help traders improve by identifying both strong and weak points. The business of trading options can itself be frustrating, because the percentage of losing trades, even for successful trading techniques, can be as high as 40 to 50 percent. Beginners can easily get discouraged if their percentage of losing trades is even higher. Yet that is precisely why a trading journal is so important. It can identify areas that need improvement. When a trading journal is used, a trader's attention can be focused on learning, rather than on feelings of frustration. And learning is a more productive focus.

Develop a Business Plan

If trading were easy, then many more people would do it. Also, if trading were easy, then someone would program a computer do it. But trading is not easy. Many people have traded for a while and then given up.

The chances for success can be increased by treating trading like a business. In formulating a plan, traders should consider these questions: How much risk am I willing to assume? How much time do I plan to spend? How much money do I hope to make? What percentage of trades do I expect to be profitable, and what percentage unprofitable? The answers to these questions are personal and will vary greatly from individual to individual. But this is the process of planning a new business. Can you imagine a new business that opens without a budget estimating sales, expenses, and net profits? Trading is no different. Trading is a business, and a business needs a plan. A good business plan for trading has four key elements:

Sufficient initial capital. There is no specific rule about the amount of capital required to start trading. However, capital must be sufficient to withstand losses during the learning phase. Keep in mind that capital devoted to trading is risk capital. It does not include other capital, such as emergency savings, long-term investments for retirement, or targeted savings such as savings for a home.

A plan for managing initial capital. *Managing capital* means dividing resources into small enough units so that one losing trade or a short series of losing trades will not impair the ability to continue. A new trader should have enough capital to provide for a realistic opportunity for net profits to be realized on an initial series of trades. Although there is no guaranty about how many trades is enough to test a trading system, 10 trades seems like a reasonable number.

Adequate time allocated to carry out the plan. As discussed above, keeping current with market conditions and knowing whether those conditions are about to signal a trading opportunity requires study and reflection. Consequently, traders must plan their schedule to include the time necessary to get the information they need. For some, reading the morning newspaper and looking at charts on the weekends is sufficient. Others require updates more frequently. As a market-forecasting technique evolves, so too will a trader's time commitment. That time commitment may increase or decrease, but the important element is consistency. If a trader knows what the time commitment is, then it is possible to look back at the end of a week or a month and evaluate whether enough time was devoted to the business of trading.

A realistic profit target. A realistic profit target gives a trader something to shoot for, and it gives a trader a great sense of satisfaction if the goal is achieved. Beginning traders, of course, should set lower goals than experienced traders. In fact, beginning traders should not expect to do much better than break even for the first several months. Over time, however, the profit target should increase both in absolute terms and in percentage terms.

Although each trade should have a specific profit target when initiated, the profit target of the trading business plan should be set for a series of trades, such as 10 trades, or for a period of time, such as 6 months, and not for individual trades. There is absolutely no certainty that any individual trade will yield a profit. That is why each trade should also have a stop-loss point when initiated.

A typical measure of profit, profit as a percent of invested capital, is unsatisfactory for trading, because it does not include the amount of time involved. Consider a trader with $50,000 of trading capital who earns $10,000 net profits before taxes during one year. On the one hand this profit is 20 percent of invested capital. On the other hand, if this trader spends 10 hours per week studying the market, or 520 hours per year, then $10,000 amounts to less than $20 per hour "wages." Seen in this light, the profit is not so impressive. Nevertheless, having a profit goal is an important part of planning. Setting a profit target is subjective. Every trader should think hard about how much, realistically, he or she hopes to make; and every part of the business plan should be consistent with that target.

EXAMPLE OF A BEGINNING TRADER

Consider Laurel, a health-care professional in Boston who has followed the stock market since college. Laurel has no credit card debt, and in addition to her Individual Retirement Account (IRA) and her 401-K plan at work, she has a small but growing investment portfolio divided into two separate accounts. One account was established to save for a condominium which she hopes to buy in the not-too-distant future. The other account is for "other investments."

One of Laurel's dreams has always been to trade, and she thinks that now is the time to take the plunge. While her work is demanding, she believes that she can set aside 4 to 6 hours per week to concentrate on trading. She estimates that this will be 30 minutes per day on weekdays and 2 to 4 hours on weekends. For capital, she plans to take three-quarters of the money in her "other investments" account along with extra savings over the last few months that were set aside in anticipation of her trading venture. Some additional capital is also available, because she has decided not to take a vacation this year. After all, starting a new business requires sacrifices! Assuming that Laurel's initial trading capital is $20,000, we can see how she might formulate a trading plan.

Although Laurel has experience investing, she is new to trading. Her first task is to find a short-term trading technique that truly becomes her own. There are several books on the subject of trading that she can choose from. Many include explanations of technical analysis, some discuss computer-aided trade selection, and others involve predicting market movements by daily or weekly cycles. Laurel must devote the time necessary to finding a system that she can adopt as her own. After all, it is her money at risk. She will make the decisions, and the profits or losses will accrue to her.

Laurel also needs a method of getting up-to-date information so that she can monitor existing positions and look for new trading opportunities. If her trading system relies on charts, she must have a source for these charts. She must also have access to current prices. CBOE's Web site at http://www.cboe. com supplies 20-minute-delayed quotes on all listed securities options at no charge. Many brokerage firms offer real-time option quotes to customers via touch-tone phone, the Internet, or both. Before initiating her first real trade, Laurel should test her abilities by paper trading, as discussed above.

When she is ready to trade for real, Laurel should plan for both successful and unsuccessful results in her first series of trades. She should set a risk limit for her first 10 trades that is substantially below her initial trading capital. Ten trades should be sufficient for Laurel to judge whether her trading technique works as well in the real market as it did on paper. If Laurel establishes an initial risk limit of $7,000, or 35 percent of her $20,000 trading capital, for example, she should select trades with a reasonable stop-loss point—$500 to $700 per trade. By doing this, if all 10 trades result in losses, Laurel should still have enough of her start-up trading capital left that she can try again when she has revised her trading plan.

With $7,000 as her initial risk limit on 10 trades, Laurel might plan her first trades to be the purchase of three options in the $5 to $15 price range with a stop-loss point $2 below the purchase price. While the capital at risk in such a trade is $1,500 (for three $5 options) to $4,500 (for three $15 options), the goal of having a stop-loss point is to close a losing trade with a loss of no more than $600 plus commissions. There is no guaranty, of course, that a position will be closed at or above Laurel's stop-loss point. If a large adverse market move occurs, it is possible that Laurel's order to close a position might be executed at a substantially worse price or not at all, in which case the full purchase price of the option would be lost. Such an experience would be a hard introduction to trading. It is an experience, however, that Laurel must be psychologically prepared to accept if it happens.

There are no strict rules on target profits. Yet Laurel should still plan to make more on a trade than the loss at her stop-loss point. If she plans to make 50 percent more than the maximum stop-loss amount of $600, for example, then she must look for trades that, in her judgment, have a realistic possibility of reaching $900 before commissions. Another example: If Laurel buys three $10 options, she should feel confident that, if her forecast is realized, these options will rise to at least 13½ plus an additional amount to cover commissions.

In the beginning, Laurel should consider entering limit-price closing orders immediately after initiating trades. If she initiates a position by purchasing three options at 10 each, for example, she could immediately enter an order with her broker to sell them at 13¾ (her profit target of 13½ plus ¼ for commissions). If such a sell order is not executed, Laurel can always instruct her broker to cancel it and change the limit price or "go to the market." Such limit-price closing orders impose discipline to take profits, and such discipline does not usually come naturally to beginners. As she develops the ability to close positions on instinct, whether at a profit or at a loss, Laurel may no longer need this enforced-discipline technique.

Laurel should also estimate the number of trades needed to achieve her annual profit target. To do this, she must estimate a profit/loss ratio, an average profit per profitable trade, and an average loss per losing trade. Assume, for example, that Laurel hopes to make net profits of $10,000 during her first year of trading. Assume also that she expects 60 percent of her trades to be profitable and average $900 of profit net of commissions, and that she expects 40 percent of her trades to be unprofitable with an average loss of $600 including commissions. From these assumptions, Laurel can use the formula in Table 17–2 to calculate that she needs to make approximately 33 trades per year, or nearly 3 per month, to achieve her goal.

The calculation in Table 17–2 is helpful, because it is another way that Laurel can monitor her progress. If she only makes one trade in a particular month, then she is behind in her business plan! There are many trading

**Table 17–2 Estimating the Number of Trades Required to Achieve a
                    Profit Target**

Assumptions
      Profit target for year   = $10,000
      Percentage of profitable trades   = 60%
      Average profit per profitable trade = $ 900
      Percentage of unprofitable trades   = 40%
      Average loss per unprofitable trade = $ 600
      Total number of trades per year   = T

Problem: Estimate number of trades per year

      Profits on profitable trades – losses on losing trades = $10,000
                              Profits on profitable trades = T × 0.60 × $900
                     Losses on unprofitable trades = T × 0.40 × $600

Solving for T
      (T × 0.6 × $900) – (T × 0.4 × $600)   = $10,000
              (T × $540) – (T × $240)   = $10,000
                  T × ($540 – $240)   = $10,000
                                    T = $10,000/$300 = 33

opportunities, and a trader who is spending the time required to find them should be able to do so. If Laurel spends 4 to 6 hours per week as she plans, then it is reasonable for her to expect to find three trading opportunities per month. Also, if three out of five trades are profitable, she is on plan in that regard. However, if the average profit per profitable trade is $400, then she is behind plan.

Only time will tell whether or not Laurel becomes a successful trader. But one thing is clear: she will not have to rely on some magical, inborn intuition. If she enjoys the process of watching the market and looking for trading opportunities, if she works at a measured pace, and if she trades with discipline, then she has every chance of succeeding. Traders must have the confidence that their trading technique will achieve net profits after a series of trades, and they must have the discipline to implement their technique consistently.

SUMMARY

Trading is an endeavor involving a series of short-term purchase and sale transactions that are intended to profit from price changes. Trading is difficult to learn and even more difficult to implement, because it involves a style and pace of thinking that is different from many other activities. Emotions can also interfere with the learning process. This means traders must strive for a healthy, objective trading psychology. They can foster this attitude within themselves by employing the concept of "percentage thinking," which means accepting the fact they will have a percentage of profitable trades and a percentage of losing trades. Psychologically, this helps a trader take losses in stride and close losing positions objectively when the forecast changes or when a stop-loss point is reached. Traders must also develop a market-forecasting technique that they are confident will make more correct forecasts than incorrect ones. Their forecasts should also include a subjective judgment about the future level of implied volatility. Although reasoned trades can result in losses, a series of reasoned trades should have a better chance of showing a net profit than a series of lucky trades. Despite the amount of effort that trading requires, focusing on one's trading activity should not be an obsession. Trading should be only one part of a well-balanced life that includes other important interests.

A trading journal is one tool that helps maintain objectivity and discipline while monitoring trading activity. It includes the elements of planning, opening, and closing a trade. A trading journal is intended to identify why particular trades succeed or fail and to help traders focus on areas that need improvement. A trading business plan is another tool. Sufficient initial capital, management of that capital, adequate time to study the market, and a reasonable profit target are all important to the plan.

There are no guaranties of success, but anyone who attempts to make trading a business by starting with sufficient capital, by working at a measured pace, and by striving to trade with discipline has a chance of succeeding.

This book has reviewed several topics involved in trading index options, the basics of options, option price behavior, strategy analysis and selection, managing positions, and the psychology of trading. The computer program OP-EVAL3™ that accompanies the text is a tool designed to help with the process.

Index option traders should include three elements in their forecast: index level, time period, and implied volatility. It is also important to have realistic expectations for the profit potential of a strategy. Once a position is established, traders should be aware of position management alternatives in case the market forecast changes or is incorrect.

Traders must have confidence that their trading technique will achieve net profits after a series of trades, and they must have the discipline to implement that technique consistently. It is essential to be guided by objectivity rather than by emotion. By striving to acquire the necessary skills, anyone can learn how to trade.

Index